AF560327

# Foreign Direct Investment and Indian Economy

# Foreign Direct Investment and Indian Economy

SUVRANSHU PAN

*Foreword by*
PROF. RAJ KUMAR SEN

**REGAL PUBLICATIONS**
New Delhi - 110 027

FOREIGN DIRECT INVESTMENT
AND INDIAN ECONOMY

ISBN 978-81-8484-238-8



*Typeset by*
RAHUL COMPOSERS
New Highway Apartments, Lakshmi Niwas
760, Pocket-D, Lok Nayak Puram, New Delhi - 110 041

***Printed in India at***
MAYUR ENTERPRISES
WZ Plot No. 3, Gujjar Market, Tihar Village, New Delhi - 110 018

*Published by*
REGAL PUBLICATIONS
F-159, Rajouri Garden, New Delhi - 110 027 • Phone : 45546396
E-mail : regalbookspub@yahoo.com

# Contents

# *Foreword*

It is always a pleasure and privilege for a teacher and research guide to foreword a book and specially for one which is based on a research work successfully completed by one of his research scholars who happened to be his student in the post-graduate classes too. Since the days of economic reforms which happens to be one of the main epochs of Indian economy, FDI or foreign direct investment has played an important role in chartering its course of development over time during the last two decades or so. One of the major factors why the Indian economy did not suffer a major setback during the 2007 meltdown of the world economy is the huge entry of FDI into the IT and other sectors of the Indian economy. In the initial stages of economic reforms FDI replaced foreign aid on which India depended for the first four decades of her planned development. It has also been mention that the FDI are necessary as the domestic capital fail short of the require investment necessary for a satisfactory role of growth urgently needed for to cover the deficit in this front and for poverty alleviation by ensuring a high rate of income generation. Of course a welcome to the FDI also means the entry of undesirable elements and culture at the same time .but it is expected that with a maturity in the development process, the Indian economy will also be able to keep her foot firm on her soil, a feature desired to take place by the father of the nation.

The present book is a product of rigorous work and research in the area of crucial importance not only for India in particular but also for all developing countries in general. This book will also be useful not only for academicians and researchers but also for any serious student of the Indian economy specially for the period since economic reforms. I wish every success to the commendable academic endeavour of my research scholar.

DR. RAJ KUMAR SEN
*Chairman,*
International Institute for Development Studies (IIDS)
*Former Professor of Economics,*
Rabindra Bharati University
*Former Managing Editor,*
*Artha Beekshan* and Former President,
Bengal Economic Association
*Former Managing Editor,*
Indian Economic Journal
*Former President,*
Indian Economic Association (IEA)

# *Preface*

One can not just ignore the growing importance of *Foreign Direct Investment (FDI)* in the era of globalization. Foreign direct investment has become one of the crucial areas for the Indian economy as well since its initiation based on the new economic strategy. India's increasing openness to foreign direct investment has contributed importantly to its exceptional growth performance. Since 1985 when India had started her openness, FDI has contributed to higher investment and productivity growth, and has created jobs and a dynamic export sector.

*Foreign Direct Investment and Indian Economy* is an important addition to the growing literature on the role and importance of FDI since the initiation of economic reforms in India in 1991 with a specific focus on its impact on Indian economy. This book is based on my research work on the same theme for which I was awarded Ph.D. in Economics in 2006 from Rabindra Bharati University, Kolkata. This book is distributed over seven broad chapters, namely, Concept and Means, Importance of Foreign Direct Investment with Respect to India, Nature and Magnitude of FDI Flows in India, Impacts of Foreign Direct Investment on Indian Economy, FDI in India: Their Anticipated and Actual Roles, FDI Inflows into India: Survey Results, and Conclusions and Policy Prescriptions. Based on empirical study with a focus on post-economic reforms period, this book will provide significant insights to the growing impact of FDI on the Indian economy. It is expected that this book will be quite useful for the students, researchers, academicians and policy-makers in particular and for the interested people in general.

The book was always a dream I cherished and I am grateful to all the people who have directly and indirectly contributed in making my dream a reality. There are a few people to whom I would like to express my heart-felt gratitude on pen and paper. First and foremost, I shall remain deeply indebted to my respected teacher Professor Raj Kumar Sen of Rabindra Bharati University, Kolkata, under whose able guidance this study has been carried out. His constant encouragement and support throughout my work and his immense patience and meticulous reading of the drafts is really appreciable. I am profoundly grateful to him for all he has done for me.

I would also like to express my gratitude to late Prof. Alak Ghosh (Presidency College, Kolkata), Prof. V. Shanmugasundaram (Indian Economic Association), Prof. Harm Zebregs (IMF), Prof. Jenifer Vita (World Bank), Prof. P.R. Gopala Rao (Indian Economic Association), Prof. Ratan Kumar Ghosal (The University of Calcutta), Dr. Bina Roy (Indian Statistical Institute, Kolkata) and Dr. Ashim Karmakar (Jadavpur University, Kolkata), for being very encouraging and reassuring me time and again that I can do it. I am also thankful to all the faculty members of Kashipur Michael Madhusudan Mahavidyalaya, Purulia, West Bengal for being helpful. In addition, the progress of study contained in this book was presented in various seminars. I thank all the participants of those seminars for their constructive comments.

I also acknowledge the officials of New Secretariat Building (NSB), Kolkata; Indira Gandhi Institute for Development and Research (IGIDR), Mumbai; Indian Statistical Institute (ISI), Kolkata; University of Kerala, Thiruvananthapuram; State Institute of Panchayat and Rural Development (SIPRD), Kalyani; The World Bank, Washington; Bengal Economic Association (BEA), Kolkata; Indian Institute of Public Administration (IIPA), New Delhi; Indian Economic Association (IEA); Secretariat for Industrial Assistance (SIA), Government of India, New Delhi; Aquinus College, Colombo and Reserve Bank of India (RBI), Kolkata for sharing useful information and data with me regarding foreign investment inflow and outflow of India.

Special thanks are also due to R.D.S. Bhatia of Regal Publications, New Delhi for publishing this book in a meticulous manner. My friends Somnath Hazra (CTRAN Consulting, Bhubaneswar), Saikat Bhattacharyya (Bangabasi College School, Kolkata) and Niladri De EIILM, Kolkata) have supported me at various stages of my work. I am thankful to them for that.

I thank all my family members specially my wife Pratyusha and daughter Ahili for being very affectionate and supportive of me always. I must acknowledge my deep debt to my parents who are an integral part of all I have achieved in life. They have encouraged and supported me throughout my academic carrier and I owe everything to them. There are no words to express my feelings for them. They are my world and in fact beyond any acknowledgement.

SUVRANSHU PAN

# Abbreviations

| | | |
|---|---|---|
| ADR | : | American Depository Receipts |
| AoA | : | Agreement on Agriculture |
| B2B | : | Business to Business |
| BoP | : | Balance of Payments |
| CCI | : | Controller of Capital Issues |
| CMIE | : | Centre for Monitoring Indian Economy |
| CMP | : | Common Minimum Programme |
| EPZ | : | Export Processing Zone |
| FCCB | : | Foreign Currency Convertible Bond |
| FDI | : | Foreign Direct Investment |
| FERA | : | Foreign Exchange Regulation Act |
| FII | : | Foreign Institutional Investments |
| FIPB | : | Foreign Investment Promotion Board |
| FIPC | : | Foreign Investment Promotion Council |
| FPI | : | Foreign Portfolio Investment |
| FTZ | : | Free Trade Zone |
| GATS | : | General Agreement on Trade in Services |
| GDP | : | Gross Domestic Product |
| GDR | : | Global Depository Receipts |
| IDP | : | Investment Development Programme |
| IDRA | : | Industrial Development and Regulation Act |
| IFDA | : | International Food Service Distributors' Association |

| | | |
|---|---|---|
| IMF | : | International Monetary Fund |
| IPO | : | Initial Public Offerings |
| IRDA | : | Insurance Regulatory and Development Authority |
| ISAE | : | Institute Di Studi E Analuse Economica |
| JV | : | Joint Ventures |
| LPG | : | Liberalisation, Privatisation and Globalisation |
| MAT | : | Minimum Alternate Tax |
| MIGAP | : | Multilateral Guarantee Agency Protocol Investment |
| MNCs | : | Multinational Corporations |
| MNE | : | Multinational Enterprises |
| MPT | : | Marginal Propensity to Tax |
| MRTPA | : | Monopolies and Restrictive Trade Pratices Act |
| NIC | : | National Information Centre |
| NIP | : | New Industrial Policy |
| NRI | : | Non-Resident Indian |
| OCB | : | Overseas Corporate Bodies |
| OECD | : | Organisation for Economic Corporation and Development |
| OEDC | : | Oil Exporting Developing Countries |
| OGL | : | Open General Licence |
| PAU | : | Project Appraisal Unit |
| R&D | : | Research and Development |
| RBI | : | Reserve Bank of India |
| RIE | : | Recognized Investment Exchange |
| SAP | : | Structural Adjustment Programme |
| SEBI | : | Securities and Exchange Board of India |
| SEZ | : | Special Economic Zone |
| SFC | : | Standing Finance Committee |
| SIA | : | Secretariat of Industrial Assistance |
| TDFS | : | Technical Development Fund Scheme |
| TEC | : | Technical Evaluation Committee |

| | | |
|---|---|---|
| TIFAC | : | Technology Information for Costing and Assessment Council |
| TNC | : | Trance National Corporations |
| UNCTAD | : | United Nations Conference on Trade and Development |
| WBIDC | : | West Bengal Industrial Development Corporation |
| WTO | : | World Trade Organisation |
| WOS | : | Wholly Owned Subsidiaries |

CHAPTER

# 1

# *Concept and Means*

## 1.1. BACKGROUND

The recent spurt in the flow of Foreign Direct Investment (FDI) to the developing country like ours has tremendous impact on the productivity *vis-a-vis* efficiency of the economy during the period of liberalization. In fact, it is well known that one of the crucial objectives of LPG (liberalization, privatization and globalization) has been to achieve competitive efficiency in respect of allocations of resources and productivity. The remarkable increase in foreign direct investment flows to developing countries over the last decade has drawn attention on whether this source of financing enhances overall economic growth for India also or not.

India's increasing openness to foreign direct investment has contributed importantly to its exceptional growth performance. FDI has contributed to higher investment and productivity growth, and has created jobs and a dynamic export sector. It has been found that in the current stage of economic reform, FDI is viewed as 'good cholesterol' because it can confer the benefits and true emphasis on social sector in India. The protagonists are emphatic on how FDI relaxes the triad constrains of saving, technology and market on growth dynamics and further how FDI-related 'externalities' and 'spillover' over the local production chains result in the outward movement of the national production function over time. In short, FDI is a powerful solution to the problem of low-level equilibrium trap.

Foreign direct investment and economic growth has been a central theme of the development literature in the past two decades. In fact, the last two or three decades have witnessed marked changes in the global organisation of industry with far-reaching effects for the evolving patterns of integration of developing countries into world economy. Foreign direct investment affects resource allocation in several ways. The presence of MNC affiliates may affect capital accumulation, industrial structure and performance, trade propensity and many other structural characteristics of the host economy.

The ongoing economic reforms in the area of foreign investment have improved India's attraction as a foreign investment destination in the preparation of the international community. The *Global Competitiveness Report, 2010* listed several encouraging parameters for the Indian economy as an investment destination. Among the main competitive advantages of India, highlighted by the Report, are licensing of technology, availability of suppliers, median income tax rate, export promotion and quality of business environment. In the overall growth competitiveness, India's position has improved in 2011 compared with 1991.

India considers liberalisation of capital account as a process and not as a single event. While relaxing capital controls, India makes a clear distinction between inflows and outflows with asymmetrical treatment between inflows (less restricted), outflows associated with inflows (free) and other outflows (more restricted). Foreign direct investment is encouraged through a progressively expanding automatic route and a shrinking case-by-case route. Capital outflows (FDI) in the form of Indian joint ventures abroad are also permitted through both automatic and case-by-case routes.

Since the beginning of the 1990s, foreign direct investment in India has increased dramatically compared to foreign portfolio investment (FPI). The distribution of FDI flows across the twenty-eight states, six union territories and one national capital territory (Delhi), however, is highly uneven; only a small number attract comparatively large amounts of foreign capital. Thus, what has been the nature and magnitude of the FDI flows in India both before and after liberalisation process set-up in 1991?

The sweeping reforms of 1990-91 have certainly affected the external sector favourably. Foreign direct investment, through its favourable impact, boosts India's trade performance with export promotion and import substitution. The share of FDI in India's GDP has been increased over the year. Though the percentage of FDI flows into Indian economy is not remarkably high as it has been expected but its direct involvement to the production process may make it attractive to the Indians. For the sake of Indian economic performance what are the impact of FDI on human capital development, domestic input market and economic welfare in India between 1991 and 2011?

Foreign direct investment coming from multinational corporations having experience, standing and efficiency can confer great benefits on the less development countries where they operate. They, by providing capital, supplement the domestic resources, provide the much needed foreign exchange resources for essential capital goods imports; provide necessary and up-to-date technology and knowledge and general employment and incomes in the host countries. They can benefit the consumers by offering better quality goods at lower prices due to the high levels of efficiency in their production process. In brief, foreign direct investment supplements domestic savings to achieve higher levels of investment and facilitate import of capital goods and technology, which are not domestically available and thus promote the diversification of economic structure and its efficiency. Apart from finance and technology, foreign direct investment brings with it marketing and management skills which are so scarce and undeveloped in less developed and developing countries. Thus, does FDI playing a supplementary role to the domestic investment in India particularly when there is dearth of domestic savings?

To find a plausible answer to the above questions is professionally interesting as well as policy relevant. In the ultimate analysis, the policy relevance of the answers lies in providing the impact of foreign direct investment on Indian economy since liberalisation policy reforms has been taken place with both welfare foundations and justification. To derive this policy implication is the basic motivation for the study.

## I.II. CONSTITUTION OF THE STUDY

This study aims at empirical assessment of the impact of foreign direct investment on Indian economy. The broad area and nature and scope of this study are given below.

### I.II.I. Broad Area of the Study

In our study we intend to cover the following areas:

(i) The nature and magnitude of flow of foreign direct investment in India both before and after liberalisation;

(ii) The percentage of foreign direct investment flows in all the three sectors of the economy in India;

(iii) The impact of foreign direct investment on the performance of all three sectors including infrastractural development in India; and

(iv) The impact of foreign direct investment on human capital development, domestic input market and economic welfare in India between 1991 and 2011.

### I.II.II. Nature and Scope of the Study

First of all, India is an open economy with federal structure of government and mixed economic system. Throughout the 1990s and the first decade of 2000s, the role assigned to foreign capital in India has been guided by the considerations of financing a level of current account deficit that is sustainable and consistent with the absorptive capacity of the economy. It becomes necessary to empirically evaluate each country's experience in terms of the specific role assigned to foreign investment in the process of development. And, foreign direct investment is not and cannot be an exception to this explanation and prediction.

Broadly speaking, foreign direct investment is a part of external sector reforms in India. Thus, in sharp contrast to the late 20th century scenario when direct investment become extremely important, accounting for more than 50 per cent of the private capital flows in the 1990s, FDI enters mostly to emerging market economies to meet their development goals.

So far as the literature on this area is concerned there are very few studies on FDI in India which have concentrated mainly on the determination of the industry specific flow of FDI. Most of the researchers have been concentrated on the FDI flow and its distributional aspects in India. But the impacts of these rising flows in every aspects of the economy have been neglected. Throughout this study we shall analyze the impact of FDI flows on Indian economy specially in the post-liberalisation period.

Second, capital flows in the form of FDI have been widely believed to be an important source of growth in recent years. Since the 1970s, imperfections in goods and factor markets, presence of scale economies and government restrictions on output, trade and entry have come to be recognised as creating market structures where foreign capital in the form of FDI contributes to growth.

Analytically, FDI policies generally take into consideration the conditions that could crowd-in domestic investment. Since trade is an important vehicle for growth, FDI could also contribute to growth by promoting exports. Despite the usual concerns that inappropriate technology is generally transferred to the foreign affiliates, empirical assessments suggest that technology—both public and private—that accompany FDI are complementary and inter-firm collaboration helps in augmenting growth.

Thus, in this study, we also want to investigate the impact of FDI on India's trade performance on the basis of secondary data. To fill up the research gap on growth of trade performance of India, this study on foreign direct investment found some scope on the relevant field.

Third, foreign direct investment is sought by developing countries to overcome capital constraint. Capital is essential for achieving higher economic growth and development. However, the flow of FDI to developing countries is extremely skewed, since countries such as China and Brazil receive a major portion of the flows. FDI flows depend on domestic investment environment as well as on external economic factors. While external economic factors are outside the control of developing countries, they can strengthen domestic environment to attract higher investment.

Considering the above factors for attracting FDI flows in the Indian economy, this study may find out the environmental structure need for it. In our study we seek to investigate the impact of FDI flows on economic welfare in India basically on the basis of secondary data and partly from our findings in the primary data as well.

## I.III. REVIEW OF LITERATURE

In what follows, a detailed review of literature is presented with a view to understanding how the questions raised above have been theoretically and empirically analysed in the literature, both in the context of India and elsewhere in the world.

For analytical purposes, the review of literature is broadly divided into international and Indian studies. Under these studies, major theoretical, empirical and descriptive approaches to analysing impact of foreign direct investment on Indian economy are covered. The purpose of this review of literature is to identify researchable issues, or research gaps, to be focussed in the study.

Review of literature has been analysed according to different aspects of foreign direct investment both for international and Indian studies. In their analysis researchers mainly worked on (a) FDI, productivity and technology transfer, (b) economic reforms and FDI, (c) FDI in developing countries, (d) FDI *vs.* debt and exchange rate, (e) cross-country analysis, (f) infrastructural issues, (g) correlation with other economic variables, and (h) FDI in India, etc.

### I.III.I. International Studies

FDI increases the rate of technical progress in the host country through a 'contagion' effect from the more advanced technology and management practices used by foreign firms (*Findley*, 1978). FDI is an important vehicle for the transfer of technology, contributing relatively more to growth than domestic investment. However, the higher productivity of FDI holds only when the host country has a minimum threshold stock of human capital. So, FDI contributes to economic growth only when a sufficient absorptive capability of the advanced technologies is available in the host economy (*Borensztein et. al.*, 1998).

The export-promoting effect of FDI on the economies of the South-East Asian countries is accentuated by the fact that production by the foreign-owned factories normally constitutes quite a large proportion of the output of the economies where they are established. There is a class of goods whose multi-stage production process is such that firms producing them are tempted to undertake direct investment in regions characterized by (i) large differences in relative factor endowments within the region, and (ii) low economic distances between points in the region (*Itoh*, 1998). The extent of multinational activity has led to renewed interest within Europe in the impact of FDI on employment, investment and trade, and the structure of economic growth. The growth of FDI suggested that such investments are likely to be an important channel for the diffusion of ideas and technologies (*Barrell et. al.*, 1997).

The investors of FDI have an informational advantage over domestic savers because they gain crucial inside information about the productivity of firms under their control (*Razin et. al.*, 1999). FDI is observed to be a predominant form of capital flows to emerging economies, especially when they are liquidity-constrained internationally during a global financial crisis. In such a situation, capital should have efficiently flown out rather than in, and FDI becomes a social loss-generating phenomenon (*Sadka et. al.*, 2000).

As transaction costs increase the cost of direct investment, foreign investors should be averse to investing in countries with higher transaction costs, and will therefore gravitate toward states with more effective or efficient legal regimes. Working with host countries, the new approach would establish a more direct and meaningful dialogue with foreign investors and recognize that legislative reform is a long and tedious process subject to a continuous cycle of incremental change and trial and error (*Hewko*, 2002; *Pan et. al.*, 2007).

The context of India-Singapore economic relations is basically deals with the supply side factors of FDI from Singapore which could be useful in identifying the strategies required to attract Singapore's FDI into India. Through this services-related FDI critically affects the host countries absolute advantage and international competitiveness (*Tan*, 1997). Third world MNEs constitute a 'second wave' of outward investment activity, which is fully consistent with net outward FDI being associated with later stages of economic development. Globalisation, interface between trade and FDI are actively related to each other for a developing country (*Dunning*, 1998).

The standard neoclassical approach is not particularly useful if we want to understand FDI flows to developing countries (*Zebregs*, 1998). In some cases, domestic firms may increase productivity simply by observing nearby foreign firms. In other cases, diffusion may occur from labour turnover as domestic employees move from foreign to domestic firms (*Aitken et. al.*, 1999).

Aid fatigue and fiscal pressures in the industrial countries have made it more difficult for developing countries to attract official capital flows. Foreign direct investors whose assets are in the form of buildings, plants, machinery and other facilities, none of which can be easily liquidated, tend to act on the premise that investment decisions represent a lasting commitment (*Pfeffermann*, 1997).

The weight applied to consumer welfare is between one-seventh and one-quarter of the weight applied to the output of state-owned enterprises. It can be established through this view that the political process in China as trading off the social benefits of increased trade and FDI against the losses incurred by state-owned enterprises due to such liberalisation (*Branstetter et. al.*, 2002). A model of FDI-economic growth suggests that FDI does promote China's economic growth and the physical marginal product of foreign capital seems to be significantly larger than that of domestic capital (*Zhang*, 2001). During the 1990s, China's growth was largely supported by FDIs coming mainly from Asia, and by the exports they were generating. In the post-east Asian crisis period, the structural problems in the Chinese economy, linked with the legacy of Dengist reforms, are becoming apparent (*Fabre*, 1999).

There is the importance of profit repatriation in generating different effects of FDI in developed as compared to less developed economies like India on net international debt, trade and the real exchange rate (*Gazioglou et. al.*, 2001). The sovereign risks associated with debt finance are shown to be generally less severe than the ones that come with FDI. FDI is chosen only if the foreign investor is more efficient in running the project, if the project is risky, and if the foreign investor has a good outside option which deters creeping expropriation (*Schnitzer*, 2002). The striking correlation between real exchange rates and foreign direct investment broke down for Japanese FDI in the 1990s, as the real exchange rate appreciated while FDI plummeted. Using bank-level and firm-level data sets, it was found that financial difficulties at banks were economically and statistically important in reducing the number of FDI projects by Japanese firms into the United States (*Klein et. al.*, 2002; *Pan*, 2011).

Welfare does not change monotonously with FDI and foreign investment may decrease national welfare due to the transfer of capital returns to foreigners. This implies that after the opening of the economy to foreign investors, domestic producers will no longer be able to act in the R & D sector (*Reis*, 2001). A number of problems are faced in evaluating foreign investments that are not present when evaluating domestic investments. These extra problems include the presence of exchange-rate and country risks, the need to consider taxes at home and abroad, the frequent need to account for subsidized financing, and so on (*Levi*, 1990). Multi-product firms use trade costs to reduce inter-variety competition by placing production of some varieties abroad. Since the varieties are differentiated, all varieties are sold in all markets. Thus while FDI displaces some exports, it also creates trade via reverse imports. This naturally leads to parallelism in the trade and FDI patterns (*Baldwin et. al.*, 2001). By pursuing an open and pro-active trade and industrial strategy, Asian tiger countries have been able to realise the benefits of FDI. However, resource-rich transnational companies have brought about a higher level of market concentration (*Mien*, 1999). But tax competition for FDI can have adverse effects on corporate tax revenue. In fact, these effects may have already become evident in the sharp decline in corporate tax revenue in some member-countries of the OECD (*Gropp et. al*, 2001).

FDI has contributed to higher investment and productivity growth, and has created jobs and a dynamic export sector.

Market size, labour costs, quality of infrastructure, and government policies are the determining factors in attracting FDI for both China and India (*Tseng et. al.*, 2002). The fiscal treatment is one of the main factors determining a country's competitiveness and it seems to be also one of the major determinants of FDI flows in industrialized countries. Within the European Union area, whenever very heterogeneous tax schemes coexist, member-states show different performances in terms of FDI inflows (*ISAE*, 2001).

The selection of an appropriate foreign market servicing mode is clearly an important element of the competitiveness of a firm operating in international markets. This choice is often limited due to constrains imposed on firms by their products, host market conditions, so their own financial and managerial constraints. FDI and exports have a strong correlation in the developing countries as well as the developed countries (*Buckley*, 1995; *Pan et. al.*, 2007).

The causal relationship between FDI and economic growth may be fairly heterogeneous across countries. It has been found that while traditional tests seem to suggest a significant and uniform impact on growth from FDI, the causal relationship between investments, both foreign and domestic, and economic growth in developing countries is highly heterogeneous (*Nair-Reichert et. al.*, 2001). Although FDI is expected to boost long-run growth in the recipient economy via technological upgrading and knowledge spillovers, it is shown that the extent to which FDI is growth-enhancing depends on the degree of complementarity and substitution between FDI and domestic investment (*de Mello*, 1999).

Governments do not respond to public pressure by altering the pattern of their aid, but rather by seeking to persuade the electorate to accept the pattern of aid which they have already decided to adopt. And thus the aid-giving process is by no means as exclusively characterized by market leadership on the part of the state (*Mosley*, 1985). As current government policy is maintained, perceived risk abates thus leading to a gradual appreciation of asset prices and a gradual decrease in their conditional variance. This may be viewed as the volatility analogue of the 'peso premium' for assets subject to large, infrequent price drops (*Cherian et. al.*, 2001).

An informed discussion of proposals on how to deal with the instability of international capital flows requires an understanding of the environment in which the financial system operates and of the problems it must solve. FDI inflows usually are of a size, time duration, and speed that can contribute to creating and amplifying macro-economic and financial disequilibrium in emerging market economies (*Mussa*, 2000). Economic growth may protect the environment in the long-run, but causes environmental degradation in the economic take-off stage. To shorten in sciences and technology lag for developing countries, FDI turns as a growing source today (*Deming*, 1999).

When mode choice (licensing *versus* FDI) is fixed, a subsidy to multinational production increases the rate but decreases the size of innovations. But when mode can switch, the rate and size of innovations both increase, provided the subsidy is not too large (*Glass et. al.*, 2002). While substantial support exists for positive spillovers from FDI, there is no consensus on causality. For FDI, free trade zones, political/economic stability, infrastructure quality and market size are important (*Lim*, 2001).

**I.III.II. Indian Studies**

The resilience of foreign direct investment during financial crisis may lead many developing countries to regard it as the private capital inflow of choice. Although there is substantial evidence that such investment benefits host countries, they should assess its potential impact carefully and realistically. FDI allows the transfer of technology and also promotes competition in the domestic input market (*Loungani et. al.*, 2001). The MNC/ supplier interactions that can help increase the productivity and efficiency of local firms (*Lall*, 1980). FDI has become one of the crucial areas for the growth of Indian economy since she initiated her economic reforms based on the LPG strategies in 1991. The new millennium has observed the continuation, if not the enhancement of the importance of FDI for such economies including India (*Pan et. al.*, 2007).

India has sought to increase inflows of FDI with a much liberal policy since 1990 after four decades of cautious attitude to it. One of the objectives of the current reforms of policies is to remove impediments for export-oriented manufacture in general and to attract MNEs to locate efficiency-seeking FDI in the country. In a developing country such as India that seeks FDI as a development resource, the focus of the FDI policy should be on maximisation of its contribution to India's development rather than on maximisation of the magnitude of inflows by itself. While in general it is admitted that host governments' policies may play an important role in extracting the benefits of FDI for development, a more exact analysis of the relative role of different policy measures in shaping the magnitudes and quality of FDI inflows is not available (*Kumar*, 1998; 2000; 2001).

The liberalisation package of 1991 had a significant impact on the FDI flows into the country. By attracting a critical quantum of FDI which can accelerate the growth process of the economy by bringing in more capital, technology and market access, the problem of low level equilibrium trap can be solved (*Radhakrishnan et. al.*, 2000). But lack of transparency especially in the Indian financial sector could have created low trust relations for investors. The inability of Indian bureaucracy to create conditions for smooth fund flows and also the fallout from the East Asian crisis may have made investors cautious (*Hegde et. al.*, 2001). External openness does provide significant opportunities for growth, but it also carries big risks. External openness by itself does not assure growth unless it is part of a larger strategy for economic growth focusing on investment in physical and human capital (*Nayar*, 2001).

In relation to foreign investment one concern particularly of developing countries has been regarding the import intensity of production. It is feared that foreign firms tend to have higher import intensity. From the angles of volatility and impact on capital formation and growth it is necessary to decide the forms of capital flows are preferable to others. Opening up of capital account need not preclude the imposition of moderate controls, either price-based or regulatory, on capital flows (*Rangarajan*, 1993; 2000).

By truncating the powers of nation-states, the proposed foreign investment regime raises several important issues. One critical question relates to the implications of lifting of controls over the movement of all forms of capital. Another fundamental issue is the future of the post-war multilateral framework built essentially around sovereign states having inviolable rights over their economic domains (*Dhar et. al.*, 1998).

The neo-liberal regime in India has so far failed to improve the macro-economic management of the economy and to achieve a better level of macro-economic capability. Inflows and outflows of FDI were also rather feeble in the South-Asian region (*Bagchi*, 1999). India's experience with financial sector de-regulation has been far from happy and has shown the limitations of the assumptions made by the Narasimham Committee. Integration of global capital flows with domestic money market was to widen the access of domestic firms to global capital, supposedly cheaper (*Khanna*, 1999; *Pan*, 2007, 2011).

FDI flows from Japan to other Asian countries including India to changing industrial structure and to trade flows. FDI from Japan has helped cost reduction and export promotion in the host countries and created a large trade surplus with Asian countries for Japan (*Goldar et. al.*, 1999). Japanese FDI are different from European FDI for India. The differential behaviour between the two groups of firms was particularly sharp with regard to the variables representing international orientation. It could be attributed mainly to the Japanese practice of vendor development (*Siddharthan*, 1999).

FDI involves a capital flow into the host country and thereby it supplements other forms of savings. In the case of joint ventures FDI also results in the mobilisation of domestic savings for productive purposes. FDI helps to promote exports as the foreign investor would normally be more conversant with foreign markets and would have their own well-established market networks (*Satyanarayan*, 1995). For 'greenfield' FDI, in which a company is starting a new enterprise from scratch is particularly true for poorer countries like India. But the impact of investment in industrial countries is likely to be much more muted, as they have continuous access to capital markets and most FDI flows involve the purchase of an existing enterprise (*IMF*, 2001). The displacement effect of FDI on domestic enterprise is closely related to the 'non-economic' question of 'national self-reliance' that figured prominently in the discourse of nationalists in former colonial and semi-colonial countries (*Chandra*, 1999).

The implications of a surge in FDI for the developing countries can be analysed with the help of an open economy macro-model. Capital raised in the host economies has of late become an important source of financing for investment projects in some developing countries (*Jana*, 2003). This has been specifically recognised in the trade policy reforms initiated in India since 1991 and these measures have exerted positive influence on India's foreign trade in general and competitiveness of India's exports in particular (*Hajra et. al.*, 1997). As regards the factors influencing the inflows, empirical results indicate that macro-economic fundamentals are equally important in attracting FDI inflows, implying thereby that the macro-economic policies have to be appropriate and they have to provide incentives for attracting foreign investment (*Gopinath*, 1997).

Foreign investment by augmenting the foreign exchange supply on capital account supposedly narrows down the balance of payments gap on the current account (*Patel*, 1984). But the benefits of globalisation have been reaped by the countries which have created the required infrastructure. In India due to unfavourable infrastructure the FDI could not reach the expected level. At the same time, the continuation of unfavourable trade balance and BOP has contradicted the argument of those who advocated the openness of the economy for MNCs through liberalisation (*Khatkar et. al.*, 1997).

NRIs have carved an important niche in the service sector and in information technology across the world. It is in these sectors perhaps that the Indian government can look at creative policy responses that, while maintaining a level playing field, seek to turn India into an attractive investment destination for NRIs (*Choudhary*, 2001). From another analysis on FDI in India, it has found that both exports and FDI, besides domestic factors, have made important contributions to China's growth, but in India as inflows of FDI are small, it may not have contributed as much to the increment in its growth (*Bhalla*, 1999).

FDI affects resource allocation in several ways. The presence of MNC affiliates may affect capital accumulation, industrial structure and performance of the host economy (*Banik et. al.*, 2001). As foreign investors are significantly risk averse they tend to reduce fresh commitments in the face of increasing conditional uncertainty or volatility in the prices of stocks as also in the event of devaluation of the local currency (*Joshi*, 1995).

The distribution of central investments, which may be expected to have a much more immediate impact on regional growth than transfers, has received much less attention than the foreign investment (*Ravi Kumar*, 2000). An increment of foreign investment in net total capital inflows thus indicates betterment in the balance of payment situation. If the capital account surplus of the balance of payments arises due to increase in foreign investment, it is treated as a better indication in the sense that the country doesn't have to bear any debt-burden in the future (*Bhukto*, 1998). But in these days, FDI is being used less for construction of new factories in the developing countries like India, while mergers and acquisitions have become more common (*Mishra et. al.*, 2001).

India can get great advantage if Indian resources are combined with foreign resources for the rapid transformation of Indian economy (*Mehta et. al.*, 1997). MNCs and their impacts play a minor role in short but the major one in long-run. The potential for market-oriented FDI is enormous, especially as the effects of economic liberalisation are taking hold (*Sharma et. al.*, 1997). The factors which lead to internal concentration also lead by according dominant firms certain monopolistic advantages, to greater success in investing abroad (*Malhotra et. al.*, 1985).

Foreign investments in plantation have tended to export their products like cotton, coffee and cocoa as raw materials for further processing and manufacturing in industrialised countries. Movement of capital from developed countries into the environmental resources of developing countries is a new phenomenon and presents a hope that international trade and investment would lead to a relative equalization of factor prices and income levels between the nations (*Agarwal*, 1979; *Pan, et. al.* 2007).

A Japanese firm's new investment in Indian economy is positively correlated with its own previous investment in that economy and also with the current/planned investments by competitors (*Mody et. al.*, 2001). Foreign aid to India merely substitutes for spending that the government would have undertaken anyway; the funds freed by earmarked aid are spent elsewhere (*Jha et. al.*, 1999). FDI benefits domestic industries by providing opportunities for technological upgradation, access to global managerial skills and practices, better utilisation of human and natural resources (*Gupta*, 2003).

From the review of literature above, it is apparent that there is a need to fill the research gap through a systematic empirical study in an effort to find answers to the research questions raised earlier in the Indian context. Thus, the study undertakes a systematic analysis of the economic impact of foreign direct investment inflows on Indian economy since 1991.

## I.IV. METHODOLOGY AND ORGANIZATION OF THE STUDY

The methodology of the study is both descriptive and prescriptive. The descriptive methodology is used to analyse indices of foreign direct investment for measuring foreign investment policy reforms in India; suggest a simple model for analysing the aggregate impact of FDI on Indian economy; to construct an empirical model for the purpose of estimating the economic implication of foreign direct investment for India with emphasis on econometric specification of the model and technique of estimation; and for drawing implications for welfare-oriented FDI for India. The prescriptive methodology is used to integrate the economic theory and policy of foreign direct investment in India through empirical impact analysis. Thus, the methodology is contributory to the theoretical, empirical and policy aspects of the impact of foreign direct investment on Indian economy.

This study will try to concentrate on the impact of FDI on Indian economy especially in the post-reform period. Attempts will be made to show the correlation between FDI and GDP in India with the help of available and published secondary data. A regression analysis will be done through panel data on FDI to find the impact of it on human development, domestic market and welfare in India.

To ascertain the actual situation regarding FDI flows in India and West Bengal a survey has been conducted to collect the primary data from 200-300 samples in West Bengal. The survey will be for categories of FDI in metro cities, middle-towns and villages (both irrigated and non-irrigated areas) all over West Bengal.

The data on FDI, FPI, exports, imports, growth rate, sectoral distribution of FDI, saving-investment gap, national income, GDP and welfare performance are collected from national and international sources. The international sources include the World Bank publications (e.g. *World Economic Surveys, World Development Report,* etc.), International Monetary Fund publications (e.g. *International Financial Statistics*), UNCTAD publications (e.g. *World Investment Report,* etc.). The national sources include the Government of India publications (e.g. *Foreign Trade Statistics of India, Pre-budget Economic Surveys, National Account Statistics, SIA Newsletter,* etc.), Reserve Bank of India publications (e.g. *RBI Bulletin, Report on Currency and Finance,* etc.), CMIE publications under Economic Intelligence Services and Tata Services Limited publication (e.g. *Statistical Outline of India,* etc). Data collected from sample survey also will be used to analyze the actual situation of FDI flows in West Bengal as well as in India.

The rest of the materials in this book is organised in the following way:

Chapter II will concentrate on the importance, advantages and disadvantages of foreign direct investment for developing countries.

Chapter III will concentrate on the analysis of the flow of nature and magnitude of foreign direct investment in India: (a) before 1947, (b) between 1947 and 1991, (c) between 1991 and 2001, and (d) after 2001.

Chapter IV will be devoted to examine the impacts of the FDI on Indian economy since liberalisation.

Chapter V will concentrate on the analysis of the expected and actual role of foreign direct investment in India and West Bengal.

Chapter VI will represent the results of sample survey and its comparison with macro results.

Chapter VII will present the conclusions and policy prescriptions of this book.

The tables, end notes, references and bibliography in this book are organised as follows.

First, all chapter-specific tables are presented inside the sub-sections whenever required. Second, all end notes are given at the end of their respective chapters. Third, all references of the book are given at the end of each chapter. Fourth, at the end of the book we present Fifth, abbreviations are present at the start of the book, list of bibliography and an index.

## References


Agarwal, J.P. (1979), "FDI in Natural Resources of Developing Countries—Review and Prospects", *The Indian Economic Journal,* Vol. 27, No. 2, October-December, pp. 48-62.

Aitken, Brian J. and Ann E. Harrison (1999), "Do Domestic Firms Benefit Direct Foreign Investment? Evidence from Venezuela", *American Economic Review,* Vol. 89, No. 3, June, pp. 605-18.

Bagchi, A. K. (1999), "Globalization, Liberalization and Vulnerability: India and Third World", *Economic and Political Weekly,* Vol. XXXIV, No. 45, November 6-12, pp. 3219-30.

Baldwin, Richard E. and Gianmarco I.P. Ottaviano (2001), "Multiproduct Multinationals and Reciprocal FDI Dumping", *Journal of International Economics,* Vol. 54, No. 2, August, pp. 429-48.

Barrel, Ray and Nigel Pain (1997), "FDI, Technological Change, and Economic Growth within Europe", *The Economic Journal,* Vol. 107, November, pp. 1770-86.

Bhalla, A.S. (1999), "The Impact of Globalization on China and India" in *Fifty Years of Development Economics* by A. Vasudevan, D.M. Nachane and A.V. Karnik, Himalaya Publishing House, New Delhi.

Bhukta, Anindya (1997), "Foreign Direct Investment in India: An Exaggerated Picture?" pp. 381-94.

Borensztein, E.J. De Gregorio and J-W Lee (1998), "How Does FDI Affect Economic Growth?" *Journal of International Economics,* Vol. 45, No. 1, June, pp. 115-35.

Branstetter, L.G. and R.C. Feenstra (2002), "Trade and TDI in China: A Political Economy Approach", *Journal of International Economics,* Vol. 58, No. 2, December, pp. 335-58.

Buckley, Peter J. (1995), *Foreign Direct Investment and Multinational Enterprises,* Macmillan Press Ltd.

Chandra, Nirmal Kumar (1999), "FDI and Domestic Economy: Neoliberalism in China", *Economic and Political Weekly,* Vol. XXXIV, No. 45, November 6-12, pp. 3195-12.

Cherian, Joseph A. and Enrico Perotti (2001), "Option Pricing and Foreign Investment under Political Risk", *Journal of International Economics,* Vol. 55, pp. 359-77.

Choudhary, Biplove (2001), "Role of Foreign Direct Investment in the Chinese Economy with Special Reference to the Overseas Chinese: Its Implication for India", *China Report—A Journal of East Asian Studies,* Vol. 37, No. 4, October-December.

De Mello, Luiz R. (1999), "Foreign Direct Investment-led Growth: Evidence from Time Series and Panel Data", *Oxford Economic Papers*, Vol. 51, pp. 133-51, Oxford University Press.

Dhar, Biswajit and Sachin Chaturvedi (1998), "Multilateral Agreement on Investment: An Analysis", *Economic and Political Weekly*, Vol. XXXIII, No. 15, April 11-17, pp. 837-49.

Dunning, John H. (1998), *Globalization, Trade and Foreign Direct Investment*, Elsevier, pp. XI + 291.

Fabre, Guilhem (1999), "China in the East Asian Crisis", *Economic and Political Weekly*, Vol. XXXIV, No. 45, November 6-12, pp. 3191-94.

Findley, Ronald (1978), "Relative Backwardness, Direct Foreign Investment and Transfer of Technology: A Simple Dynamic Model", *Quarterly Journal of Economics*, Vol. 92, pp. 1-16.

Gazioglou, S. and W.D. McCausland (2001), "An International Economic Analysis of FDI and International Indebtedness", *The Indian Economic Journal*, Vol. 48, No. 4, April-June, pp. 82-91.

Goldar, Biswanath and Ishigami, Etsuro (1999), "Foreign Direct Investment in Asia", *Economic and Political Weekly*, Vol. XXXIX, No. 22, May 29-June 4, pp. M 50-M 60.

Gopinath, T. (1997), "Foreign Investment in India: Policy Issues, Trends and Prospects", *RBI Occasional Papers*, Vol. 18, Nos. 2 and 3, June-September, pp. 453-70.

Gropp, Reint and Kristina Kostial (2001), "FDI and Corporate Tax Revenue: Tax Harmonization or Competition?" *Finance and Development*, Vol. 38, No. 2, June, pp. 10-13, IMF.

Gupta, Subrata (2003), "Role of Foreign Direct Investment and Multinational Corporations—The Indian Context", *Artha Beekshan*, Vol. 11, No. 4, March, pp. 24-37.

Hajra, Sujan and David L. Sinate (1997), "Fifty Years of India's Foreign Trade: Issues and Perspectives", *RBI Occasional Papers*, Vol. 18, Nos. 2 & 3, June-September, pp. 421-52.

Hegde, Dinesh and Sorab Sadri (2001), "India's Economic Reforms: An Examination of the Effect of Liberalization in Selected Segments", *IASSI Quarterly*, Vol. 20, No. 2, October-December, pp. 5-29.

Hewko, John (2002), "FDI: Does the Role of Law Matter?" *Transition Newsletter*, Vol. 13, No. 2, March-April, pp. 11-13, The World Bank.

IMF (2001), *World Economic Outlook*, World Economic and Financial Surveys, October, pp. 145-73.

ISAE (2001), "The Impact of Taxation on FDI Flows in the European Union Member-States", *Istituto Di Studi E Analise Economica*, June, Annual Report on the State of the European Union.

Itoh, Motoshige (2000), "FDI, International Trade and Transfer of Technology : A Case Study in South-East Asia", in John Piggott and Alan Woodlant (eds): *International Trade Policy and the Pacific Rim*, International Economic Association, Vol. 120, Sydney.

Jana, Siuli (2003), "A Model on Foreign Direct Investment in the Developing Countries", *Artha Beekshan*, Vol. 11, No. 4, March, pp. 38-43.

Jha, Shika and Vinaya Swaroop (1999), "Foreign Aid to India—What Does It Finance?" *Economic and Political Weekly*, Vol. XXXIV, No. 19, May 8-14, pp. 1142-46.

Joshi, Himanshu (1995), "Stock Market Risk and Foreign Portfolio Investments—An Empirical Investigation", *RBI Occasional Papers*, Vol. 16, No. 4, December, pp. 301-12.

Khanna, Sushil (1999), "Financial Reforms and Industrial Sector in India", *Economic and Political Weekly*, Vol. XXIV, No. 45, November 6-12, pp. 3231-41.

Khatkar, R.K., S.D. Chamola and R.C. Hasija (1997), "Globalization : Multinational Corporation in India", *Kautilya : The Journal of Haryana Economic Association*, Vol. XVII, Nos. 1 and 2, pp. 53-60.

Klein, Michael W, Joe Peek and Eric S. Rosengren (2002), "Troubled Banks, Impaired FDI: The Role of Relative Access to Credit", *American Economic Review*, Vol. 92, No. 3, June, pp. 664-82.

Kumar, Nagesh (1998), "Liberalization and Changing Patterns of Foreign Direct Investments—Has India's Relative Attractiveness as a Host of FDI Improved?" *Economic and Political Weekly*, Vol. XXXIII, No. 22, pp. 1321-29.

Kumar, Nagesh (2000), "Economic Reforms and Their Macro-economic Impact", *Economic and Political Weekly*, Vol. XXXV, No. 10, March 4-10, pp. 803-12.

Kumar, Nagesh (2001), "FDI, Regional Economic Integration and Industrial Restructuring in Asia: Trends, Patterns and Prospects", *RIS Occasional Paper*, No. 62, New Delhi.

Kumar, Nagesh (2001), "WTO Regime, Host Country Policies and Global Patterns of MNE Activity: Recent Quantitative Studies and India's Strategic Response", *Economic and Political Weekly*, Vol. XXXVI, No. 1, January 6-12, pp. 39-50.

Lall, S. (1980), "Vertical Interfirm Linkages in LDCs: An Empirical Study", *Oxford Bulletin of Economics and Statistics*, Vol. 42, pp. 203-26.

Levi, Maurice D. (1990), *International Finance: The Markets and Financial Management of Multinational Business*, International Edition.

Lim, Ewe-Ghee (2001), "Determinants of, and the Relation Between, Foreign Direct Investment and Growth: A Summery of the Recent Literature", *IMF Working Paper*, WP/ 01/175.

Loungani, Prakash and Assaf Razin (2001), "How Beneficial is FDI for Developing Countries?" *Finance and Development*, Vol. 3, No. 2, IMF, pp. 6-9, June.

Malhotra, Anju and Autar S. Dhesi (1985), "FDI in Manufacturing from an LDC: India", *The Indian Economic Journal*, Vol. 32, No. 3, January-March, pp. 36-41.

Mehta, Surender and Randhir Khatri (1997), "Socio-Cultural Environment and Role of Multinational Corporations in Indian Economic Development", *Kautilya : The Journal of Haryana Economic Association*, Vol. XVII, Nos. 1 & 2, pp. 67-81.

Mein, Bernard Tai Khium (1999), "Foreign Direct Investment and Pattern of Trade: Malayasian Experience", *Economic and Political Weekly*, Vol. XXXIV, No. 22, May 29-June 4, pp. M72-M77.

Mishra, Deepak; Ashoka Mody and Antu Panini Murshid (2001), "Private Capital Flows and Growth", *Finance and Development*, Vol. 38. No. 2, June, pp. 2-5, IMF.

Mody, Ashoka and Yoko Kinoshita (2001), "Private Information for Foreign Investment in Emerging Economies", *Canadian Journal of Economics*, Vol. 34, No. 2, pp. 448-64.

Mosley, Paul (1985), "The Political Economy of Foreign Aid: A Model of the Market for a Public Good", *Economic Development and Cultural Change*, Vol. 33, No. 2, January, pp. 373-93.

Mussa, Michael; Alexander K. Swoboda; Jeromin Zettelmeyer and Olivier., Jeanne (2000), "Moderating Fluctuations and Capital Flows to Emerging Market Economies", In Peter Kenen and Alexander Swoboda (eds): *Reforming the International Monetary and Financial System*, IMF, pp. 72-142, 155-74.

Pan, S. and Sen, R.K. (2007), *Foreign Direct Investment and Trade in India*, Deep & Deep Publications Pvt. Ltd., New Delhi.

Pan, S. (2011), "Is Globalization Reducing Poverty and Inequality in India? A theoretical Overview", in R.K. Sen (ed): *Modern Indian Economy*, pp. 326-59, Deep & Deep Publications, New Delhi.

Panchamukhi, P.R. (2000), "Social Impact of Economic Reforms in India—A Critical Appraisal", *Economic and Political Weekly*, Vol. XXXV, No. 10, March 4-10, pp. 836-47.

Patel, Meena (1984), "Private Foreign Investment and Balance of Payments Effects in India during 1960-70", *The Indian Economic Journal*, Vol. 31, No. 3, Jan-Mar., pp. 62-69.

Pfeffermann, Guy (1996), "Prospects for Increasing Foreign Direct Investment in Low-Income Countries"; in Zubair Iqbal and Ravi Kanbur's *External Finance for Low-Income Countries*, IMF, pp. 194-206.

Radhakrishnan, K.G. and Jaya Prakash Pradhan (2000), "Foreign Direct Investment in India: Policy, Trends and Determinants", *Productivity*, Vol. 41, No. 3, October-December, pp. 454-62.

Rangarajan, C. (1993), "Maximising Foreign Investment", in Uma Kapila : *Recent Developments in Indian Economy with Special Reference to Structural Reforms (Part-II)*, Vol. 5, pp. 59-66.

Ravi Kumar, T. (2000), "Public Investment and Regional Disparities", *Economic and Political Weekly*, Vol. XXXV, No. 41, October 7-13, pp. 3683-87.

Razin, Assaf, Efraim Sadka and Chi-Wa Yuen (1999), "Excessive FDI under Assymetric Information," *NBER Working Paper*, No. 7400.

Reis, Ana Balaco (2001), "On the Welfare Effects of Foreign Investment," *Journal of International Economics*, Vol. 54, No. 2, August, pp. 441-27.

Sadka, E., Assaf Razin and Chi-Wa Yuen (2000), "An Information-based Model of FDI: The Gains from Trade Revisited", in Isard, Razin and Rose (eds.) : *International Finance and Financial Crises (Essays in Honour of Robart P. Flood, Jr.)*, IMF, Kluwer Academic Publishers, pp. 59-120.

Satyanarayan, B. (1995), "Foreign Direct Investment in LDCs (with Special Reference to India)", *IASSI Quarterly*, Vol. 13, No. 4, April-June, pp. 73-79.

Schnitzer, Monika (2002), "Debt *vs*. FDI: The Impact of Sovereign Risk on the Structure of International Capital Flows", *Economica*, Vol. 69, No. 273, p. 41.

Sharma, R.C., Karampal Singh and Raakesh Vashishta (1997), "Multinational Corporation and Their Impact on Indian Economy", *Kautilya*, Vol. XVII, Nos. 1 and 2, pp. 75-81.

Siddharthan, N.S. (1999), "European and Japanese Affiliates in India : Differences in Conduct and Performance", *Economic and Political Weekly*, Vol. XXXIV, No. 22, pp. M61-M65, May 29-June 4.

Tan, Joseph L.H. (1997), "Singapore's FDI in Indochina and Myanmar: Opportunities and Challenges", *RIS Occasional Paper*, No. 50, New Delhi.

Tseng, Wanda and Harm Zebregs (2002), "Foreign Direct Investment in China: Some Lessons for other Countries", *IMF Policy Discussion Paper*, PDP/02/3.

UNCTAD (2010), *Global Competitiveness Report*, New York.

Zebregs, Harm (1998), "Can the Neoclassical Model Explain the Distribution of Foreign Direct Investment across Developing Countries?" *IMF Working Paper*, WP/98/139.

Zhang, K.H. (2001), "Roads to Prosperity: Assessing the Impact of Foreign Direct Investment on Economic Growth in China", *International Economics*, Vol. LIV, No. 1, February, pp. 113-24.

CHAPTER

# 2

# Importance of Foreign Direct Investment with Respect to India

## II.I. INTRODUCTION

Foreign direct investment is the investment by multinational companies in physical assets such as the establishment of local manufacturing plant. Physical foreign direct investment in new manufacturing plants and sales subsidiaries, or the acquisition of established business, provide the multinational company with a more flexible approach to supplying foreign markets. Foreign direct investment (FDI) is preferred primarily for the reason that it goes directly to increase the capital formation of the recipient country.

In a developing country such as India that seeks FDI as a development resource, the focus of the FDI policy should be on maximisation of its contribution to India's development rather than on maximisation of the magnitude of inflows by itself. Liberalizing foreign direct investment was an important part of India's reforms, driven by the belief that this would increase the total volume of investment in the economy, improve production technology and increase access to world markets.

The main objective of this chapter is to describe the major determinants of foreign direct investment in India. Through this chapter we also discuss the theories, the policies, the importance, advantages and disadvantages of foreign direct investment. In particular, a detailed accounts of the various FDI policies since 1947 and particularly since 1991 are presented with a view to understand the major elements of the foreign investment policy reforms measures in India.

## II.II. THEORIES OF FDI

Theories of FDI assert that the basis for such investment lies in the transactions cost of transferring technical and other knowledge, and market imperfections. Needless to say that in a world of perfect markets, the multinational enterprises would not exist and there would be no FDI. Some important theories on FDI are as follows:

### (a) Hymer-Kindleberger Theory

According to this theory (1969), the foreign-owned firm would make an investment in the host country only if it possesses some compensating advantage which allows it to compete on equal terms with indigenous firms. This is, however, not a sufficient condition for FDI since the firm has the option of licensing the advantage (technology) to an indigenous producer or exporting the product to the host country. Clearly, certain other conditions have to be satisfied for FDI to arise. Some of these conditions are : (i) the advantage is internally transferable (it can be exploited by a subsidiary of the present firm without any additional cost to the parent firm or to the subsidiaries already exploiting it); (ii) it is more profitable for the foreign-owned firm to exploit the advantage itself than to license it to an indigenous producer (because of imperfections in the market for knowledge and heavy firm to firm transfer costs of the advantage); and (iii) exporting the product to the host country is not possible or unprofitable due to tariff or transport cost barriers.

### (b) Kojima's Theory

According to this theory (1978), Kajima argued that there is an inherent difference between FDI originating in the west and that in Japan. He was developed a theoretical framework which integrates trade theory with FDI. This theory presents the triple effect of the Japanese-type FDI: investment, trade and industrial restructuring with mutual benefit. The triple effect can be seen in the textiles industry typically, but not so much in the automobiles and electrical appliances industries, which contributed to upgrade local industry 'to some extent' (it is still at a low level) but much less in the exports of these manufactures. The 1997 'Asian economic crisis' tells us that the fundamental weakness in these countries is that of their own industrial structure which lacks a strong basis of local supporting industry. Since 1980 as Japanese FDI have changed fundamentally, questions can be raised on the applicability of this theory in recent years.

### (c) Dunning's Electic Theory

This theory (1988) explains both the ways in which overseas markets are served by enterprises of different nationalities and the industrial and geographical composition of such activities. According to this theory, a firm will make a direct investment in a foreign country if the following three conditions are satisfied : (i) it possesses some ownership advantages *vis-a-vis* firms of other nationalities in serving particular markets; (ii) it is more beneficial for the firm to use the advantages itself than to sell or lease them to foreign firms; and (iii) it is profitable for the enterprise to utilize these advantages in conjunction with at least some factor inputs outside the home country. While the electric theory provides a good explanation for the decision of firms to invest abroad, it seems to us that the theory does not cover the competitive FDI induced by trade restrictions.

### (d) Buckley-Casson Theory

This theory (1991) is based on three simple postulates : (i) firms maximise profits in a world of imperfect markets; (ii) when markets in intermediate products are imperfect there is an incentive to bypass them by creating internal markets (within the firm); and (iii) internalisation of markets across national boundaries generates MNEs. This theory also predicts that unless transport costs are very low, returns to scale at the plant level are high, or the comparative advantage of one location is very significant, the international acquisition and exploitation of knowledge will normally involve international production through a worldwide network of basically similar plants.

### (e) Author's View

The above theories are mainly indicated the existence of multinational enterprises and their performances in host and abroad on the regards of foreign investment. Inflow and outflow of such investments channelize basically in the imperfect market economies. Throughout this book, what we have found is that the impacts of FDI in host economies are multidimensional. It is positively related with the performance of growing GDP, national income and wealth, market volatility, risk factor and production function. All these impact analysis are portrayed in Chapter IV of this book.

### II.II.I. FDI *vs.* External Public Debt

Foreign capital comes in the form of FDI, FPI or in the form of external public debt. Two idealized forms of transferring foreign capital are considered in India—a combination of a credit and licensing agreement ('debt finance'), and foreign direct investment. In India, FDI also came in the form of external public debt. Since 1960 onwards, the idea of FDI was come into existence which is markedly different from external public debt.

External public debt and FDI give different rights to the foreign investor and thus are subject to different risks. In case of external public debt, the investor has a well defined right on a fixed monetary payment. If the host country defaults on its debt repayment, this may trigger international sanctions such as exclusion from world capital markets or restrictions on international trade. In case of FDI, the investor has a property right on the physical assets of its investment in the host country, but these assets are prone to nationalisation. Again, this is an unambiguous act of expropriation, and, as in case of debt repudiation, it may be punished by international sanctions.

There is a second risk involved in FDI. Even if the assets are not nationalised, the returns from the investment may be adversely affected by sovereign acts of the host country such as changes in the tax law, specific import or export duties, or other charges which the investor has to pay. In contrast to debt repudiation or outright nationalisation, such forms of 'creeping expropriation' that are designed to capture the return stream of a particular investment project are less visible and are not a clear-cut violation of international trade and investment agreements. Hence, it is much more difficult to deter them by international sanctions. The investor can use its control rights only to protect the returns from its investment. For example, it can respond to changes in taxation by transferring some of its production to other plants abroad, possibly at some cost.

In India, we consider how the value of the investment to the foreign investor and to the host country depends on who is in control, what type of goods are produced, and what kind of technology is used for production. It is shown that, if the return streams that can be generated under the control of the host country and the foreign direct investors are the same, there is a clear tendency towards debt finance. Debt finance is more efficient, it is more likely to be viable, and it enables a larger share of the surplus to be given to the foreign investor. However, if the foreign investor is more efficient in running the project, then FDI may become the preferred mode of investment.

In case of debt finance, it may happen that the host country is forced into liquidity default in a bad state of the world. If the foreign investor is unable to observe the state of the world and to distinguish between liquidity default and strategic default, then there will be an inefficient punishment of the debtor country with positive probability in equilibrium. Since the return on FDI varies with the state of nature 'liquidity default' is not a problem. This makes FDI comparatively more attractive.

From the 'electric theory of FDI' (*Dunning,* 1981), it is found that information asymmetries and market failures in the market for technology make it difficult to transfer technological know-how through licensing. Thus, if the technology is very sophisticated, transaction cost considerations suggest that FDI is the optimal form of investment.

## II.III. IMPORTANCE OF FOREIGN DIRECT INVESTMENT TO DEVELOPING COUNTRIES

All over the world, FDI is seen as an important source of non-debt inflows. It is increasingly being sought as a vehicle for technology flows and as a means of building interfirm linkages in a world in which multinational corporations (MNCs) are primarily operating on the basis of a network of global interconnections. India can achieve very dynamic growth based on labour-intensive manufacturing that combines the vast domestic workforce, including skilled managerial and engineering labour, with foreign capital, technology and markets.

Foreign direct investment enables the foreign investor in acquiring a lasting and controlling interest in the company concerned. Direct investment includes equity capital and a portion of the re-invested earnings of the company allocable to the foreign investor on the basis of proportion of foreign equity held by him to the total equity of the company. In the case of the branches of foreign companies operating in India, their net position was taken as foreign direct investment. The forms of FDI into India have discussed below.

### II.III.I. Forms of FDI in India

Foreign direct investment (FDI) to and by India up to 1999-2000 comprise mainly equity capital. In line with international best practices, the coverage of FDI has been expanded since 2000-01 to include, besides equity capital reinvested earnings (retained earnings of FDI companies) and 'other direct capital' (inter-corporate debt transactions between related entities). Data on equity capital include equity of unincorporated entities (mainly foreign bank branches in India and Indian bank branches operating abroad) besides equity of incorporated bodies. Data on reinvested earnings for the latest year are estimated as average of the previous two years as these data are available with a time lag of one year. In view of the above revision, FDI data are not comparable with similar data for the previous years. In terms of standard practice of balance of payments (BoP) compilation, the above revision of FDI data would not affect India's overall BoP position as the accretion to the foreign exchange reserves would not undergo any change. The composition of BoP, however, would undergo changes. These changes relate to investment income, external commercial borrowings and errors and omissions. In case of reinvested earnings, there would be a contra entry (debit) of equal magnitude under investment income in the current account. 'Other capital' reported as part of FDI inflow has been carved out from the figure reported under external commercial borrowings by the same amount. 'Other capital' by Indian companies abroad and equity capital of unincorporated entities have been adjusted against the errors and omissions for 2000-01 and 2001-02.

Foreign direct investment is permitted as under the following forms of investments:

(a) Through financial collaborations,
(b) Through joint ventures and technical collaborations,
(c) Through capital markets via Euro issues, and
(d) Through private placements of preferential allotments.

These foreign direct investments in India included investment in (i) branches of foreign companies operating in India, and (ii) foreign direct enterprises.

### *(A) Forbidden Territories*

Foreign direct investment is not permitted in the following industrial sectors:

(a) Arms and ammunition
(b) Atomic energy
(c) Railway transport
(d) Coal and lignite
(e) Mining of iron, manganese, chrome, gypsum, sulphur, gold, diamonds, copper, and zinc.

### *(B) Foreign Investment through GDRs (Euro Issues)*

Foreign investment through Global Depository Receipts (GDRs) is treated as foreign direct investment. Indian companies are allowed to raise equity capital in the international market through the issue of GDRs. GDRs are designated in dollars and are not subject to any ceilings on investment. An applicant company seeking Government's approval in this context should have consistent track record for good performance (financial or otherwise) for a minimum period of 3 years. This condition would be relaxed for infrastructure projects such as power generation, telecommunication, petroleum exploration and refining, ports, airports and roads.

*Use of GDRs* : The Proceeds of the GDRs can be used for financing capital goods imports, capital expenditure including domestic purchase/installation of plant, equipment and building and investment in software development, prepayment or scheduled repayment of earlier external borrowings, and equity investment in joint ventures (JV)/WOSs in India.

### (C) Automatic Approval by RBI

The Reserve Bank of India accords automatic approval within a period of two weeks (provided certain parameters are met) to all proposals involving:

(i) foreign equity upto 50 per cent in 3 categories relating to mining activities;
(ii) foreign equity upto 51 per cent in 48 specific industries; and
(iii) foreign equity upto 74 per cent in 9 categories.

Where the item (iii) includes items also listed in item (ii), 74 per cent participation shall apply. The lists are comprehensive and cover most industries of interest to foreign companies. Investment in high-priority industries or for trading companies primarily engaged in exporting is given almost automatic approval by the RBI.

*Opening an Office in India* : Opening an office in India for the aforesaid incorporates assessing the commercial opportunity for self, planning business, obtaining legal, financial, official, environmental, and tax advice as needed, choosing legal and capital structure, selecting a location, obtaining personnel, developing a product marketing strategy and more.

### (D) The FIPB Route

Foreign Investment Promotion Board (FIPB) approves all other cases where the parameters of automatic approval are not met. Normal processing time is 4 to 6 weeks. Its approach is liberal for all sector and all types of proposals and rejections are few. It is not necessary for foreign investors to have a local partner, even when the foreign investor wishes to hold less than the entire equity of the company. The portion of the equity not proposed to be held by the foreign investor can be offered to the public.

There is no restriction on the number of Euro-issue to be floated by a company or a group of companies in the financial year. A company engaged in the manufacture of items covered under the New Industrial Policy (NIP) whose direct foreign investment after a proposed Euro-issue is likely to exceed 51 per cent or which is implementing a project not contained in NIP, would need to obtain prior FIPB clearance before seeking final approval from Ministry of Finance.

### (E) Restrictions

However, investment in stock markets and real estate will not be permitted. Companies may retain the proceeds abroad or may remit funds into India in anticipation of the use of funds for approved end uses. Any investment from a foreign firm into India requires the prior approval of the Government of India.

## II.III.II. Determinants of FDI in India

Foreign direct investment is sought by developing countries to overcome capital constraint. Capital is essential for achieving higher economic growth and development. However, the flow of FDI to developing countries like India is extremely skewed, since countries such as Brazil and China receive a major portion of the flows. FDI flows depend on domestic investment environment as well as on external economic factors. While external economic factors are outside the control of developing countries, they can strengthen domestic environment to attract higher investment.

In the context of India it is hypothesized that FDI flows into the country are determined by the following set of factors:

### (i) Quality of Infrastructure

Quite often in academic discussions, it has been held that infrastructural bottlenecks in our country have slowed down the actual FDI flows as well as widened the gap between the actual and approved FDI inflows. The stock of infrastructural base in India has been structured as the combined expenditure of the centre and state governments on economic services which include expenditure on energy, transport and communication services, technology and environment, electricity, gas and water and other economic services. Growth and development of the infrastructural base is expected to encourage the inflow of FDI.

### (ii) Domestic Market Size

The domestic market size has a critical impact on the inward flow of FDI into the country. The huge and fast growing domestic market of India acts as a positive incentive for foreign investments in India. The market size has been proxies by the gross domestic product.

### (iii) Change in Market Size

The change in market size is a significant consideration entering into the choice—function of foreign investors to invest in India. Theoretically, it is expected that expansion of domestic market would have a positive impact on FDI inflows.

### (iv) Openness of the Economy

The degree of openness of the economy is one of the major determinants of FDI flows into the country. It is supposed that openness of the economy impact positively on the FDI inflows.

### (v) Deep Links with Global Market

As world became a global village, deep links with global market increase FDI flows into the country. This type of opening of the economy is measured by the percentage ratio of export plus import to GDP.

### (vi) Exchange Rate

A continued devaluation of domestic currency is *a priori* expected to depress the profitability position of foreign investors. It is found that (a) this may curtail the quantum of dividends, royalty, technical fees, etc. repatriated by them, and

(b) most of the FDI companies have high import-elasticity of sales. Hence, erosion of the value of domestic currency leads to high cost of production.

### *(vii) Capital Formation*

Domestic capital formation is one of the major determinants for attracting FDI. Economies with higher capital formation are expected to be fertile grounds for attracting FDI. As far as the case of FDI in India is concerned, capital formation has been taken as gross fixed capital formation.

### *(viii) Probability of Earning Higher Profits*

Foreign direct investment is also determined by host country's probability or confidence of earning relatively higher profits. It reflects the perception of the prospective foreign investor about the host country's economy.

### *(ix) Debt-Service Ratio*

Debt-service ratio indicates the extent of pre-emption of investible resources for servicing the debt. A fall in the debt-service ratio could attract large non-debt creating inflows. Thus, debt-service ratio has a negative relationship with attracting FDI.

### *(x) Rate of Inflation*

High inflationary pressures will erode the profitability of foreign investment, increase the cost of production and introduce distortions in the host country's economy. As a consequence, a negative relationship has been hypothesized between the rate of inflation and the flow of foreign investment.

### *(xi) Foreign Exchange Reserves*

The high level of foreign exchange reserves in terms of the import cover reflects the strength of the external payments position and helps to improve the confidence of the perspective investors. Therefore, a positive relationship is postulated between the foreign exchange reserves and inflow of FDI.

### *(xii) Labour-Intensive Production*

A reliable and skilled work force in India produced labour-intensive manufacturing production. These skills and productivity of labour prevent foreign investors to invest in India. Thus labour-intensive manufacturing production process has a negative relationship with FDI inflows.

### *(xiii) Gross Fiscal Deficit*

High gross fiscal deficit in the face of high unplanned expenditure would be a cause for worry as it tends to vitiate macroeconomic environment. Gross fiscal deficit has a negative relationship with the flow of foreign direct investment.

### *(xiv) Regime Shift*

The regime shift undoubtedly helped to sharply increase foreign direct investment flows into the country. The reforms in India have helped remove the entry barriers. With the liberalisation process, an exit policy also helps foreign firms to enter into India. But FDI regime in India is still quite restrictive.

### *(xv) Degree of Transnationalization of Production*

The degree of transnationalization of production means the extent to which exchange of capital takes place for purposes of production. This means as degree of transnationalization increases, inflow of FDI also increases.

### *(xvi) Social and Political Stability*

Social and political stability is one of the major determinants of FDI flows into the country. A country with its social and political stability attracts more FDI compare to others.

### *(xvii) Stringent Labour Laws*

Large firms in India are not allowed to retrench or layoff any workers, or close down the unit without the permission of the state government. While the law was enacted to monitor unfair retrenchment and layoff, in effect it has turned out to be a provision to public sector employees. Most importantly, the continuing barrier to the dismissal of unwanted workers in Indian establishments with 100 or more employees paralyses firms in hiring new workers.

### *(xviii) Lack of Decision-Making*

Lack of decision-making authority with the state

governments is also a hurdle for FDI flows. The reform process so far has mainly concentrated at the central level. India has yet to free up its state governments sufficiently so that they can add much greater dynamism to the reforms.

### *(xix) Archaic Land Laws*

The urban land (ceiling and regulation) act of 1976 prevents enterprises from selling surplus land in major cities without the permission of the state government. It further undermines the rational use of land by specifying an upper limit on the size of landed property that an individual, a group of people, or a company can own. So, archaic land laws prevent free flows of FDI into India.

### *(xx) Lack of Clear-cut Policies*

Lack of clear-cut and transparent sectoral policies for FDI is another deterrent of these flows. Expeditious translation of approved FDI into actual investment would require more transparent sectoral policies, and a drastic reduction in time-consuming red-tapism.

Except the above major determinants of foreign direct investment for India as well as for other developing countries, there are also some other factors which have a negative or positive impacts on FDI. These are : (i) a tradition of prudent fiscal management, (ii) guarantees of their right to repatriate both income and capital, (iii) poor performance of competitiveness, and (iv) corporate tax rates, etc. Now we should discuss the advantages and disadvantages of FDI in the next two sub-sections.

## II.III.III. Advantages of Foreign Direct Investment in India

Capital flows in the form of foreign direct investment have been widely believed to be an important source of growth in recent years. Since the 1970s, imperfections in goods and factor markets, presence of scale economics and government restrictions on output, trade and entry have come to be recognised as creating market structures where foreign capital in the form of FDI contributes to growth. It is eminently plausible that FDI flows might not have existed but for the presence of these imperfections.

The basic reason for increasing FDI flows into the developing countries like India is that it has some advantages for the host economy. These advantages are :

### (i) Growing Source of Finance

FDI could provide a relatively stable and growing source of finance for the host country. FDI flows have tended to be considerably less volatile than other types of capital inflows for middle-and-high income countries. So, FDI becomes a stagnant source of finance and promise a variety of potential benefits to the receipient countries.

### (ii) Filling Savings Gap

FDI viewed as a way of filling gaps between the domestically available supplies of savings, foreign exchanges, government revenues, and human capital and the desired level of these resources necessary to achieve growth and development targets. Thus, FDI involves a capital flow into the host country and thereby it supplements other forms of savings. In the case of joint ventures FDI also results in the mobilisation of domestic savings for productive purposes.

### (iii) Export Promotion

FDI helps to promote exports as the foreign investor would normally be more conversant with foreign markets and would have its own well-established market networks. Sometimes exports are made to the home country i.e., to that country from where the FDI originated. Moreover, FDI promote exports by setting up assembling plants and helping host firms access international markets for exports.

### (iv) Creat Linkages

FDI benefits through production linkages between foreign affiliates and domestic firms. These linkages can be of three forms—backward, forward and horizontal.

(a) *Backward Linkages* : It exist when foreign affiliates acquire goods or services from domestic firms. This improves productivity of local firms.

(b) *Forward Linkages* : It exist when foreign affiliates sell goods or services to domestic firms. This increases the improvement of technology transfer from foreign firms to local firms.

(c) *Horizontal Linkages* : These Linkages involve interactions with domestic firms engaged in competing activities.

Linkages raise output and employment in linked supplier enterprises. Linkages can be powerful channels for diffusing knowledge and skills between firms. Strong linkages can promote production efficiency, productivity growth, technological and managerial capabilities and market diversification in supplier firms. They increase the local integration and 'rooting' of TNCs and make them less footloose.

### *(v) Higher Wages*

Multinational corporations raise employment by establishment of new firms. It finds to pay higher wages than domestic enterprises and can offer valuable training opportunities to workers.

### *(vi) Integrate Countries*

FDI flows provide one mechanism for helping to integrate poorer countries into the global economy. As FDI coming more freely than before, the trade performance between countries now increased day-by-day. This taken the less developed economies coming closer to the industrial countries as world becomes a global village.

### *(vii) Long-term Commitment*

FDI has always been preferred by countries because of its long-term commitment. FDI is less volatile and small powerful hot money than foreign institutional investments (FII) and that is why FDI is more preferable than any other foreign investments now-a-days.

### *(viii) Balances Trade Deficit*

FDI provides the much needed foreign exchange to help bridge the balance of trade deficit. Indeed, in the wake of the debt crisis, FDI has come to be viewed as an increasingly important source of external finance for developing countries.

### (ix) Increase Productivity and Efficiency

The spillover efficiency occurs when advanced technologies and managerial skills embodied in FDI are transmitted to domestic plants simply because of the presence of multinational firms. The productivity of the local firms improves as FDI provide technical assistance to their local suppliers and customers. The competitive pressure exerted by the foreign affiliates may also force local firms to operate more efficiency and introduce new technologies earlier than when would otherwise have been the case.

### (x) Affects Growth

Long-run growth rate depends positively on FDI. FDI affects growth directly, by increasing the stock of physical capital in the recipient economy and indirectly, by inducing human capital development and promoting technological upgrading. The impact of foreign direct investment on growth is expected to be two-fold—through capital accumulation and through knowledge transfers.

### (xi) Protecting Secrecy

Direct investment may be preferred to the granting of a license for a company to produce a product if secrecy is important. A firm can be motivated to choose direct investment over licensing by a feeling that, while a licensee will take precautions to protect patent rights, it may be less conscientious than the original owner of the patent.

### (xii) Two-way Gains of FDI

The expected gains from FDI are in line with the traditional trade proposition are of two-fold. These are: (a) conventional gains that stem from opening up the economy to the flow of capital, thereby allowing a more efficient intertemporal allocation of consumption and investment, and (b) intrinsic gains associated with the superior micro-management by FDI investors.

### (xiii) Low Cost of Product

The Indian consumers also stand to gain from FDI because they get a number of articles of daily use at a relatively low cost. This is because of more competition within the industries itself.

These companies are trying their best to produce at an economic price to provide best after sales service, and again, to produce new brands which are according to the likings of the consumers.

### *(xiv) Managerial Revolution*

FDI kindle a managerial revolution in India through professional management and the employment of highly sophisticated management techniques. This is clear from the point of view that MNCs have a high percentage of their own management staff which is highly qualified and which helps a lot to Indian management stuff too.

### *(xv) Access to Foreign Markets*

Through FDI, India now enter into the world markets. Since 1991, India has been established herself as one of the most accessable economy to the foreign markets. So, through FDI India's access to the world market is more acceptable in these days.

### *(xvi) Raise Domestic Investment*

FDI policies generally take into consideration the conditions that could crowd in domestic investment.

Thus, FDI brings huge advantages with little or no downside in the form of new capital, technology, managerial expertise, and access to foreign markets. Direct investment in India since economic reforms should be actively sought. According to *Dunning's electric theory of international production,* a firm will make a direct investment in a foreign country if the following three conditions are satisfied:

(a) it possesses some ownership advantages *vis-a-vis* firms of other nationalities in serving particular markets;

(b) it is more beneficial for the firm to use the advantages itself than to sell or lease them to foreign firms; and

(c) it is profitable for the enterprise to utilize these advantages in conjunction with at least some factor inputs outside the home country.

The greater the economies of production and marketing favour a foreign location; the greater is the inducement for FDI.

In the next sub-section we discuss some of the harmful effects of FDI for developing countries.

### II.III.IV. Disadvantages of Foreign Direct Investment in India

The Government of India has set on ambitious target in actual FDI inflows a year. In favour of this announcement by India Government, there are lots of international investors who would flock to India, especially now that they see that India has a lot of safety for them compared to other developing countries, for example. These increasing flows of FDI may create some problems for the host economies.

The basic disadvantages of foreign direct investment to India and other developing countries are as follows:

#### *(i) Profit Transferred*

The main harmful effect of FDI is that national Research and Development (R & D) becomes unprofitable. This implies that profits are transferred to foreigners and that nationals lose the opportunity to invest.

#### *(ii) Decrease National Welfare*

Foreign direct investment may decrease national welfare due to the transfer of profits to foreigners, even when the increase in the rate of growth has a positive effect on welfare. That is, after the opening of the economy to foreign investors, domestic producers will no longer be able to act in the R & D sector. This has a negative effect on national income which decreases the host economy's national welfare.

#### *(iii) Excessive Costs*

Linkages with foreign companies may also involve excessive costs for a host economy even under relatively open conditions. The reason lies in the size and market power of foreign affiliates. Exclusive linkages with large, monopsonistic foreign affiliates can lead to anti-competitive practices and unfair terms and conditions for suppliers.

#### *(iv) Fear of Colonialism*

As the flows of FDI coming in maximum numbers to the developing countries, the fear of colonialism rises. FDI in India are mainly coming from industrially developed and powerful countries. If they enter into all sectors of the economy, local firms may be dominated and ruined by the foreign firms very soon.

### *(v) Recurring Constraint*

FDI results in the import of raw materials and spare parts and thus causes a recurring constraint on the limited foreign exchange resources of host countries. Sometimes, it does not result in significant exports to offset the import burden. Used machinery has been shipped from the headquarters plant, which does not result in any technological gain to the host country.

### *(vi) Biased Against Domestic Manufactures*

It is argued that often import protection and export subsidies have to be provided to a foreign invested enterprise to keep it finally viable. This causes further distortions and often bias against domestic manufacturers. Firms may strike considerable linkages in protected industries in which there are inadequate incentive to invest in technological capabilities. Then there is a difference between judicious, highly selective and temporary protection to foster technological learning and open-ended protection to firms—domestic or foreign—that deters learning and upgrading.

### *(vii) Political Trouble*

Political trouble has followed FDI where it has come predominantly from one home country and the host country has been merely the recipient of foreign investment without any other major benefits.

### *(viii) Less Beneficial for Economic Development*

The entry of FDI through the takeover of domestic firms is less beneficial for economic development. At the heart of these concerns is that foreign acquisitions so not add to the productive capacity but simply transfer ownership and control from domestic to foreign hands. It is also feared that such acquisitions may reduce competition in domestic markets.

### *(ix) Less Important Vehicle*

Foreign investors can be deemed to select the technologies

embodied in FDI-related capital accumulation depending on specific productive and institutional characteristics of the recipient economy. In this case, FDI may be a less important vehicle for cross-border knowledge transfers and the elimination of technological gaps between leaders and followers than previously thought.

***(x) Endogeneity Problems***

The cross-country regressions faced endogeneity problems. The correlation between FDI and growth rate could arise from an endogenous determination of FDI, i.e., FDI itself may be influenced by innovations in the stochastic process governing growth rates.

For the above disadvantages of FDI, economies may (i) be less efficient in the use of the new technologies embodied in FDI-related capital accumulation, (ii) have difficulty to assimilate capital and technology-intensive improvements, or (iii) that the latter are not much more modern or productive than the ones existing in the recipient economy.

## II.IV. EVALUATION OF FOREIGN DIRECT INVESTMENT IN INDIA : AN OVERVIEW

On the eve of launching the National Economic Reforms in July 1991, India was faced with a host of acute economic problems. These problems includes possibility of defaulting on international commitments or losing of access to external credit markets, rising current account deficit, falling rate of economic growth, high inflationary pressures, depletion of foreign currency reserves, scarcities of essential commodities and breakdown of fiscal discipline. The problems above are apparent from the basic data on the Indian economy around 1991, as published in the various pre-budget economic surveys of the Government of India.

For instance, the falling economic growth was evident in the declining size and annual growth of GDP at factor cost and constant prices (1980-81 prices) from 10.60 per cent during 1988-89 to 5.40 per cent during 1990-91 and further to 0.80 per cent during 1991-92.[1] This falling trend in the annual growth was also witnessed in trade sector in GDP with a drastic decline from 7 per cent during 1988-89 to 2.30 per cent in 1991-92.[2] The overall decline in the growth of many sectors of the economy on the eve of the reforms was also reflected in the sharp fall in the annual growth of per capita income. For instance, the annual growth of per capita income which stood at 8.45 per cent during 1988-89, fell to just 3 per cent in 1990-91 and dipped even further to become negative at –1.08 per cent in 1991-92.[3]

In addition, gross domestic saving as percentage of GDP also shows a declining trend from 23.1 in 1990-91 to 22.5 in 1993-94. So far as the gross domestic capital formation as a percentage of GDP was concerned, this also declined from 26.3 in 1990-91 to 23.1 in 1993-94. The figures also reveal that public sector savings as a percentage of gross domestic savings had declined from 2.0 per cent during 1988-89 to 1.0 per cent in 1990-91.[4]

Moreover, the performance of the external sector was equally poor. There was a steep fall in the annual growth of both exports and imports. The annual growth of exports in million US$ was negative (–1.50 per cent) during 1991-92 as compared to 15.60 per cent in 1988-89. Similarly, the annual growth of total imports in million US $ which were 13.60 per cent in 1988-89, but showed a negative rate of –19.40 per cent during 1991-92.[5] As a consequence, total current deficit as a percentage of total GDP increased from 2.30 per cent during 1988-89 to 3.20 per cent in 1990-91.[6]

Thus, the problems confronted by the national economy on the eve of the reforms had their origin in almost all the sectors. Consequently, the reforms had to be formulated and implemented to open-up foreign direct investment in the Indian economy for all-round development of the national economy. Here we shall discuss the policies taken by Indian government for foreign direct investment since independence in the next points.

### II.IV.I. Policy Review on FDI : Since Independence

Since independence, the policy on foreign investment was formulated essentially within the broad ambit of industrial policy as embodied in the Industrial Policy Resolutions. As stated in the Prime Minister's statement in the Parliament in 1949, the foreign investment policy would be based on the principles of effective Indian control, non-discrimination, giving opportunities to foreign investors to remit their return on foreign investment and fair compensation in the event of nationalisation. The Industrial Policy Resolution of 1948 acknowledged the need for foreign capital to supplement the domestic savings in financing higher levels of investment. However, it advocated an effective Indian control over the management of such foreign capital to ensure its regulation in the national interest.

Till seventies, the Government of India's approach towards FDI was based on three principal regulations, viz., the Industrial Development and Regulation Act (IDRA, 1951); the Monopolies and Restrictive Trade Practices Act (MRTPA, 1969); and the Foreign Exchange Regulation Act (FERA, 1973). IDRA provided for an elaborate licensing system for establishment of new industrial units or expansion of existing units. Towards the end of the third Annual Plan in the late sixties, there was an acute pressure on the external payment situation.

During 1970s, the Government gave effect to MRTPA to ensure against concentration of economic power and restrictive trade practices. FERA was designed to control foreign investment and restrict the operation of foreign companies in India like limiting the participation of foreign companies' up to 40 percent of paid-up capital. This policy brought in its wake a highly regulated policy frame as regards, among other things, management of foreign capital. Further, a process of Indianisation was introduced in the sense that these companies were required to dilute their non-resident shareholding within two years to the levels prescribed by the Reserve Bank, which was placed generally at 40 per cent. However, companies involved in export activities, manufacturing activities involving sophisticated technology, skills are exempted from this dilution clause. These companies were allowed foreign share holding up to 74 per cent. In the Industrial Policy Statement (1977), the regulatory regime was prohibiting foreign collaboration in certain industries, because it was perceived that indigenous technology in these industries had sufficiently developed.

However, during the eighties there was increasing disenchantment with the growth of economy marked by inefficiency, low productivity, and technological obsolescence attributed to the dirigistic model of industrialisation pursued till then. This led to policy re-orientations focused on 'growth with productivity' marked by a touch of liberalisation and half-hearted opening up of the economy to the external world. In view of the weakening of balance of payments position and in the context of the emerging new international situation, where foreign capital markets have begun to play critical role in flow of resources, foreign investment policy was revised in the early 1980s to encourage direct and portfolio investment by NRIs/OCBs and investors in Oil Exporting Developing Countries (OEDCs), which were flush with funds in the wake of the first oil shock.

Normally, where the required foreign technology was of a highly sophisticated nature or where the project was predominantly export-oriented, foreign equity participation at a higher levels was considered on merits of each case. Policies relating to foreign investment introduced in 1980s were:

### *(A) Direct Investment Policies*

(i) 40 per cent equity on repatriation basis for investments in new issues of new/existing companies in manufacturing sector;

(ii) 100 per cent equity participation in housing and real estate development with a lock-in period of 3 years and a ceiling of 16 per cent on remittable profit;

(iii) *Sick unit scheme* : NRIs/OCBs are allowed to make investment on repatriation basis up to 100% subject to certain condition like lock-in period of 5 years and the shares of the company should have been quoted below par for 2 years;

(iv) 100% equity participation by NRIs on repatriation basis under the air taxi scheme;

(v) 40 per cent equity participation on repatriation basis in private banks; and

(vi) 100 per cent equity participation on non-repatriation basis in any company, proprietary or partnership concerns engaged in any industrial, commercial or trading activities.

### (B) Portfolio Investment Policies

(i) NRIs/OCBs were allowed to acquire up to 1 per cent of paid-up capital of an Indian company with an aggregate ceiling of 5 per cent for all NRIs/OCBs; and

(ii) Portfolio investment from OEDCs were allowed in new companies engaged in (a) exports, (b) manufacturing activities covered under the Industrial Policy of 1973, (c) hotels, (d) hospitals, and (e) shipping.

Thus, 1980s witnessed a gradual but dissemble sign of easing of restrictions on foreign investment inflows.

### II.IV.II. Pre-reform Policies on FDI in India

Government of India in its pre-budget economic survey in 1989-90 had announced various procedural and related matters in respect of foreign investment. These measures, *inter alia*, included simplification of remittance procedures, equality participation permissible up to 40 per cent (with higher limits for investment in selected areas), exemption from dilution formula, simplified visa and travel regulations, and rationalisation of taxation, exchange control, licensing and rules relating to appointment of foreign technicians, managers, etc. Specially liberal provisions have been made for investment in areas of technology upgradation and exports. A 'Fast Track Mechanism' has also been set-up, from the middle of 1988, for expanding investment from Japan, the UK, the USA, the Federal Rupublic of Germany and France through speedy redressal of matters of policy, procedures and specific problems of foreign investors.

Before 1990, foreign direct investment in India has played only a minor role as a source of external finance. The bulk of foreign capital flows to India is in the form of loans, suppliers' credits, portfolio investment in equity shares, debentures, etc. and also in the form of FDI. As regards the policy relating to FDI, changes have been made from time to time in response to the changing economic environment. A number of procedural simplifications have been introduced in the years 1990-91. The areas of procedural liberalisation include industrial licensing, procedures for collaboration approvals, appointment of directors and technicians, visa requirements, custom procedures, repatriation of funds, etc.

In 1990-91, there has been a grater emphasis on encouragement of increased flow of technology from abroad and more equity participation by foreign companies. With a view to facilitating investments from some of the major investing countries, informal inter-ministerial groups have been set-up. These are popularly known as 'fast track' groups. Under the existing policy, foreign direct investment is generally welcome in areas of hi-tech, sophisticated technologies and substantial exports.

### II.IV.III. FDI Policy in India—In the Beginning of Reforms

Since July 1991, the Government has consistently pursued the objective of attracting larger volumes of foreign investment to augment the resource availability in infrastructural and other critical areas of the economy. A number of policy measures, detailed in the two *Economic Surveys* (1991-92, 1992-93) were taken to attract both direct and portfolio investment from foreign investors. Among the new measures announced include the extension of the rate of tax of 30 per cent in respect of short-term capital gains to the foreign institutional investments (FIIs) and the permission given to foreign brokers to do business in India on behalf of the FIIs. The efforts at mobilising non-debt creating foreign capital inflows have begun to yield results.

Policy towards foreign investment was liberalised in 1991 to permit automatic approval for foreign investment up to 51 per cent equity in 34 industries. The Foreign Investment Promotion Board (FIPB) was also set-up to process applications in cases not covered by automatic approval. During 1992-93 several additional measures were taken to encourage investment flows: FDI, FPI, NRI investment and deposits and investment in global depository receipts. They are given below:

(i) The dividend-balancing condition earlier applicable to foreign investment up to 51 per cent equity is no longer applied except for consumer goods industries.
(ii) Existing companies with foreign equity can raise it to 51 per cent subject to allowed in exploration,

production and refining of oil and marketing of gas. Captive coal mines can also be owned and run by private investors in power.

(iii) NRIs and Overseas Corporate Bodies (OCBs) predominantly owned by them are also permitted to invest up to 100 per cent equity in high priority industries with repatriability of capital and income. NRI investment up to 100 per cent of equity is also allowed in export houses, trading houses, star trading houses, hospitals, EOUs, sick industries, hotels and tourism-related industries and without the right of repatriation in the previously excluded areas of real estate, housing and infrastructure. Foreign citizens of Indian origin are now permitted to acquire house property without the permission of the RBI.

(iv) Disinvestment of equity by foreign investors no longer needs to be at prices determined by the Reserve Bank. It has been allowed at market rates on stock exchanges from 15 September 1992 with permission to repatriate the process of such disinvestments.

(v) India has signed the Multilateral Investment Guarantee Agency Protocol for the protection of foreign investment on 13 April 1992.

(vi) Foreign companies have been allowed to use their trade marks on domestic sales from 14 May 1992.

(vii) Provisions of the Foreign Exchange Regulation Act (FERA) have been liberalised through the ordinance dated 9 January 1993 as a result of which companies with more than 40 per cent of foreign equity are also now treated on par with fully Indian-owned companies.

### II.IV.IV. FDI Policy in the Reform Phase : 1991 to 2010

In the early part of 1991, India underwent a major macro-economic crisis characterised by high inflation, large fiscal and current account deficits, and an unsustainable burden of domestic and foreign debt. In fact, there was a steep fall in foreign exchange reserves to about US $1 billion hardly sufficient to meet two week's imports, and a sharp downgrading of India's credit rating.

The sweeping structural reforms brought in by the Government of India during 1991 were in response to this macro-economic instability. The reforms were intended to accomplish a fundamental transformation in the Indian economic structure, push up the growth process and to integrate national economy with the global economic system. Structural Adjustment Programme (SAP), among other things, comprised major policy initiatives partaining to foreign investment as well as foreign technology agreements. This indicated a significant departure with the earlier policy paradigm governing inward FDI. The rationale for such a policy approach was that India can not afford to shackle foreign investment without losing the benefits of additional capital, technology, market access and growth that have been to successfully harnessed by its neighbours in East Asia. These liberalisation measures embodied in the New Economic Policy, were followed up in later years by a series of policy measures further liberalising the inward FDI policy regime.

As a part of the structural adjustment policies introduced in 1991, in the wake of a sharp external payments crisis, policies relating to foreign investment and foreign technology agreements were radically changed. A new foreign investment policy was put in place which stipulated, three tiers for approving proposals for FDI in the country, viz. (i) Reserve Bank of India's automatic approval system, (ii) Secretariat for Industrial Approvals (SIA) for proposals falling outside the powers delegated to the RBI, and (iii) the Foreign Investment Promotion Board (FIPB), specially created to invite, negotiate and facilitate substantial foreign investment.

### *(i) RBI's Automatic Approval System*

The existing companies in India with foreign equity participation wishing to increase it to 51 per cent will be granted automatic approvals provided (a) the expansion programme is in the high priority industries listed in the Industrial Policy Statement 1991, and (b) the cost of import of capital goods is covered by foreign equity. Earlier a dividend balancing clause was also in force, under which any outflow on account of dividend payments needed to we balanced by the export earnings of items over a period of 7 years from the commencement of commercial production. However, the clause was dropped in June 1992 except in the case of 22 consumer goods industries. Automatic permission will be granted for foreign technology agreements in high priority industries subject to certain conditions.

***(ii) Secretariat for Industrial Approvals (SIA)***

Proposals within the general policy framework but outside the powers delegated to the RBI would be considered by the Secretariat for Industrial Approvals.

***(iii) Foreign Investment Promotion Board (FIPB)***

Foreign Investment Promotion Board was specially created to invite, negotiate and facilitate substantially large investment by international companies that would provide access to high technology and world markets.

Foreign Institutional Investors (FIIs) such as pension funds, etc. are permitted to invest in Indian stock markets. Such investment will be subject to a ceiling of 24 per cent of the issued share capital of a company for all FIIs put together. An individual FII can invest up to 10 per cent.

In 1995, a Working Group[7] was set-up to examine the existing schemes and incentives available to NRIs for investment in India and make recommendations for attracting larger NRI investment. The Group has made various recommendations, some of which are mentioned below:

(i) Abolition of 40 per cent scheme on repatriation basis and merger of areas available for NRIs under the scheme with those available under 100 per cent repatriation schemes;

(ii) Abolution of lock-in period and ceiling on remittable profits with respect to investment in housing and real estate;

(iii) *Sick units schems* : Abolition of lock-in period of 5 years and the stipulation that shares should have been quoted at below par for 2 years;

(iv) Removal of sectoral restrictions on direct investment by NRIs/OCBs; and

(v) Increase of individual NRI/OCB ceiling to 5 per cent and doing away with the requirement of general body approval for aggregate ceiling of 24 per cent.

Some of the recommendations of the Working Group have been implemented. They are:

(a) OCBs are allowed to sell/transfer shares/bonds/debentures of Indian companies acquired with repatriation benefits through stock exchange under the portfolio investment schemes.
(b) Foreign investors are allowed to disinvest equity shares through stock exchanges in India.
(c) Permission is also granted to foreign investors for disinvestment of listed equity shares through private placement subject to certain stipulations.
(d) Restrictions relating to the 5 year lock-in period for issue of equity shares on preferential basis are removed except in those cases where preferential issue of securities is in favour of promoters.

Thus, the period from 1947 to 2010 had four phases: (a) from independence to the emergence of crisis in the late 1960s (1947-66), which was marked by a cautious approach to foreign capital, (b) from 1967 till the second oil shock in 1979, characterised by a highly regulated regime, (c) from 1979 to 1990 with progressive attention of regulations, and (d) the first two decades of the reform periods 1991 to 2010, signifying liberal foreign investment environment.

### II.IV.V. Foreign Investment Promotion Board

The Government of India has set-up a special Board known as the Foreign Investment Promotion Board (FIPB) in 1991. This specially empowered Board in the office of the Prime Minister is the only agency dealing with matters relating to FDI as well as promoting investment into the country. It is chaired by the secretary of industry (Department of Industrial Policy and Promotion).

(a) *Objective of FIPB :* Its objective is to promote FDI into India by undertaking investment promotion activities in India and abroad by facilating investment in the country through international companies, non-resident Indians and other foreign investors.

(b) *Clearance of Proposals* : Early clearance of proposals submitted to it through purposeful negotiation and discussion with potential investors. Reviewing policy and put in place appropriate institutional arrangements, transparent rules and procedures and guidelines for investment promotion and approvals. The Foreign Investment Promotion Board is expected to meet every week to ensure quick disposal of the cases pending before it. It endeavours to ensure that the Government's decisions on FDI proposals are communicated to the applicant within six weeks. Foreign investment proposals received by the board's secretariat should be put up to the Board within 15 days of receipt and the Administrative Ministers must offer their comments either prior to and/or in the meeting of the FIPB. It would function as a transparent effective and investor-friendly single window providing clearance for investment proposals.

(c) *Functions of FIPB* : Foreign Investment Promotion board is functioning :

(i) to ensure expeditious clearance of the proposals for foreign investment;

(ii) to review periodically implementation of the proposals cleared by the Board;

(iii) to review, on a continuance basis, the general and sectoral policy regimes relating to FDI and in consultation with the Administrative Ministers and other concerned agencies, evolve a set of transparent guidelines for facilitating foreign investment in various sectors;

(iv) to interact with the Industry Association/Bodies and other concerned government and non-governmental agencies on relevant issues in order to facilitate increased inflow of FDI;

(v) to undertake investment promotion activities including establishment of contact with and inviting selected international companies to invest in India in the appropriate projects; and

(vi) to interact with the Foreign Investment Promotion Council (FIPC) being constituted separately in the Ministry of Industry.

## II.IV.VI. India's Regulatory Environment for Inward FDI, 1991-2010

| *Year* | | *Description of Measures Adopted/Industries Liberalised* |
|---|---|---|
| 1991 | : | Abolishment of mandatory licensing system. |
| | : | Opening of areas previously closed to foreign investors including power generation. |
| | : | Establishment of Foreign Investment Promotion Board. |
| 1992 | : | Movement of partial convertibility of rupee (current account). |
| | : | Adoption of Export-Import Policy, involving a phased reduction of both tariffs and quotas. |
| 1993 | : | Full ownership allowed in certain industries previously closed to or restricted for foreign investors. |
| | : | Adoption of national treatment principle. |
| | : | Partial opening of financial industry to FDI. |
| | : | Rupee becomes fully convertible (current account). |
| 1994 | : | Telecommunications industry opened to FDI. |
| 1995 | : | Cable television network opened to FDI. |
| | : | A Working Group set-up for examination of schemes and incentives available to NRIs for investment in India, some of whose recommendations have been implemented subsequently. |
| 1997 | : | Expansion of scope of automatic approval route. |
| | : | Increase in foreign equity participation from 51 to 74 per cent under automatic approval (100 per cent in case of NRIs). |
| 1998 | : | 100 percent foreign equity allowed in several infrastructural areas under the automatic route, subject to a ceiling of Rs. 1500 crores. |
| 1999 | : | GDR/ADR guidelines further liberalised. |
| | : | Establishment of Foreign Investment Implementation Authority (FIIA) to expedite approvals as well as implementation of foreign investments. |
| | : | Opening up of domestic private insurance sector to foreign investment. |

2000 : Reduction of the negative list to a limited number of industries.

: Permission to 100 per cent foreign investment in film industry.

: Fixation of upper limit for foreign equity participation at 74 per cent in advertising sector.

: Hydrocarbon industry— specially, refining sector has been allowed for 100 per cent FDI, against existing limit of 49 per cent.

: Adoption of exim policy 2000-01 providing for, *inter alia*, scrapping of quantitative restrictions on import of 714 items, and introduction of a scheme of Special Economic Zones (SEZs).

: Permission of 100 per cent in IT industry.

2001 : Permission of FDI up to 100 per cent for development of integrated townships, including housing, commercial premises, hotels, resorts, city and regional level urban infrastructure facilities such as roads and bridges, mass rapid transit system and manufacture of building materials.

: Allow private sector participation up to 100 per cent in the defence industry with FDI permissible up to 26 per cent.

: FDI up to 49 per cent from all sources is permitted in private sector banks under the automatic route.

2002 : Reserve Bank permitted reinvested earnings with equity capitals as part of FDI in India.

2003 : Other capital also came into the account of FDI to ensure global status and parity in foreign investments.

2004 : India has experienced floods and sudden stops of capital flows.

2005 : Followed a consistent policy on allowing capital inflows in general and on capital account management in particular.

2006 : Net private financial flows to emerging and developing economies increased in the first half and then declined.

2007 : Global meltdown occurs worldwide due to price hike in steel ore and impact foreign investment badly.

: At the height of the global financial crisis net private financial flows declined.

2008 : The resumption of capital flows has triggered familiar concerns in EMEs about macro-economic and financial stability.

2009 : Sparked off a vigorous debate internationally on the policy approach to capital flows at the country level and at the international level.

2010 : There is a ceiling on the FII investment in sovereign and corporate debt (quantity variable) and there is also a withholding tax (price variable).

: The rupee appreciated by 13 per cent in nominal terms but by as much as 19 per cent in real terms because of the inflation differential between India and her trading partners.

: Large capital inflows lead to currency appreciation unrelated to fundamentals and trigger a 'Dutch Disease' syndrome for Indian economy.

### II.IV.VII. Liberalisation of FDI Norms in India

On September 10, 2000, the Government further liberalised on FDI norms, permitting 100 per cent FDI in special economic zones and some telecom sector activities. In the liberalised regime, off-shore venture capital funds and companies have been allowed to invest in domestic venture capital understanding. It provides for a review of the existing sectoral policy and sectoral equity cap for FDI and investment by NRIs and Overseas Corporate Bodies (OCBs).

FDI up to 100 percent is allowed through the automatic route for all manufacturing activities in special economic zones expect for certain categories. These include arms and ammunition, explosives and allied items of defence equipments, defence aircraft and warships, atomic substances, narcotics and psychotropic substances, hazardous chemicals, distillation and brewing alcoholic drinks, cigarettes, cigars and manufactured tobacco substitutes.

FDI upto 100 per cent has been allowed in the telecom sector for ISPs not providing gateways (both for satellite and submarine cables), infrastructure provides dark fiber electronic mail, and voice mail. FDI up to 100 per cent is for what subject to the condition that such companies would divest 26 per cent of their equity in favour of Indian public in five years if these companies are listed in other parts of the world. Moreover, these services would be subject to licensing and security requirements wherever required. The proposals for FDI beyond 49 per cent shall be considered by FIPB on case to case basis. Payment of royalty up to two per cent for exports and one per cent of domestic sales is allowed under automatic route on use of trade-marks and brand name of the foreign collaborator without technology transfer.

Payment of royalty up to 8 per cent on exports and 5 per cent on domestic sales by wholly-owned subsidiaries to offshore parent companies is allowed under the automatic route, without any restriction on the duration of royalty payments. The offshore venture capital funds and companies are allowed to invest in domestic venture. Capital undertaking as well as other companies through the automatic route, subject only to SEBI regulations and sector-specific caps on FDI.

### *(a) FDI in the Banking Sector*

The norms relating to FDI in the Indian banking sector are governed by the overall foreign investment policy as well as guidelines laid down by the Reserve Bank under various statutory provisions. Limit for FDI under Automatic Route in Private Sector Banks are :

(i) FDI upto 49 per cent from all sources is permitted in private sector banks under the automatic route, subject to conformity with the guidelines issued by the Reserve Bank from time to time.

(ii) Initial Public Offerings (IPOs), private placements, ADRs/GDRs and acquisition of shares from existing shareholders are included for the purpose of determining the above mentioned FDI ceiling under the automatic route.

(iii) Issue of fresh shares under the automatic route is not available to those foreign investors who have a financial or technical collaboration in the same or allied field. This category of investors requires FIPB approval.

(iv) The automatic route is not applicable to transfer of existing shares in a banking company from residents to non-residents. This category of investors requires approval of FIPB, followed by 'in principle' approval of the Reserve Bank. The 'fair price' for transfer of existing shares is determined by the Reserve Bank, broadly on the basis of SEBI guidelines for listed shares and the erstwhile Controller of Capital Issues (CCI) guidelines for unlisted shares. After receipt of 'in principle' approval, the resident seller can receive funds and apply to the Reserve Bank for obtaining final permission for transfer of shares.

(v) Under the Insurance Act, the maximum foreign investment in an insurance company has been fixed at 26 per cent. Application for foreign investment in banks which have joint venture/subsidiary in insurance sector should be made to the Reserve Bank. Such applications will be considered by the Reserve Bank in consultation with Insurance Regulatory and Development Authority (IRDA).

(vi) Foreign banks having branch presence in India are eligible for FDI in the private sector banks subject to the overall cap of 49 per cent with the approval of the Reserve Bank.

### *(b) FDI in the Development of Township*

Government permitted FDI upto 100 per cent for development of integrated townships, including housing, commercial premises, hotels, resorts, city and regional level urban infrastructure facilities such as roads and bridges, mass rapid transit systems and manufacture of building materials. Development of land and providing allied infrastructure will form an integrated part of township's development.

FDI in the development of integrated township will be subject to the following guidelines:

(i) The foreign company intending to invest, shall be registered as an Indian Company under Companies, Act 1956 and will henceforth be allowed to take up land assembly and its development as a part of

Integrated Township Development. These cases would be processed by FIPB under the exclusive cell of Ministry of Urban Development and Poverty Alleviation.

(ii) Once their proposal has been approved, the investing foreign company should achieve clear milestones.

(iii) A minimum lock-in period of three years from completion of minimum capitalisation shall apply before repatriation of original investment is permitted.

(iv) US $10 million for a wholly owned subsidiary and US $5 million for joint ventures with Indian partners shall be the minimum capitalisation norm. The funds would have to be brought in upfront.

(v) The core business of the company should be integrated township development with a record of successful execution of such projects seeking to make investment elsewhere.

(vi) The developer will retain the lands for community services such as (a) schools, (b) shopping complex, (c) ration shop, (d) hospital/dispensary, and (e) community centres. These services will be developed by developer himself and shall be made operational before the houses are occupied.

(vii) Land with assembled area for peripheral services such as police stations, milk booths will be handed over free of cost to the Government/local authority/agency as the case may be.

### *(c) FDI in the Production of Arms and Ammunitions*

In the defence industry foreign direct investment has been permitted up to 26 per cent out of 100 per cent private sector participation. The guidelines for licensing production of arms and ammunitions are :

(i) In consultation with Ministry of Defence, license applications will be considered by the Department of Industrial Policy and Promotion, Ministry of Commerce and Industry.

(ii) In consultation with Ministry of Defence, cases involving FDI will be considered by the FIPB and licenses given by the Department of Industrial Policy and Promotion.

(iii) Indian companies/partnership firms are eligible to apply for the production of arms and ammunities.

(iv) For the FDI, there would be no minimum capitalization. A proper assessment, however, needs to be done by the management of the applicant company depending upon the product and the technology.

(v) It is not possible for all the time to give purchase guarantee for products to be manufactured by the Ministry of Defence.

(vi) Import of equipment for pre-production activity including development of prototype by the applicant company would be permitted.

(vii) Government decision on applications to FIPB for FDI in defence industry sector will be normally communicated within a time frame of 10 weeks from the date of acknowledgment by the Secretariat for Industrial Assistance in the Department of Industrial Policy and Promotion.

### *(d) Ceiling on FDI Lifted*

On July 17, 2000, the Government issued formal notifications, bringing into force decisions taken by the cabinet to liberalise the country's FDI regime. This includes lifting the Rs. 1500 crore ceiling on FDI in power sector, allowing 100 per cent owned companies to be set-up for e-commerce activities, withdrawing the dividend-balancing clause for 22 consumer industries, and permitted FDI in the petroleum refinery sector.

The Government, after a review of the FDI policy, decided to bring about the following policy changes:

(i) FDI up to 100 per cent will be allowed for e-commerce activities. This is subject to the condition that such companies would divest 26 per cent of their equity in favour of the Indian public in five years, if these companies are listed in other parts of the world.

Further, these companies would engage only in business to business (B2B) e-commerce and not in retail trading, implying the existing restrictions on FDI in domestic trading would be applicable to e-commerce as well.

(ii) It has been decided with immediate effect, to remove the condition of dividend-balancing on 22 consumer goods industries.

(iii) In view of the growing demand for power in the country and the need for more investment in this sector, the government as part of further libealisation of FDI regime, has decided to remove the upper limit for FDI in respect of projects relating to electric generation, transmission and distribution, other than atomic reactor power plants.

(iv) The government has decided to increase the level of FDI in oil refining sector under automatic route from existing 49 per cent to 100 per cent.

### II.IV.VIII. New FDI Norms

Union Government gave its nod to 100 per cent FDI for the development of integrated townships, including housing on January 4, 2009. It includes commercial premises, city and regional-level urban infrastructural facilities like roads and bridges, hotels, resorts, mass rapid transit systems and manufacture of building materials.

The following are the highlights of the new FDI norms:

(i) Minimum capitalisation norm at US$10 million for wholly-owned subsidiary and US$5 million for joint ventures.

(ii) A minimum lock-in period of three years from completion of minimum capitalisation.

(iii) Minimum area to be developed should be 100 acres.

(iv) Foreign company to be registered as an Indian company.

(v) Such FDI cases to be processed by FIPB.

(vi) Minimum of 50 per cent of integrated project development to be completed within a period of five years from possession date.

(vii) Investors to be responsible for developing internal and peripheral development, infrastructure facilities, layout plan.

(viii) Land with assembled area for peripheral services to be handed over free of cost of the government/local authority.

(ix) Community services to be retained by developer who will develop and will be operational before occupied.

(x) FIPB may exempt conditions for companies investing in special economic zones.

(xi) Intending company must have record of successful execution of such projects elsewhere.

(xii) Investor should achieve clear milestone after approval.

(xiii) FIPB to decide in case investor intends to exit the project.

## II.V. SUMMARY AND CONCLUSION

This chapter provides with a brief introduction to the situation of foreign direct investment in India. Throughout this chapter are discussed the different forms of foreign direct investment and its main determinants for all developing countries including India. The main advantages and disadvantages of foreign direct investment in India and also in other developing countries have been analyzed in the chapter.

In the context of India it is hypothesized that FDI flows into the country are determined by the analyzed factors. Out of these determinants, some have positive and some factors have negative impacts with Indian economy. Accordingly, a composite indicator has been arrived at by giving weight to each indicator inverse to its mean, and the resultant indicator is expected to retain the negative impact.

In the next two sections, we have discussed the potential gains and harmful effects of foreign direct investment in India. If positive effects are permanent, while the negative effects are transitory, then as unprofitable firms exit, the negative productivity effects could decline. The productive advantage of foreign ownership might increase the stock of human capital if domestic workers absorb this advantage through training and learning-by-doing.

## End Notes

1. Annual growth of GDP at 1980-81 prices in 1981-82 was 6.0. In 1988-89 it was 10.5, 5.6 in 1990-91, in 1995-96 it was 7.3 but again decreased to 5.2 in 2000-01 and 5.3 in 2001-02. These figures are revised at 1993-94 prices. See *Statistical Outline of India 2001-02,* Tata Services Limited, p. 11.
2. Trade performance includes both import and exports. The percentage change in exports in 1981-82 was 2.6. In 1989-90 it increased to 15.6 but decreased to 9.2 in 1990-91 and again increased to 20.9 in 1995-96. This trend regained in 2000-01 with 20.4. The case for import, in 1981-82 was 4.4, in 1989-90 it was 8.8 but rose to 13.5 in 1990-91. In 1995-96 it reached a high of 28.0 but felled to 0.2 in 2001-02. See *Statistical Outline of India, 2001-02,* Tata Services Limited, p. 12 and 88.
3. For per capita income at factor cost see *Statistical Outline of India, 2001-02,* Tata Services Limited, pages 5 and 15. Data shows that per capita income had a low rate of growth in Rs. 1741 in 1980-81 to Rs. 5365 in 1990-91, but since then it increase sharply to Rs. 10,160 in 1995-96 and Rs. 17,188 in 2000-01.
4. Gross domestic saving as percentage of GDP in 1980-81 was 18.9. In 1990-91 it rose to 23.1, in 1995-96 it was 25.1 but declined to 22.3 in 1999-2000. And in case of gross domestic capital formation as percentage of GDP in 1980-81 was 20.3 but rose to 26.3 in 1990-91. In 1995-96 it was 26.8 but declined to 23.3 in 1999-2000. For further details see *Statistical Outline of India, 2001-02,* Tata Service Limited, pp. 24-27.
5. *Statistical Outline of India, 2001-02,* Tata Services Limited, PP. 12 an 88.
6. Current deficit in 1990-91 was Rs. 7215 crores but in 1999-2000 it increased to Rs. 67,596 crores and in 2000-01 it is Rs. 77,370 crores. Fiscal deficit as percentage of GDP in 1990-91 was 8.3 and decreased to 4.1 in 1995-96, 5.4 in 1999-2000 and 5.1 in 2000-01. For more details see pages 194, 196 and 202 of *Statistical Outline of India 2001-02,* Tata Services Limited.
7. Working Group for examination of the schemes and incentives available to NRIs for investment in India (Chairman Shri O.P. Sodhani).
8. Dunning, J.H. (1988), *Explaining International Production,* Union Hyman, London. It explains both the ways in which overseas markets are served by enterprises of different nationalities and the industrial and geographical composition of such activities.

## References

Aitken, Brian J. and Ann E. Harrison (1999), "Do Domestic Firms Benefit from Direct Foreign Investment? Evidence from Venezuella", *American Economic Review,* Vol. 89, No. 3, June, pp. 605-18.

Baldwin, Richard E. and Gianmarco I.P. Ottaviano (2001), "Multi-product Multinationals and Reciprocal FDI Dumping", *Journal of International Economics*, Vol. 54, No. 2, August, pp. 429-48.

Branstetter, Lee G. and Robert C. Feenstra (2002), Trade and Foreign Direct Investment in China: A Political Economy Approach, *Journal of International Economics*, Vol. 58, No. 2, December, pp. 335-58.

De Mello, Luiz Jr. (1999), "Foreign Direct Investment-led Growth: Evidence From Time Series and Panel Data", *Oxford Economic Papers*, Vol. 51, pp. 133-51, Oxford University Press.

Dunning, J.H. (1981), *International Production and Multinational Enterprise*, London: George Allen & Unwin.

GOI, Economic Survey, Various Issues, New Delhi.

IMF (2001), *World Economic Outlook*, World Economic and Financial Surveys, pp. 145-73, October.

Kumar, Nagesh (2000), "Economic Reforms and Their Macro-economic Impact", *Economic and Political Weekly*, Vol. XXXV, No. 10, March 4-10, pp. 803-12.

Pan, S. and Sen, R.K. (2007), *Foreign Direct Investment and Trade in India*, Deep & Deep Publications, New Delhi.

Pan, S. (2008), "FDI and India's External Sector Development", in Raj, F. (ed.): *Indian Economy: Economic Ideas, Development and Financial Reforms*, pp. 200-13, Deep & Deep Publications, New Delhi.

——, (2011), "Is Globalization Reducing Poverty and Inequality in India? A Theoretical Overview ", in R.K. Sen (ed.), *Modern Indian Econocy*, pp. 236-59, Deep & Deep Publications, New Delhi.

Pfeffermann, Guy (1997), Prospects for increasing Foreign Direct Investment in Low-income Countries, in Zubair Iqbal and Ravi Kanbur (eds.): *External Finance for Low-Income Countries*, IMF, pp. 194-232.

Rangarajan, C. (2000), "Capital Flows : Another Look", *Economic and Political Weekly*, Vol. XXXV, No. 50, December 9-15, pp. 4421-27.

RBI (1996), "Census of India's Foreign Liabilities and Assets as on March 31, 1992", *RBI Bulletin*, September, pp. 409-57.

Satyanarayan, B. (1995), "Foreign Direct Investment in LDCs (with Special Referance to India)", *IASSI Quarterly*, Vol. 13, No. 4, April-June, pp. 73-79.

UNCTAD (2001), *World Investment Report, 2001: Promoting Linkages*, United Nations, Bookwele, Delhi.

Zhang, K.H. (2001), "Roads to Prosperity: Assessing the Impact of Foreign Direct Investment on Economic Growth in China", *International Economics*, Vol. LIV, No. 1, February, pp. 113-25.

CHAPTER

# 3

# *Nature and Magnitude of FDI Flows in India*

## III.I. BACKGROUND

India was a latecomer to economic reforms, embarking on the process in earnest only in 1991, in the wake of an exceptionally severe balance of payments crisis. Liberalizing foreign direct investment was one of the important parts of India's reforms. It was driven by the belief that this would increase the total volume of investment in the economy.

The purpose of foreign direct investment is now more clearly defined as being to help countries to attain economic independence at a high rate of growth. This requires positive action on their part, as well as cooperation from the developed countries. Capital inflows in the form of FDI are generally welcome in a developing economy.

FDI inflows are generally considered more permanent in character for India. Since Swamiji's visit to USA in the early nineteenth century, India emerged as a strong destination for FDI investors. In the early decades of twentieth century FDI came to India in a little amount in the form of foreign aid up to 1947 (pre-independence period). Since then the yearly turnover of FDI jointly influenced the Indian economy with FPI (Foreign

Portfolio Investment) up to 1970 (post-independence period). Since 1970s, imperfections in goods and factor markets, presence of scale economies and Indian government restrictions on output, trade and entry have come to be recognized as creating market structures where foreign capital in the form of FDI contributes to growth (pre-reform period) up to 1990. And then came the new economic reforms into Indian economy which embarks a huge amount of FDI to the country (reform period).

Foreign direct investment flows to India are now one of the major macro-economic indicators of growth. In this chapter, we are interested to find out the nature and magnitude of FDI flows (both inflows and outflows) to and from India.

## III.II. PROPOSED COVERAGE OF FDI TO INDIA

In the recent past, there have been discussions in various floras regarding the coverage of foreign direct investment (FDI) statistics in India, which mainly include equity capital, *vis-a-vis* the data published by some other countries which include equity capital, reinvested earnings and other capital.

In an effort to bring the reporting system of FDI data in India into alignment with international best practices, the Department of Industrial Policy and Promotion (DIPP), Ministry of Commerce and Industry, Government of India (GOI), in consultation with the Reserve Bank of India, constituted a committee in May 2002. The Committee comprised officials from the Reserve Bank and the DIPP. The Committee studied the relevant conceptual and methodological issues and identified the data gaps involved in order to make necessary recommendations for strengthening the collection, compilation and reporting FDI data.

The Committee submitted its Report in October 2002 recommending that the FDI statistics should include, besides equity capital, 'reinvested earnings' (retained earnings of FDI companies) and 'other direct capital' (inter-corporate debt transactions between related entities) in accordance with the international best practices. The Committee also recommended that the steps be taken jointly by the Reserve Bank and the DIPP to expand the coverage of FDI statistics in India.

As a follow-up action to the submission of FDI Compilation Report, a Technical Monitoring Group (TMG) was constituted by DIPP in November 2002 for speedy implementation of the recommendations made by the Committee. The TMG had representatives from the Reserve Bank, DIPP, Department of Economic Affairs (DEA), Department of Company Affairs (DCA) and National Informatics Centre (NIC). The main focus of the TMG was to identify various components of FDI, which are operationally feasible and capture their components in a specified institutional framework and within a specified time period. TMG submitted its first Action Taken Report on June 27, 2003.

After reviewing the international best practices as also some select country experiences, the TMG concluded that inclusion of *fourteen* items in Indian FDI data under three major heads would, by and large, comply with the reporting system in line with international best practices. The items were:

**A. Equity Capital**

(1) Equity capital of unincorporated entities;
(2) Non-cash acquisition against technology transfer, plant and machinery, goodwill, business development and similar considerations;
(3) Control premium;
(4) Non-competition fees.

**B. Reinvested Earnings**

(5) Reinvested earnings of incorporated entities;
(6) Reinvested earnings of unincorporated entities;
(7) Reinvested earnings of indirectly held direct investment enterprises.

**C. Other Capital**

(8) Short-term and long-term inter-corporate borrowings;
(9) Trade credit;
(10) Suppliers credit;
(11) Financial leasing;
(12) Financial derivatives;

(13) Debt securities; and
(14) Land and buildings.

Against this background, the Reserve Bank and the DIPP jointly decided to expand the coverage of data on FDI, both inflow and outflow for 2000-01 and 2001-02 and continue. The revised data on FDI include all items indicated under equity capital (except non-cash acquisitions). The equity capital of unincorporated entities includes the equity capital of foreign banks' branches in India. All items under the reinvested earnings have been included except reinvested earnings of indirectly held direct investment enterprises. Data under other capital relate to short-term and long-term borrowing, trade credit (more than 180 days), suppliers' credit (more than 180 days), and financial leasing.

Thus, out of fourteen items, the FDI data do not include the following six items, viz., (i) non-cash acquisitions, (ii) reinvested earnings of indirectly held direct investment enterprises, (iii) short-term trade credit, (iv) financial derivatives, (v) debt securities, and (vi) land and building. The TMG is exploring the feasibility of including these items in future and accepted in the second phase of the first decade of 2000s.

## III.III. PATTERNS OF FOREIGN DIRECT INVESTMENT FLOWS TO EMERGING MARKETS

Over the last century capital flows to emerging markets have followed a boom-bust pattern, notwithstanding the large regional and compositional variations. The major boom in capital flows that started around 1870s continued till the outbreak of the First World War. This was the period of *laissez faire,* marked by significant international flows of goods, labour and capital across nations, mainly directed towards infrastructure, especially utilities and railroads. Most of the foreign investment during this period was long-term with about two-thirds in the form of portfolio flows and the remaining being in the form of direct investment. The weak communication infrastructure and information-base led investors to prefer debt instruments. This is in sharp contrast to the late 20th century scenario when direct investment became extremely important, accounting for more than 50 per cent of the private capital flows in the 1990s. The boom ended with the onset of World War I. The ensuring years (1920-31) saw a modest revival of capital flows, mostly to emerging market economies to meet their development goals.

The period from 1945 to 1972 was marked by large capital flows among different industrialised countries, with capital flowing to emerging markets only at the margin. The period since 1973, however, witnessed different phases:

(a) 1973-82 : boom in capital flows to developing countries averaging at about US $ 163 billion per annum,
(b) 1983-89 : stagnation in capital flows at about US $ 103 billion per annum,
(c) 1990-97 : dramatic surge in capital flows, with the peak of US $ 344 billion in 1997,
(d) 1997-1999 : sharp deceleration in the aftermath of South-East Asian crisis,
(e) 2000-01 : moderate recovery in 2000 but heightened uncertainty amidst global recessionary conditions and tendency for flight to safety, and
(f) 2002-10 : steady business by foreign companies both home and abroad until global meltdown take place in 2007 worldwide.

Capital flows during 1973-82 was associated with the recycling of oil revenues as this was the period of first two oil shocks. Bank loans to developing country governments, firms and banks were the main form of capital flows accounting for almost 57 per cent of total flows. Capital flows to developing economies almost stagnated at around US$ 105-110 billion between 1983 and 1989. By the end of the decade, aggregate FDI flows into developing countries were one-eighth of the flows into developed countries (US$ 18.1 billion as against US$ 161.2 billion). FPI flows were rather limited (practically zero), given the underdeveloped and non-existent nature of developing country equity markets. The disadvantages of contractual foreign capital as opposed to FDI became clearly evident during the external debt crisis of the 1980s. The earlier aversion to FDI—reflected in restrictive national FDI policies stipulating ownership norms, operational restrictions viz., positive, negative and restricted lists, performance requirements viz., export obligation—declined over time. In the competition to attract FDI, a combination of preconditions and incentive package assumed increasing importance in the liberalisation of FDI policy.

The 1990s saw a return of foreign direct investment flows to emerging markets with better economic performance and relatively open capital accounts to the pre-1914 levels. The composition of capital flows, however, altered significantly over time. For the first time since 1982, private flows exceeded official finance in 1991-92 with their share rising from 42.6 per cent in 1990 to a peak of 90.1 per cent in 1996, before dropping to 82.1 per cent in 1999 but further increase to 87.3 per cent in 2001. This also reflected a growing preference on the part of developing countries for non-debt flows. Although portfolio inflows remained important, it is foreign direct investment that showed a six-fold jump from about US $ 35 billion in 1991 to $ 185 billion in 1999. The share of FDI in developing country's GDP rose from around 0.8 per cent to 2.5 per cent over the same period.

The private sector receives more than 65 per cent of the total flows (a trend similar to the 1870-1913 period), unlike the other two period of surges (1920s and 1970s) when the share of the private sector had fallen to around 20 per cent. Asia and Latin America accounted for around 70 per cent of the total flows to emerging markets with Middle East and Sub-Saharan Africa getting a minimal share. FDI occupied the dominant position for Asia while portfolio flows were more significant in Latin America.

It is generally believed that the boom in capital flows of the late 20th century can no way match the degree of integration that prevailed during the gold standard era. As a percentage of the world total, foreign investment in developing economies was 45 per cent in 1914 as against only 22 per cent in 1992 and 29.61 per cent in 2001. Following the financial crisis of 1997, private capital flows to emerging markets declined sharply (specially in case of bank loans, bonds and equity) owing to uncertainty and risk aversion of investors. FDI continued its rising trend in absolute terms, though as a share in global FDI, it increase slightly from 34.2 per cent in 1995 to 39.2 per cent in 2000 and but further decrease to 29.6 per cent in 2009 (Table 3.3).

In developing country, private capital flows saw a modest recovery in 2000 to US$ 257 billion; however, it still remains about 15 per cent below the peak 1997 level. For the first time in over a decade, FDI showed a decline though it still continues to be the dominant component of private capital in all regions. The slowdown in FDI was maximum in Asia and Western Hemisphere reflecting slowdown in mergers and acquisition activity in Asia and completion of large-scale privatisation projects in Latin America. Unlike FDI, FPI flows have shown a rising trend for the past two years reaching US$ 48 billion in 2000. With the growing linkages between emerging markets and US market stock prices, equity flows are guided apparently less by diversification motives and remain concentrated in few countries—particularly Brazil, China, Mexico and Turkey—that received more than 80 per cent of the flows. The future scenario remains uncertain with the absence of any counter cyclical trend in capital flows to emerging markets as in the past.

## III.IV. EVOLUTION OF INDIAN GOVERNMENT'S POLICY TOWARDS FDI SINCE INDEPENDENCE

Foreign direct investment today is seen as an instrument to facilitate and support domestic investment for achieving a higher level of economic development. In this section we briefly review the evolution of India's policy towards FDI over the past five-and-a-half decades. The evolution of India's policy has been observed as follows:

### (a) Early Post-Independence Period (1948-67): Import Protection and Receptive Attitude to FDI

Soon after independence, India embarked on a strategy of import substituting industrialisation in the framework of development planning with a focus on development of local capability in heavy industries including the machinery manufacturing sector. The scope of import substitution extended literally to almost everything that could be manufactured in the country. The domestic industry was accorded considerable protection in the form of high tariffs and quantitative restrictions on imports. In order to channel country's scarce investible resources (the savings rate was just over 10 per cent in 1950) according to plan priorities, an industrial approval (licensing) system was put into place in the country that regulated all industrial investments beyond a certain minimum. A number of key industries were embarked for further development in the public sector either in view of their strategic nature or anticipated lack of initiative in the private sector because of large capital requirements. As a part of the development plans large investments were made in human resources creating activities such as expansion of educational, especially the technical and engineering, facilities and creation of a scientific and technological infrastructure in the form of a network of national and regional laboratories in the country. The government also made investments in development of institutional infrastructure for industrial development such as term lending and capital markets development.

As the domestic base of 'created' assets, viz., technology, skills, entrepreneurship was quite limited, the attitude towards FDI was increasingly receptive. FDI was sought on mutually advantageous terms though the majority local ownership was preferred. Foreign investors were assured of no restrictions on the remittances of profits and dividends, fair compensation in the event of acquisition, and were promised a 'national treatment'. The foreign exchange crisis of 1957-58 led to further liberalisation in the government's attitude towards FDI.

In a bid to attract foreign investment to finance foreign exchange component of projects, a host of incentives and concessions were extended. The protection accorded to local manufacture acted as an important locational advantage encouraging market seeking FDI. A large number of enterprises serving Indian market through exports started establishing manufacturing affiliates in the country. This was the period (late 1950s and early 1960s) when western multinational enterprises started showing real interest in India.

### (b) From 1968 to 1979: Restrictive Attitude to Protect the Domestic Base of 'Created' Assets

Investment made in machinery fabrication facilities,

manpower development, scientific and technological infrastructure made in the previous period had led to development of certain 'created' assets in the country. For instance, certain capabilities for process and product adaptations had been built up in the country. A number of local design engineering and project management consultants had accumulated considerable expertise while acting as sub-contractors for western prime consultants. A considerable plant fabrication capability had been built up in the country. A number of local design engineering and project management consultants had accumulated considerable expertise while acting as sub-contractors for western prime consultants.

In this period, locally available skills and capabilities needed some sort of infant industry protection as these were not able to stand competition from more established industrialized country sources. Constraints on local supply of capital and entrepreneurship had begun to ease somewhat. On the other hand, outflow on account of remittances of dividends, profits, royalties, and technical fees, etc., abroad on account of servicing of FDI and technology imports from the earlier period had grown sharply and had become a significant proportion of the foreign exchange account of the country.

These factors prompted the government to streamline the procedures for foreign collaboration approvals and adopt a more restrictive attitude towards FDI. Restrictions were put on proposals of foreign direct investments unaccompanied by technology transfer and those seeking more than 40 per cent foreign ownership. The government listed industries in which FDI was not considered desirable in view of local capabilities. The permissible range of royalty payments and duration of technology transfer agreements with parent companies were also specified for different items. The guidelines evolved for foreign collaborations required exclusive use of Indian consultancy services wherever available.

The renewals of foreign collaboration agreements were restricted. From 1973 onwards the further activities of foreign companies (along with those of local large industrial houses) were restricted to a select group of core or high priority industries. In the same year a new Foreign Exchange Regulation

Act (FERA) came into force which required all foreign companies operating in India to register under Indian corporate legislation with up to 40 per cent foreign equity. Exceptions from the general limit of 40 per cent were made only for companies operating in high priority or high technology sectors, tea plantations, or those producing predominantly for exports.

### (c) The 1980s : Cautious Deregulation

Towards the end of the 1970s India's failure to significantly step up the volume and proportion of her manufactured exports in the background of the second oil price shock began to worry the policy-makers. It led to the realisation that international competitiveness of Indian goods had suffered from growing technological obsolescence and inferior product quality, limited range, and high cost which in turn were due to the highly protected local market. Another limiting factor for Indian manufactured exports lay in the fact that marketing channels in the industrialised countries were substantially dominated by MNEs. The government intended to deal with the situation by putting emphasis on the modernisation of industry with liberalised imports of capital goods and technology, exposing the Indian industry to foreign competition by gradually liberalising the trade regime, and assigning a greater role to MNEs in the promotion of manufactured exports. This strategy was reflected in the policy pronouncements that were made in the 1980s.

These covered liberalisation of industrial licensing (approval) rules, a host of incentives, and exemption from foreign equity restrictions under FERA to 100 per cent export-oriented units. Four more export processing zones (EPZ) were set-up in addition to the two existing ones, namely, those at Kandla (set-up in 1965) and at Santacruz (set-up in 1972) to attract MNEs to set-up export-oriented units. The trade policies gradually liberalised the imports of raw materials and capital goods by gradually expanding the list of items on the Open General License (OGL). During 1984-85 alone, 150 items and 200 types of capital goods were added to OGL list. Tariffs on imports of capital goods were also slashed. Imports of designs and drawings and capital goods were permitted under a liberalised Technical Development Fund Scheme (TDFS).

By an increasingly receptive attitude towards FDIs and foreign licensing collaborations, the liberalisation of industrial and trade policies was accompanied. Approval systems were streamlined. A degree of flexibility was introduced in the policy concerning foreign ownership, and exceptions from the general ceiling of 40 per cent on foreign equity were allowed on the merits of individual investment proposals. The rules and procedures concerning payments of royalties and lump sum technical fees were relaxed and withholding taxes were reduced.

The approvals for opening liaison offices by foreign companies in India were liberalised. New procedures were introduced enabling direct application by a foreign investor even before choosing an Indian partner. A *'fast channel'* was set-up in 1988 for expediting clearances of FDI proposals from major investing countries, viz. Japan, Germany, USA and UK.

### (d) 1990s : Full-Scale Liberalisation and Integration with World Economy

The Indian government initiated a programme of macro-economic stabilisation and structural adjustment supported by the IMF and the World Bank in June 1991. As a part of this programme a New Industrial Policy (NIP) was announced on July 24, 1991 in the parliament which has started the process of full scale liberalisation and intensified process of integration of India with the global economy. The NIP and subsequent policy amendments have liberalised the industrial policy regime in the country, especially, as it applies to FDIs beyond recognition.

The industrial approval system in all industries has been abolished except for 18 strategic or environmentally sensitive industries. In 34 high priority industries FDI up to 51 per cent is approved automatically if certain norms are satisfied. FDI proposals do not necessarily have to be accompanied by technology transfer agreements. Trading companies engaged primarily in export activities are also allowed up to 51 per cent foreign equity. To attract MNEs in the energy sector, 100 per cent foreign equity was permitted in power generation. International companies were allowed to explore non-associated natural gas and develop gas-fields including laying down pipelines and setting up liquefied petroleum gas (LPG) projects. A new package for 100 per cent export-oriented projects and companies in export processing zones was announced.

A Foreign Investment Promotion Board (FIPB) authorised to provide a single window clearance has been set-up in the prime minister's office to invite and facilitate investments in India by international companies. The existing companies are also allowed to raise foreign equity levels to 51 per cent for proposed expansion in priority industries. The use of foreign brand names for goods manufactured by domestic industry which was restricted has also been liberalised. India became a signatory to the convention of the Multilateral Investment Guarantee Agency (MIGA) for protection of foreign investments. In Foreign Exchange Regulation Act of 1973 has been amended and restrictions placed on foreign companies by the FERA has been lifted. Companies with more than 40 percent of foreign equity are now treated on par with full Indian owned companies. New sectors such as mining, banking, telecommunications, highways construction and management have been thrown open to private, including foreign owned, companies.

These relaxations and reforms of policies have been accompanied by active courting of foreign investors at the highest level. The international trade policy regime has been considerably liberalised too with lower tariffs on most types of importables and sharp pruning of negative list for imports. The rupee was made convertible first on trade and finally on current account.

### (e) 2000 to 2010 : Second Generation Liberal FDI Policy

Governments are continuously making additional reforms for further liberalisation of FDI. Such measures include ending of state monopoly in insurance, opening up of banking and manufacturing industry to competition and gradual disinvestment of public sector enterprises. Foreign investors are being allowed to own bigger stakes in projects like chemicals and chemical products, basic metals and metal products, electricity production and distribution, construction, transport and storage and advertising, where the ceiling on foreign ownership has been raised to 74 per cent from 51 per cent. Foreign equity of up to 51 per cent is permitted in textiles and telecommunication services. Wholly foreign owned ventures are now allowed in mining and the film industry. India is gradually moving to a regime where, except for a short negative list, most investment proposals are given automatic approval, provided the proposed foreign equity is within the specified ceiling. Foreign exchange controls have also been relaxed. But in 2007 the world economy faced a financial meltdown which restricts most of the foreign enterprises to rethink about foreign investment worldwide. Though in India, this global financial crisis is not affected very much as because of the strong and watchful monetary and fiscal policies by the government.

## III.V. INWARD FLOWS OF FDI TO INDIA

*Foreign direct investment is an international investment by an entity resident in one country in an enterprise resident in another economy that is made with the objective of obtaining a lasting interest.* The lasting interest implies the existence of a long-term relationship between the direct investor and the enterprise and a significant degree of influence on the management of the enterprise. Direct investment involves both the initial transaction that establishes the relationship between the two entities and all subsequent capital transactions between them and among affiliated enterprises, both incorporated and unincorporated.

India is an 'underperformer' in case of attracting foreign direct investment. But India became more open in terms of capital flows into the country with the economic reform policies have been taken since July, 1991. In the next few sections we are discussing the position of India in the global economy.

### III.V.I. India's Stand in the World Economy

India as a developing economy is growing up steadily in these days. In the Eleventh Five Year Plan, Indian government aimed to achieve the target of growth rate at 9.3 per cent. Though currently, India is far behind to this regard. Total GDP growth which was 5.7 per cent in 1990-91 shows some uprising trend in 1994-95 with 7.3 per cent and in 2001-02 with 7.8 per cent. But in 2008-09, it declines to 8.0 and in 2009-10 it was 7.4 per cent (Table 3.1).

From Table 3.1 it is also found that sectoral growth of GDP is also not up to the mark with some declining trend in-between

TABLE 3.1

**India : Major Macro-economic Indicators**

| Season | Total GDP Growth (% per year) | Sectoral Growth of GDP (% per year) | | | Combined Fiscal Deficit of Central and State Govts. (% of GDP) | Gross Savings | | Gross Capital Formation | |
|---|---|---|---|---|---|---|---|---|---|
| | | Agiriculture | Industry | Services | | Private Sector (% of GDP) | Public Sector (% of GDP) | Private Sector (% of GDP) | Public Sector (% of GDP) |
| (1) | (2) | (3) | (4) | (5) | (6) | (7) | (8) | (9) | (10) |
| 1990-91 | 5.7 | 3.8 | 7.0 | 6.7 | 9.4 | 22.0 | 1.1 | 14.7 | 9.3 |
| 1991-92 | 1.3 | –1.1 | 1.0 | 4.8 | 7.0 | 20.1 | 2.0 | 13.1 | 8.8 |
| 1994-95 | 7.3 | 5.3 | 10.3 | 7.1 | 7.1 | 23.2 | 1.7 | 14.7 | 8.7 |
| 1995-96 | 7.3 | –0.3 | 12.3 | 10.5 | 6.5 | 23.1 | 2.0 | 18.9 | 7.7 |
| 2001-02 | 7.8 | 8.8 | 7.7 | 7.2 | 6.4 | 21.5 | 1.7 | 14.7 | 7.0 |
| 2008-09 | 4.0 | 0.1 | 6.6 | 4.8 | 9.4 | 24.0 | –0.9 | 16.1 | 7.1 |
| 2009-10 | 5.4 | 5.7 | 3.3 | 6.5 | 9.6 | 25.1 | –1.7 | 15.8 | 7.1 |

*Note* : Public sector capital formation minus public sector savings does not equal the fiscal deficit because the definition of public sector for estimate of savings and capital formation includes non-departmental enterprises. Estimates of public sector savings and capital formation distinguishing general government from non-departmental enterprises are not readily available for recent years.

*Source* : *Economic Surveys, 2001-02 and 2009-10*, Ministry of Finance, Government of India, 2002 and 2010.

the year 1990-2010. Sectoral growth of agriculture, industry and services was 3.8 per cent, 7.0 per cent and 6.7 per cent in 1990-91 respectively. In 2009-10, these figures turned to 5.7 per cent, 3.3 per cent and 6.5 per cent respectively. Gross savings in private sector was 22.0 per cent of GDP and in public sector was 1.1 per cent of GDP in 1990-91. These now change to 25.1 per cent and –1.7 per cent of GDP in 2009-10 respectively. In case of capital formation, the figure was 14.7 per cent of GDP for private sector and 9.3 per cent of GDP for public sector in 1990-91. This is now moves to 15.8 per cent and 7.1 per cent respectively in 2009-10.

As far as the case of capital flows over three decades in India is concerned, capital account balance of India was

TABLE 3.2

**India : Capital Flows over Three Decades**

*(in Mn. of U.S. Dollars)*

| | *1980s* | *1990s* | *2000s* | *% Change over Decade* | |
|---|---|---|---|---|---|
| | | | | *1980-90* | *1990-2000* |
| Capital Account Balance | 6,154 | 39,317 | 77,689 | 538.86 | 97.60 |
| External Assistance | 6,616 | 14,871 | 15,153 | 124.77 | 1.90 |
| Commercial Borrowings* | 1,136 | 10,349 | 17,780 | 811.00 | 71.80 |
| Deposit by Non-resident Indians | 854 | 11,349 | 14,664 | 1,228.92 | 29.21 |
| Portfolio Investment | — | — | 18,498 | — | — |
| FDI | 366 | 1,396 | 15,580 | 281.42 | 1,016.05 |
| Other | –2,818 | 1,262 | –3,986 | 144.78 | 415.85 |
| Current Account Balance | –287 | –44,140 | –43,141 | 15,279.79 | 2.26 |
| Change in Reserves (– increase) | –5,866 | 4,823 | –34,548 | 182.22 | 182.22 |

*Note* : *Includes US $ 4.2 billion from Resurgent India Bond in 1998.
*Source* : RBI, *Handbook of Statistics of the Indian Economy*, 2010.

TABLE 3.3

**FDI Inflows by Host Regions**

(*US $ Billion*)

| | 1989-94 (*ann. avg.*) | 1995 | 1996-99 (*ann. avg.*) | 2000 | 2001-04 (*ann. avg.*) | 2005 | 2006-08 (*ann. avg.*) | 2009 |
|---|---|---|---|---|---|---|---|---|
| (1) | (2) | (3) | (4) | (5) | (6) | (7) | (8) | (9) |
| I. World | 200.1 | 331.1 | 384.9 | 477.9 | 692.5 | 1,075.2 | 1,270.8 | 760 |
| II. Developed Countries | 137.1 | 203.5 | 219.7 | 271.4 | 483.2 | 829.8 | 1,005.2 | 500 |
| III. Developing Countries | 59.6 | 113.3 | 152.5 | 187.4 | 188.4 | 222.0 | 240.2 | 225 |
| Share (%) | 29.8 | 34.2 | 39.6 | 39.2 | 27.2 | 20.7 | 18.9 | 29.6 |

*Source* : *World Investment Report*, 2001 and *UNCTAD Press Release* of 21st January 2010.

### TABLE 3.4
## Global Financial Flows

| *To Counties* | *Net Private Capital Flows (US $ Mn)* | | *FDI (US $ Mn)* | | *Portfollio Investment Flows* | | | | *Bank and Trade-related Lending (US $ Mn)* | |
|---|---|---|---|---|---|---|---|---|---|---|
| | | | | | *Bonds (US $ Mn)* | | *Equity (US $ Mn)* | | | |
| | *1990* | *2009* | *1990* | *2009* | *1990* | *2009* | *1990* | *2009* | *1990* | *2009* |
| *(1)* | *(2)* | *(3)* | *(4)* | *(5)* | *(6)* | *(7)* | *(8)* | *(9)* | *(10)* | *(11)* |
| India | 1872 | 8306 | 162 | 3351 | 147 | 1919 | 105 | 2116 | 1458 | 920 |
| Bangladesh | 70 | 118 | 3 | 135 | 0 | 0 | 0 | 11 | 67 | –28 |
| China | 8107 | 60828 | 3487 | 44236 | –48 | 3330 | 0 | 8457 | 4668 | 4805 |
| France | — | — | 13183 | 23045 | — | — | — | — | — | — |
| Germany | — | — | 2532 | –344 | — | — | — | — | — | — |
| Indonesia | 3235 | 10863 | 1093 | 4677 | 26 | 3120 | 312 | 298 | 1804 | 2769 |
| Malaysia | 769 | 9312 | 2333 | 5106 | –1239 | 2503 | 293 | –489 | –617 | 2192 |
| Mauritius | 86 | 771 | 41 | 53 | 0 | 600 | 0 | 24 | 45 | 94 |
| Netherlands | — | — | 12352 | 8725 | — | — | — | — | — | — |
| Pakistan | 182 | 2097 | 244 | 713 | 0 | 375 | 0 | 252 | –63 | 757 |
| Philippines | 639 | 4164 | 530 | 1222 | 395 | 2631 | 0 | 73 | 286 | 238 |
| Russian Fed. | 5562 | 12453 | 0 | 6241 | 310 | 5460 | 0 | 1206 | 5252 | 454 |
| Saudi Arabia | — | — | 1864 | — | — | — | — | — | — | — |
| South Africa | — | 3610 | — | 1725 | — | 623 | — | 1393 | — | –131 |
| Sri Lanka | 54 | 574 | 43 | 430 | 0 | 50 | 0 | 98 | 11 | –4 |
| Thailand | 4399 | 3444 | 2444 | 3745 | –87 | 1726 | 449 | –308 | 1593 | –1719 |
| U.K. | — | — | 32518 | 38081 | — | — | — | — | — | — |
| U.S.A. | — | — | 47918 | 93448 | — | — | — | — | — | — |

*Source* : *World Development Indicators*, 2010, World Bank.

US $ 6,154 million in 1980s and US $ 39,317 million in 1990s. This is changed to US $ 77,689 million in the first decade of 2000s. External assistance also moves from US $ 6,616 million in 1980s to US$ 15,153 million in the first decade of 2000s. Comparing with these, foreign direct investment has increased from US$ 366 million in 1980s to US $ 15,580 million in the first decade of 2000s. This means, a huge increase in the percentage change over decade from 281 in 1980-90 to 1016 in 1990-2000 (Table 3.2).

Global foreign direct investment almost quadrupled between 1995 and 2010. However, FDI flows to developing countries grew at a much slower rate over this period, doubling to US$ 240.2 billion their share (Table 3.3). FDI inflows into developing countries virtually halted in 1998 as a result of the Asian crisis. The share of developing countries in global flows reached a peak of 39.2 per cent in 2000, declining rapidly thereafter to reach 29.6 per cent of total flows in 2009. Though absolute FDI amounts have declined in 2009-10, the share of developing countries has increased dramatically to 30 per cent (Table 3.3).

Net private capital flows increased from US $ 1872 million in 1990 to US $ 8306 million in 2009 in India. At the same time, foreign direct investment flows also increased by US $ 3189 million while portfolio investment flows increased by US $ 3783 million (US $ 1772 million as bonds and US $ 2011 as equity). But bank and trade-related lending decreased from US $ 1458 million to US $ 920 million in this period for India (Table 3.4). Table 3.4 also shows the comparative figure for other countries. China has affected most by global financial flows in this period. Net private capital flows was increased by US $ 52721 million of which FDI increased by US $ 40749 million and portfolio investment increased by US $ 11835 million in this period into China. Indonesia, Malaysia, South Africa and Russian Federation are also far ahead of India in this regard in the 1990s (Table 3.4).

### III.V.II. Composition of Capital Flows in India

With better economic performance and relatively open capital accounts, the 1990s saw a return of capital flows to emerging markets to the pre-1914 levels. Net capital flows to developing economies surged from US $ 80.5 billion in the late 1980s to US $ 344 billion in 1997. The composition of flows, however, altered significantly over time. In 1991-92, for the first time since 1982, private flows exceeded official finance with their share rising from 42.6 per cent in 1990 to a peak of 90.1 per cent in 1996, before dropping to 82.1 per cent in 1999.

Before so-called economic reforms has taken place in India, the composition of capital flows were basically depends on non-resident Indian's deposit, external assistance and commercial borrowings. In 1985, the figure was 16.3, 30.3 and 21.1 per cent of total (net) capital flows for NRI deposits, external assistance and commercial borrowings respectively. After June 1991, Indian economy has much more dependent on foreign investment (both FDI and FPI). In 1991, the percentage of FDI and FPI to total (net) capital flow were 3.4 and 0.10 respectively. In 1995, these figures rose to 46.0 and 58.3. But after that the percentage of portfolio investment was decreasing at faster rate than direct investment. In 2000, the figure was 21.2 for FDI and 29.5 for portfolio investment. At that time maximum share of capital flow goes to commercial borrowing with 53.0 per cent. Then in 2010, FDI flows slightly improved to 40.8 per cent and portfolio investment to 21.0 per cent. Net capital account as a per cent of GDP is also improved from 2.32 per cent in 2000 to 3.63 per cent in 2010 (Table 3.5).

### III.V.III. Foreign Investment Flows by Categories Including Priority Sectors

After the announcement of New Industrial Policy in 1991, there has been acceleration in the flow of foreign capital in India. As per data provided in Table 3.6, total foreign investment flows were of the order of US $ 28.30 billion, out of which about US $ 12.83 billion (45.3 per cent) were in the form of FDI and the remaining US $ 15.47 billion (57.3 per cent) were in the form of portfolio investment. This clearly shows that the preference of foreign firms was more in favour of portfolio investment and much less in the form of direct investment. Moreover, out of the total direct foreign investment of the order of US $ 12.83 billion, nearly 8.5 per cent (US $ 2.43 billion) was contributed by Non-resident Indians. Thus, the net contribution of foreign firms in direct investment was merely 38 per cent of total foreign investment flows.

TABLE 3.5

**Composition of Capital Flows in India**

*(Percentage to Total (net) Capital Flows)*

| Year | Foreign Investment | | NRI Deposits | External Assistance | Commercial Borrowings | Net Capital Account | |
|---|---|---|---|---|---|---|---|
| | Direct | Portfolio | | | | (US $ bn) | (% of GDP) |
| (1) | (2) | (3) | (4) | (5) | (6) | (7) | (8) |
| 1985 | 0 | 0 | 16.3 | 30.3 | 21.1 | 1.37 | — |
| 1990 | 1.3 | 0.08 | 21.4 | 30.7 | 31.3 | 7.19 | — |
| 1995 | 46.0 | 58.3 | 24.5 | 21.5 | 29.2 | 4.69 | 1.31 |
| 2000 | 21.2 | 29.5 | 20.3 | 8.6 | 3.0 | 10.42 | 2.32 |
| 2005 | 30.9 | 14.1 | 22.0 | 5.8 | 54.7 | 7.49 | 1.91 |
| 2010 | 40.8 | 21.0 | — | 11.8 | — | — | 3.63 |

*Source* : Calculated from *Report on Currency and Finance*, 1998-99; *RBI Bulletin*, July 2001 and, June 2010, RBI, Mumbai.

TABLE 3.6

**Foreign Investment Flows by Categories-I**

*(US $ Mn)*

| *Year* | *Direct Investment* | | | *Portfolio Investment* | | | *Grand Total* |
|---|---|---|---|---|---|---|---|
| | *Foreigners*[1] *(A)* | *NRI's (B)* | *Sub-total (C=A+B)* | *FIIs (D)* | *Others*[2] *(E)* | *Sub-total (F=D+E)* | *(G=C+F)* |
| *(1)* | *(2)* | *(3)* | *(4)* | *(5)* | *(6)* | *(7)* | *(8)* |
| 1990-91 | 66 | 63 | 129 | 4 | 0 | 4 | 133 |
| 1995-96 | 1418 | 715 | 2133 | 2009 | 739 | 2748 | 4881 |
| 2000-01 | 2057 | 639 | 2696 | 1926 | 1386 | 3312 | 6008 |
| 2005-06 | 2956 | 241 | 3179 | 979 | 849 | 1828 | 5025 |
| 2009-10 | 2400 | 62 | 2462 | –390 | 329 | –61 | 2401 |
| Total (1991-92 to 2009-10) | 10402 (37.8) | 2430 (8.5) | 12832 (45.3) | 7967 (27.2) | 7769 (27.5) | 15466 (54.7) | 28298 (100.0) |

*Notes* : 1. Foreigners include investment flows by RBI automatic route and SIA/FIPB route.
2. Others include Euro equities (GDR amounts raised by Indian Corporates) and offshore funds and others.
3. Figures in brackets are percentages of total investment.

*Source* : Compiled from Government of India, Economic Survey (2010).

As a response to the policies of liberalisation, the foreign investors were very keen to undertake portfolio investment, including GDR (Global Depository Receipts) and investment by Foreign Institutional Investors, Euro equities and others rose sharply from US $ 244 million in 1992-93 to US $ 3,567 million in 1993-94, US $ 3,824 million in 1994-95 and declined to US $ 1,828 million in 1997-98. Portfolio investment became negative in 2005-06 but it recovers in the period 2009-10 (Table 3.7).

TABLE 3.7

**Foreign Investment Inflows-II**

| *Year* | *Direct Investment* | | *Portfolio Investment* | | *Total* | |
|---|---|---|---|---|---|---|
| | *Rs. Crore (A)* | *US $ Mn. (B)* | *Rs. Crore (C)* | *US $ Mn. (D)* | *Rs. Crore (A + C)* | *US $ Mn. (B + D)* |
| 1990-91 | 174 | 97 | 11 | 6 | 185 | 103 |
| 1991-92 | 316 | 129 | 10 | 4 | 326 | 133 |
| 1992-93 | 965 | 315 | 748 | 244 | 1713 | 559 |
| 1993-94 | 1838 | 586 | 11188 | 3567 | 13026 | 4153 |
| 1994-95 | 4126 | 1314 | 12007 | 3824 | 16133 | 5138 |
| 1995-96* | 7172 | 2144 | 9192 | 2748 | 16364 | 4892 |
| 2000-01* | 13220 | 3557 | 6696 | 1828 | 19916 | 5385 |
| 2005-06* | 10358 | 2462 | –257 | –61 | –10101 | 2401 |
| 2009-10* | 9338 | 2155 | 13112 | 3026 | 22450 | 5181 |

*Note* : *Including acquisition of shares of Indian companies by non-residents under Section 29 of Foreign Exchange Regulation Act (FERA).

*Sources* : *Handbook of Statistics on Indian Economy*, Reserve Bank of India, Mumbai (2010) and *India Development Report*, 2009.

In terms of aggregate annual inflows, FDI maintained its declining trend for the second successive year after 1997-98. FDI inflows in India for the year 2005-06 (US $ 2,155 million) were lower than for the year 2000-01 (US $ 2,462 million). Inflows in the year, 2008-09, however, are showing signs of improvement. Aggregate FDI inflows have been higher (US $ 1,916 million) than the comparable period of 2008-09 (US $ 1,489 million) (Table 3.8).

Table 3.8
**Foreign Investment Flows by Categories-III**

*(US $ Mn.)*

| | 1992-93 | 1993-94 | 1994-95 | 1995-96 | 1996-97 | 1997-98 | 2000-01 | 2005-06 | 2008-09 | 2009-10 |
|---|---|---|---|---|---|---|---|---|---|---|
| (1) | (2) | (3) | (4) | (5) | (6) | (7) | (8) | (9) | (10) | (11) |
| A. Direct Investment | 315 | 586 | 1314 | 2144 | 2821 | 3557 | 2462 | 2155 | 1489 | 1916 |
| (a) RBI Automatic Route | 42 | 89 | 171 | 169 | 135 | 202 | 179 | 171 | 127 | 330 |
| (b) SIA/FIPB Route | 222 | 280 | 701 | 1249 | 1922 | 2754 | 1821 | 1410 | 987 | 1262 |
| (c) NRI | 51 | 217 | 442 | 715 | 639 | 241 | 62 | 84 | 71 | 51 |
| (d) Acquision of Shares+ | — | — | — | 11 | 125 | 380 | 400 | 490 | 304 | 273 |
| B. Portfolio Investment | 244 | 3567 | 3824 | 2748 | 3312 | 1828 | –61 | 3026 | 1916 | 296 |
| (a) FIIs* | 1 | 1665 | 1503 | 2009 | 1926 | 979 | –390 | 2135 | 1187 | –476 |
| (b) Euro Equities and ADRs/GDRs @ | 240 | 1520 | 2082 | 683 | 1366 | 645 | 270 | 768 | 619 | 696 |
| (c) Offshore Funds and others | 3 | 382 | 239 | 56 | 20 | 204 | 59 | 123 | 110 | 76 |
| Total (A + B) | 559 | 4153 | 5138 | 4892 | 6133 | 5385 | 2401 | 5181 | 3405 | 2212 |

\+ Relates to acquisition of shares of Indian companies by non-residents under Section 29 of FERA.

* Represents fresh inflow/outflow of funds by FIIs.

@ Figures include GDRs/ADRs amounts raised abroad by the Indian corporate.

*Source* : *Reserve Bank of India Bulletin*, 2002 and 2012.

Aggregate portfolio investment, comprising mainly of investment under ADR/GDR route and by Foreign Institutional Investors (FIIs), displayed a marked turnaround in 2005-06. Cômpared to a net outflow of US $ 61 million in 2000-01, portfolio investment recovered strongly in 2005-06 to post a total of US $ 3026 million. The bulk of this increase in portfolio investment was attributable to higher FII inflows. From a net outflow of US $ 390 million in 2000-01, FII investment shot up to more than US $ 2 billion in 2008-09. Higher FII investment in 2008-09 was indicative, in part, of improving investor perceptions of emerging economics after Brazilian-Asian-Russian crises. Portfolio investment, accruing through the ADR/GDR route was also much higher in 2009-10 compared to the previous year. The higher trends illustrate the improved ability of Indian corporates in mobilizing funds from overseas markets. The firm trends of inflows through ADR/GDR are also evident in the current year. In 2009-10, the inflows through this route have increased compared to the same period last year. The success in tapping resources from overseas capital markets vindicates the policy measures taken in recent times for facilitating investment under the ADR/GDR route (Table 3.8).

### III.V.IV. FDI Approvals into the Country

The process of liberalisation of capital account has been very gradual in India. Taking the cue from the crisis of 1991, India's policy on external sector had been cautious. The cautious approach to the management of the external sector is reflected in the procedures for foreign direct investment, portfolio investment, external commercial borrowings, non-resident Indian deposit and outflows. Of these foreign direct investments has been recognised as a preferred form of capital inflow. In the following few paragraphs we are trying to discuss the approval of FDI into India with different forms.

#### *(a) Country-wise Approvals of FDI*

The inflow of FDI in India is smartly dominated by USA. During the period 1991-2010, USA contributed 20.4 per cent share of FDI inflows into India. The next nine countries are Mauritius (11.9 per cent), UK (6.5 per cent), Japan (4.0 per cent), Korea (3.9 per cent), Germany (3.4 per cent), Australia (2.7 per cent), Malaysia (2.3 per cent), France (2.1 per cent) and the Netherlands (1.9 per cent). Foreign direct investment approvals into the country increased fourth-fold from Rs. 5,95,398.90 million during the period 1991-95 to Rs. 21,41,323.07 million during the period 1996-2001. NRI's investment also increased to Rs. 74,396.15 million during 1996-2001 from Rs. 27,027 million during 1991-95. In case of Euro issues (GDRs/FCCBs) the figure also goes up to Rs. 4,19,536.02 million from Rs. 64,199.40 million during the said period (Table 3.9).

Table 3.9 also shows that most of the FDI approvals came into the country during the last decade were from the European countries (40 countries) and Asian countries (34 countries). 10 African countries, 10 North American countries, 3 South American countries and 3 Osenian countries also invested directly into the country during 1991-2010 periods.

### (b) Route-wise Approvals of FDI

Foreign direct investment in India came through three routs—(i) Secretariat for Industrial Assistance (SIA), (ii) Reserve Bank of India (RBI), and (iii) Foreign Investment Promotion Board (FIPB).

Total number of foreign collaboration approvals in the year 1991 was 950 out of which 760 came through SIA route, 188 came through RBI and 2 through FIPB. Since then foreign collaboration through SIA has decreased and became lower in 1997 with 167 but increased by a little amount in 2001 with 207. Foreign collaboration through RBI route coming with a fluctuating rate and has a massive increase with 1132 in 2001. Through FIPB route, foreign collaboration reached its maximum in the year 1999 with 1432 and then decreased to 931 in 2001 (Table 3.9a).

Out of a total number of 21189 foreign collaboration approvals during the period 1991-2001, total number of technical foreign collaboration approvals was 7157. Out of this technical collaboration, 2759 came through SIA route, 4189 through RBI route and 209 through FIPB. A total of 14032 foreign collaboration approvals came involving foreign investment into the country during 1991-2001 (of which 1263 came through SIA, 3118 through RBI and 9651 through FIPB). Total amount of foreign investment in India during the period

TABLE 3.9
**Foreign Direct Investment Approved (Country-wise)**

| Sl. No. | Name of Country | 1991-95 (Rs. Mn.) | 1996-2001 (Rs. Mn.) | 2002-10 (Rs. Mn.) | Share of FDI (1991-2010) (in % of total) |
|---|---|---|---|---|---|
| | (1) | (2) | (3) | (4) | (5) |
| 1. | USA | 154216.60 | 398793.10 | 553009.70 | 20.4 |
| 2. | Mauritius | 24674.70 | 298573.76 | 323248.46 | 11.9 |
| 3. | U.K. | 37975.10 | 175846.82 | 213821.92 | 6.4 |
| 4. | Japan | 28355.30 | 78349.68 | 106704.98 | 4.0 |
| 5. | Korea (South) | 4959.20 | 93020.17 | 97979.37 | 3.9 |
| 6. | Germany | 22128.50 | 66980.65 | 89109.15 | 3.4 |
| 7. | Netherlands | 16477.80 | 67457.53 | 83935.33 | 1.9 |
| 8. | Australia | 20024.60 | 46988.60 | 67013.20 | 2.7 |
| 9. | France | 6881.50 | 52291.62 | 59173.12 | 2.1 |
| 10. | Malaysia | 14944.00 | 41878.99 | 56822.99 | 2.3 |
| 11. | Singapore | 138448.60 | 34780.20 | 48628.80 | — |
| 12. | Italy | 10758.30 | 36504.94 | 47263.24 | — |
| 13. | Israel | 41484.70 | 959.54 | 42444.24 | — |
| 14. | Belgium | 2048.70 | 39550.47 | 41599.17 | — |
| 15. | Cayman Island | 68.00 | 37312.62 | 37380.62 | — |
| 16. | Switzerland | 15098.40 | 14088.33 | 29186.73 | — |
| 17. | Canada | 14485.60 | 11414.82 | 25900.42 | — |
| 18. | Thailand | 23490.10 | 1113.95 | 24604.05 | — |
| 19. | Hong Kong | 7381.30 | 15136.61 | 22517.91 | — |
| 20. | Sweden | 5699.00 | 14689.59 | 20388.59 | — |
| 21. | Other 32 European Countries | 9307.40 | 21007.90 | 30315.30 | — |
| 22. | Other 26 Asian Countries | 25866.62 | 25615.16 | 51481.78 | — |
| 23. | Other 10 African Countries | 208.20 | 21850.42 | 22058.62 | — |

*(Contd.)*

TABLE 3.9 (*Contd.*)

| (1) | (2) | | (3) | (4) |
|---|---|---|---|---|
| 24. Other 8 North American Countries | 3147.50 | 18984.43 | 22131.93 | — |
| 25. Other 3 South American Countries | 1.30 | 189.20 | 190.50 | — |
| 26. Other 2 Osesian Countries | 526.20 | 3857.64 | 3913.84 | — |
| 27. NRI | 27027.40 | 74396.15 | 101423.55 | 3.7 |
| 28. Euro Issues (GDRs)/(FCCBs) | 64199.40 | 419536.02 | 483735.42 | 17.7 |
| Total (Rs. Mn) | 595398.90 | 2141323.07 | 2736721.97 | — |

*Source* : Calculated from *SIA Newsletter*, various issues, Govt. of India, New Delhi.

1991-2001 involved Rs. 47.7 billion inflows through SIA, Rs. 182.7 billion through RBI and Rs. 2506.2 billion through FIPB. Inflows through SIA route shows an up and down trend with Rs. 3.6 billion in 1991, Rs. 1.6 billion in 1993, Rs. 11.8 billion in 1996, Rs. 0.1 billion in 1999 and Rs. 7.9 billion in 2001. RBI operated Rs. 1.4 billion inflows in 1991, Rs. 92.7 billion in 1997 and Rs. 23.5 billion in 2001. On the other hand, FIPB had incurred Rs. 0.3 billion inflows of foreign investment in 1991, a maximum of Rs. 453.0 billion in 1997 and Rs. 237.4 billion in 2001 (Table 3.9a).

Table 3.10 shows that total 19863 foreign collaborations were approved in 1st ten post policy periods but in the second ten years (August 2001 to June 2010) the figure is 1010 which include 3590 through SIA, 6876 with RBI and 9397 with FIPB. Out of these approvals 2507 as technical and 1083 as foreign investment came for SIA route. 4121 as technical and 2755 as foreign investment came through RBI route. 209 as technical and 9188 as foreign investment inflows came into the country through FIPB.

TABLE 3.9(a)

**Foreign Collaboration Approvals (Route-wise)**

| | 1991 | 1992 | 1993 | 1994 | 1995 | 1996 | 1997 | 1998 | 1999 | 2000 | 2001 | Total 1991-2001 |
|---|---|---|---|---|---|---|---|---|---|---|---|---|
| (1) | (2) | (3) | (4) | (5) | (6) | (7) | (8) | (9) | (10) | (11) | (12) | (13) |
| 1. Total No. of Foreign Collaboration Approvals by : | | | | | | | | | | | | |
| (i) SIA | 760 | 585 | 307 | 382 | 593 | 410 | 167 | 8193 | 221 | 197 | 207 | 4022 |
| (ii) RBI | 188 | 736 | 676 | 702 | 799 | 719 | 801 | 432 | 571 | 551 | 1132 | 7307 |
| (iii) FIPB | 2 | 199 | 493 | 770 | 945 | 1174 | 1357 | 1161 | 1432 | 1396 | 931 | 9860 |
| Total | 950 | 1520 | 1476 | 1854 | 2337 | 2303 | 2325 | 1786 | 2224 | 2144 | 2270 | 21189 |
| 2. Total No. of Foreign Collaboration (Technical) Approvals by : | | | | | | | | | | | | |
| (i) SIA | 514 | 342 | 248 | 290 | 428 | 311 | 119 | 129 | 170 | 132 | 76 | 2759 |
| (ii) RBI | 147 | 485 | 441 | 501 | 552 | 424 | 416 | 401 | 324 | 286 | 212 | 4189 |
| (iii) FIPB | — | 1 | 2 | 1 | 2 | 9 | 12-5 | 65 | 4 | 0 | 0 | 209 |
| Total | 661 | 828 | 691 | 792 | 982 | 744 | 660 | 595 | 498 | 418 | 288 | 7157 |

(Contd.)

TABLE 3.9(a) (*Contd.*)

| *(1)* | *(2)* | *(3)* | *(4)* | *(5)* | *(6)* | *(7)* | *(8)* | *(9)* | *(10)* | *(11)* | *(12)* | *(13)* |
|---|---|---|---|---|---|---|---|---|---|---|---|---|
| 3. No. of FC Approvals Involving Foreign Investment by : | | | | | | | | | | | | |
| (i) SIA | 246 | 243 | 59 | 92 | 165 | 99 | 48 | 64 | 51 | 65 | 131 | 1263 |
| (ii) RBI | 41 | 251 | 235 | 201 | 247 | 295 | 385 | 31 | 247 | 265 | 920 | 3118 |
| (iii) FIPB | 2 | 198 | 491 | 769 | 943 | 1165 | 1232 | 1096 | 1428 | 1396 | 931 | 9651 |
| Total | 289 | 692 | 785 | 1062 | 1355 | 1559 | 1665 | 1191 | 1726 | 1726 | 1982 | 14032 |
| 4. Total Amount of Foreign Investment Involved: (Rs. in Billion) | | | | | | | | | | | | |
| (i) SIA | 3.6 | 4.2 | 1.6 | 3.2 | 3.0 | 11.8 | 3.2 | 7.2 | 0.1 | 1.9 | 7.9 | 47.7 |
| (ii) RBI | 1.4 | 1.8 | 6.6 | 5.3 | 5.4 | 12.5 | 92.7 | 1.9 | 9.9 | 15.7 | 23.5 | 182.7 |
| (iii) FIPB | 0.3 | 26.9 | 80.4 | 133.4 | 312.3 | 337.2 | 453.0 | 299.0 | 273.6 | 352.7 | 237.4 | 2506.2 |
| Total (In Indian Rupees) | 5.3 | 32.9 | 88.6 | 141.9 | 320.7 | 361.5 | 548.9 | 308.1 | 283.6 | 370.3 | 268.8 | 2736.6* |

*Notes* : (i) 1 billion = 100 crore.

(ii) #—Includes 94 proposals by FIPB for American Depository Receipts (ADRs)/ Global Depository (GDRs)/ Foreign Currency Convertible Bonds (FCCBs) involving investment of Rs. 483.73 billion.

(iii) @*—The amount of FDI Approved = US @ 74.29 billion (Approx.); SIA—Secretariat for Industrial Assistance, RBI—Reserve Bank of India; FIPB—Foreign Investment Promotion Board.

*Source* : *SIA Newsletter*, Vol. X, No. 9, January 2011, p. 7, Government of India, New Delhi.

TABLE 3.10

**Foreign Collaboration Approvals (Route-wise)**

*(Post-policy period)*

| | *Post-Policy Period* | | |
|---|---|---|---|
| | *1st to 10th Years (Aug. 1991-Jul. 2001)* | *11th to 20th Years (Aug. 2001-Jun. 2010)* | *Total (Aug. 1991-Jun. 2010)* |
| 1. Total No. of Foreign Collaboration Approvals: | | | |
| (i) SIA | 3590 | 116 | 3706 |
| (ii) RBI | 6876 | 431 | 7307 |
| (iii) FIPB | 9397 | 463 | 9860 |
| Total | 19863 | 1010 | 20873 |
| 2. No. of Foreign Collaboration (Technical) Approvals : | | | |
| (i) SIA | 2507 | 23 | 2530 |
| (ii) RBI | 4121 | 68 | 4189 |
| (iii) FIPB | 209 | 0 | 209 |
| Total | 6837 | 91 | 6928 |
| 3. No. of Foreign Collaboration Approvals Involving Foreign Investment: | | | |
| (i) SIA | 1083 | 93 | 1176 |
| (ii) RBI | 2755 | 363 | 3118 |
| (iii) FIPB | 9188 | 463 | 9651 |
| Total | 13026 | 919 | 13945 |
| 4. Total Amount of Foreign Investment Involved : (Rs. in Billion) | | | |
| (i) SIA | 43.5 | 3.8 | 47.3 |
| (ii) RBI | 176 | 6.6 | 182.6 |
| (iii) FIPB | 2443.5 | 62 | 2505.5 |
| Total (In Indian Rupees) | 2663 | 72.4 | 2735.4 |

*Sources* : *SIA Newsletter*, Jan. 2002 and July 2010, Government of India, New Delhi.

During January 1991 to June 2010, actual FDI inflow through governments approval (FIPB and SIA route) was Rs. 5,33,220.8 million and RBI's automatic approval under delegated power was Rs. 89,725.2 million. During this period, amount of FDI inflows on acquisition of shares was Rs. 1,22,982.3 million, RBI's various NRI's schemes was Rs. 83475.0 million and amount of ADRs/GDRs/FCCBs were Rs. 2,20,853.4 million. Since 1999, actual inflows of FDI came in the form of closing balance of advance was Rs. 35,259.6 million. As on 30th June, 2010, total actual inflows of FDI through various routes was Rs. 1,085,516.3 million (during the period 1991 to 2010) (Table 3.11).

### (c) Industry-wise Approvals of FDI

*ISID study underlines the fact* : "Liberalisation of Industrial Licensing in the form of freeing public sector reserved areas has been the single most important policy decision that influenced sectoral pattern of FDI" (Dutta-Sundaram).

The bulk of the approved inflows in 2010 have been directed to non-manufacturing sectors bringing the share of manufacturing down from 85 per cent in the stock of FDI in 2010 to just 35 per cent in cumulative approvals. Infrastructural sectors such as energy (32 per cent) and telecommunication services (23 per cent) account for the bulk of the approvals as it clear from Table 3.12. These sectors have not been open to FDI inflows before and hence, the inflows directed to them could be attributed to policy liberalisation.

During the period 1980-2009, a greater production of technology transactions of Indian enterprises take place through internal or FDI mode. The proportion of foreign collaborations that approved has gone up from just over 16 per cent in the 1970s to nearly 58 per cent during the 1990s. Therefore, liberalisation has shifted the balance between FDI and licensing in favour of FDI. Furthermore, majority foreign ownership, which was restricted to certain exceptional cases during the 1970s and 1980s because of regulations in becoming more popular again. Majority of approvals over the 1990s have been in the 50-100 per cent foreign ownership range with a third accounted for by wholly foreign owned subsidiaries.

TABLE 3.11

**Actual Inflows of Foreign Direct Investment (Route-wise) (1991 to 2010)**

*(Amount in Rs. Million)*

| Year | Actual Inflow of FDI in the Following Routes | | | | | | | Grand Total (I to VI) |
|---|---|---|---|---|---|---|---|---|
| | Govt's. approval (FIPB, SIA Route) I | RBI's Automatic Approval (Underdelegated Power) II | Amount of Inflows on Acquisition of shares III | RBI's Various NRI's Schemes IV | Amount of ADRs/ GDRs/ FCCBs V | Total (I to V) | Closing balance of Advance VI | |
| (1) | (2) | (3) | (4) | (5) | (6) | (7) | (8) | (9) |
| 1991 | 1911.8 | — | — | 1602.5 | — | 3514.3 | — | 3514.3 |
| 1992 | 4779.5 | 475.4 | — | 1496.9 | — | 6751.8 | — | 6751.8 |
| 1995 | 38694.4 | 5301.6 | — | 19705.6 | 4498.7 | 68200.3 | — | 68200.3 |
| 2000 | 101284.0 | 8672.2 | 9540.3 | 10396.2 | 34360.6 | 164253.3 | — | 164253.3 |
| 2001 | 82397.3 | 6106.5 | 40593.5 | 3594.8 | 706.3 | 133398.4 | — | 133398.4 |
| 2005 | 61894.3 | 7608.1 | 19608.3 | 3488.3 | 67011.1 | 159610.1 | 9067.8 | 168677.9 |
| 2009 | 63425.3 | 16918.0 | 20580.5 | 3488.2 | 69879.6 | 174291.6 | 19125.8 | 193417.4 |
| 2010 | 96385.9 | 32410.4 | 29621.7 | 2292.5 | 24874.5 | 185585.0 | 7066.0 | 192651.0 |
| Total (as on 30.06.10) | 533220.8 | 89725.2 | 122982.3 | 83475.0 | 220853.4 | 1050256.7 | 35259.6 | 1085516.3 |

*Source* : RBI (ECD), Central Office, Mumbai.

TABLE 3.12

**Selected Distribution of Stock of FDI in India**

(in Mn. Rupees)

| Industry Group | | FDI Stock as in March 1980 | | FDI Stock as in March 1990 | | FDI Stock as in March 2010 | |
|---|---|---|---|---|---|---|---|
| | | Value | Per cent | Value | Per cent | Value | Per cent |
| | (1) | (2) | (3) | (4) | (5) | (6) | (7) |
| I. | Plantation and Horticulture | 385 | 4.1 | 2560 | 9.5 | 5318 | 0.22 |
| II. | Mining | 78 | 0.8 | 80 | 0.3 | 43453 | 1.79 |
| III. | Petroleum and Power | 368 | 3.9 | 30 | 0.1 | 768028 | 32.47 |
| IV. | Manufacturing | 8116 | 86.9 | 22980 | 84.9 | 727840 | 30.77 |
| | Food and Beverages | 391 | 4.2 | 1620 | 6.0 | 91195 | 03.85 |
| | Textiles | 320 | 3.4 | 920 | 3.4 | 34057 | 1.44 |
| | Machinery and Machine Tools | 710 | 7.6 | 3540 | 13.1 | 27567 | 1.16 |
| | Transport Equipments | 515 | 5.5 | 2820 | 10.4 | 21874 | 0.92 |
| | Metal and Metal Products | 1187 | 12.7 | 1410 | 5.2 | 110975 | 4.68 |
| | Electricals and Electronics | 975 | 10.4 | 2950 | 10.9 | 265604 | 11.2 |
| | Chemical and Allied | 3018 | 32.3 | 7690 | 28.4 | 125860 | 5.31 |
| | Miscellaneous | 1000 | 10.7 | 2030 | 7.5 | 50704 | 2.14 |

| | | | | | | | |
|---|---|---|---|---|---|---|---|
| V. | Services | 385 | 4.1 | 1400 | 5.2 | 821728 | 34.74 |
| | Telecommunications | 0 | 0 | 0 | 0 | 551499 | 23.27 |
| | Finance and Banking | na | na | na | na | 116414 | 4.91 |
| | Hotels and Tourism | na | na | na | na | 48434 | 2.04 |
| | Air and Sea Transport | na | na | na | na | 28934 | 1.22 |
| | Consultancy | na | na | na | na | 24989 | 1.05 |
| | Other Services | na | na | na | na | 51458 | 2.17 |
| | Total | 9332 | 100.0 | 27050 | 100.0 | 2365367 | 100.0 |

*Note* : Percentages might not add up to 100 because of rounding off errors.

*Source* : (i) Kumar (1998), *Economic and Political Weekly*, Vol. XXXIII, No. 22, May 30.

(ii) *SIA Newsletter*, 2002 and 2011, Ministry of Commerce and Industry, Govt. of India.

TABLE 3.13

**Foreign Direct Investment Approved (Country-wise)**
**(Post-Policy period from 01.08.1991 to 31.12.2009)**

(*Amount in Rs. million*)

| *Sl. No.* | *Name of Industry* | *No. of Approvals* | | | *Amount of FDI Approved* | *Percentage with Total FDI Approved* |
|---|---|---|---|---|---|---|
| | | *Total* | *Tech.* | *Fin.* | | |
| | *(1)* | *(2)* | *(3)* | *(4)* | *(5)* | *(6)* |
| 1. | Fuels | 867 | 266 | 601 | 768028.37 | 28.07 |
| 2. | Telecommunications | 777 | 123 | 654 | 551499.53 | 20.16 |
| 3. | Electrical Equipment | 4370 | 1143 | 3227 | 265604.28 | 9.71 |
| 4. | Transportation Industry | 1400 | 577 | 823 | 195126.18 | 7.13 |
| 5. | Service Sector | 938 | 56 | 882 | 167872.13 | 6.14 |
| 6. | Mettallurgical Industries | 679 | 350 | 329 | 153427.34 | 5.61 |
| 7. | Chemicals (other than Fartilizers) | 1687 | 794 | 893 | 125859.63 | 4.60 |
| 8. | Food Processing Industries | 837 | 152 | 685 | 91195.01 | 3.33 |
| 9. | Hotel and Tourism | 516 | 162 | 354 | 48433.56 | 1.77 |
| 10. | Textiles (Incld. Dyed, Printed) | 720 | 149 | 571 | 34057.31 | 1.24 |
| 11. | Paper Product and Pulp | 183 | 63 | 120 | 32600.02 | 1.19 |
| 12. | Drugs and Pharmaceuticals | 467 | 229 | 238 | 28690.94 | 1.05 |

| | | | | | | |
|---|---|---|---|---|---|---|
| 13. | Consultancy Services | 704 | 103 | 601 | 24989.31 | 0.91 |
| 14. | Trading | 548 | 19 | 529 | 23734.10 | 0.87 |
| 15. | Industrial Machinery | 1388 | 818 | 570 | 23603.48 | 0.86 |
| 16. | Cement and Gypsum Products | 108 | 41 | 67 | 21039.66 | 0.77 |
| 17. | Glass | 123 | 37 | 86 | 20314.89 | 0.74 |
| 18. | Miscellaneous Machinery and Engineering | 894 | 364 | 530 | 16078.32 | 0.59 |
| 19. | Fermentation Industries | 77 | 22 | 55 | 12884.42 | 0.47 |
| 20. | Rubber Goods | 212 | 104 | 108 | 11965.67 | 0.44 |
| 21. | Commercial, Office and Household Equipment | 88 | 31 | 57 | 11601.53 | 0.42 |
| 22. | Sugar | 11 | 1 | 10 | 10535.55 | 0.39 |
| 23. | Ceramics | 225 | 60 | 165 | 8811.60 | 0.32 |
| 24. | Leather, Leather Goods and Pickers | 199 | 40 | 159 | 5625.94 | 0.21 |
| 25. | Agricultural Machinery | 48 | 32 | 16 | 4534.85 | 0.17 |
| 26. | Machine Tools | 207 | 88 | 119 | 3963.12 | 0.14 |
| 27. | Medical and Surgical Appliances | 104 | 31 | 73 | 3651.10 | 0.13 |
| 28. | Soaps, Cosmetics and Toilet Preparation | 58 | 19 | 39 | 3383.53 | 0.12 |
| 29. | Vegetable Oils and Vanaspati | 45 | 3 | 42 | 2460.73 | 0.09 |
| 30. | Earth-Moving Machinery | 69 | 41 | 28 | 2430.96 | 0.09 |

*(Contd.)*

TABLE 3.13 (*Contd.*)

| (1) | (2) | (3) | (4) | (5) | (6) | (7) |
|---|---|---|---|---|---|---|
| 31. | Fertilizers | 64 | 57 | 7 | 2468.85 | 0.09 |
| 32. | Photographic Ranfilm and Paper | 28 | 12 | 16 | 2366.87 | 0.09 |
| 33. | Boilers and Steam Generating Plants | 76 | 42 | 34 | 1471.58 | 0.05 |
| 34. | Industrial Instruments | 186 | 106 | 80 | 1281.76 | 0.05 |
| 35. | Dye-Stuffs | 21 | 4 | 17 | 1164.43 | 0.04 |
| 36. | Prime Movers other than Electrical | 61 | 38 | 23 | 917.4 | 0.03 |
| 37. | Scientific Instruments | 46 | 16 | 30 | 657.36 | 0.02 |
| 38. | Mathematical Surveying and Drawing | 6 | 2 | 4 | 383.70 | 0.01 |
| 39. | Timber Products | 17 | 2 | 15 | 338.64 | 0.01 |
| 40. | Defence Industries | 6 | 6 | 0 | 0.00 | 0.00 |
| 41. | Glue and Gelatin | 4 | 1 | 3 | 14.25 | 0.00 |
| 42. | Miscellaneous Industries | 1804 | 717 | 1087 | 50704.27 | 1.85 |
| | Grand Total | 20868 | 6921 | 13947 | 2735772.01 | 100.00 |

*Source* : Calculated from *SIA Newsletter*, June 2011.

Bulk of the FDI in India was channelised in the form of fuels (28.07 per cent) and telecommunications (20.16 per cent). The next important share of FDI from the electrical equipment (9.71 per cent), transportation industry (7.13 per cent), service sector (6.14 per cent), metallurgical industries (5.61 per cent), chemicals (other than fertilizers) (4.60 per cent), food processing industries (3.33 per cent), hotel and tourism (1.77 per cent), textiles (including dyed, printed—1.24 per cent), paper product and pulp (1.19 per cent) and drugs and pharmaceuticals (1.05 per cent) (Table 3.13).

As far as the FDI in food products in India is concerned, data shows that FDI in fish and fish preparation has increased from Rs. 85.90 crore in 1992 to Rs. 427.60 crore in 2010. In the other food categories like sugar, coca, milk, fruits, mushroom and vinegar, there are some up and down movement of FDI inflows. In fruits and fruits preparation FDI increased to Rs. 3018.55 crore in 1997 and then decreased to Rs. 766.26 crore in 2005. (Table 3.14).

### (d) State-wise Approvals of FDI

Maharashtra has emerged as a clear winner in attracting the inflow of foreign direct investment ever since 1991 when the country opened its doors to foreign capital. However, other states, like Tamil Nadu and Karnataka, are fast catching up with pro-active policies of their respective state governments. According to the data available, total FDI approval since August 1991 till June 2010 is estimated to be Rs. 2,81,333.6 crore, of which 17.32 per cent or Rs. 48,722.4 crore was cornered by Maharashtra. Delhi finished a distant second with Rs. 33,806.5 crore, accounting for over 12 per cent of total inflows (Table 3.15).

Tamil Nadu, called as the Datriot of India, managed to attract FDI worth Rs. 23,470.3 crore (8.34 per cent) while Karnataka approved FDI proposals worth Rs. 21,945 crore (7.8 per cent). Gujarat finished fifth with a share of 6.56 per cent of the total approvals aggregating Rs. 18,453.2 crore. Despite its pro-active image, Andhra Pradesh could only manage to attract Rs. 13,092.24 crore of foreign capital, which works out to Rs. 4.65 per cent of total FDI approvals during the period (Table 3.15).

TABLE 3.14

**FDI in Food Products in India**

(Rs. Crore)

| Year | Fish | Sugar | Coca | Milk | Fruit | Mushroom | Vinegar |
|---|---|---|---|---|---|---|---|
| (1) | (2) | (3) | (4) | (5) | (6) | (7) | (8) |
| 1991 | 0 | 0 | 0 | 0 | — | 0 | 0 |
| 1992 | 85.90 | 7.56 | 0 | 1.31 | 5.00 | 0.6 | 0 |
| 1993 | 50.06 | 535.19 | 0 | 20.50 | 363.58 | 110.08 | 0 |
| 1994 | 166.23 | 32.77 | 91.78 | 826.42 | 352.31 | 3096.85 | 7.43 |
| 1995 | 42.46 | 70.70 | 0 | 0 | 912.13 | 517.94 | 0.70 |
| 1996 | 91.10 | 222.95 | 969.38 | 265.30 | 119.52 | 945.79 | 0 |
| 1997 | 46.90 | 913.50 | 119.00 | 369.99 | 3018.55 | 115.33 | 0 |
| 1998 | 0 | 6.22 | 0 | 144.96 | 1623.37 | 72.24 | 50.00 |
| 2000 | 359.60 | 31.00 | 0 | 25.00 | 101.75 | 0 | 0 |
| 2005 | 0.61 | 0 | 0 | 0 | 766.26 | 16.18 | 0 |
| 2010 (Till May) | 427.60 | 139.50 | 0 | 0 | 12.17 | 0 | 0 |

*Source* : IIC's Data Tape, 2010, Indian Institute of Public Administration, New Delhi.

TABLE 3.15

**State-wise Break-up of Foreign Direct Investment (Aug. 1991 to June 2010)**

| *State* | *Total No. of Approvals* | *Amount (Rs. Crore)* | *% to Total* | *Rank* |
|---|---|---|---|---|
| *(1)* | *(2)* | *(3)* | *(4)* | *(5)* |
| Maharashtra | 4002 | 48722.40 | 17.32 | 1 |
| Delhi | 1990 | 33806.58 | 12.02 | 2 |
| Tamil Nadu | 2165 | 23470.30 | 8.34 | 3 |
| Karnataka | 1973 | 21945.00 | 7.80 | 4 |
| Gujarat | 1050 | 18453.20 | 6.56 | 5 |
| Andhra Pradesh | 1017 | 13092.24 | 4.65 | 6 |
| Madhya Pradesh | 225 | 9227.30 | 3.28 | 7 |
| West Bengal | 594 | 8808.30 | 3.13 | 8 |
| Orissa | 136 | 8229.00 | 2.92 | 9 |
| Uttar Pradesh | 740 | 4795.00 | 1.70 | 10 |
| Haryana | 784 | 3519.40 | 1.25 | 11 |
| Rajasthan | 320 | 3004.70 | 1.07 | 12 |
| Punjab | 183 | 1968.40 | 0.70 | 13 |
| Kerala | 265 | 1527.80 | 0.54 | 14 |
| Pondicherry | 115 | 1242.29 | 0.44 | 15 |
| Himachal Pradesh | 97 | 1173.90 | 0.42 | 16 |
| Goa | 177 | 970.62 | 0.35 | 17 |
| Bihar | 47 | 739.50 | 0.26 | 18 |
| Chhattisgarh | 46 | 632.70 | 0.22 | 19 |
| Chandigarh | 59 | 161.97 | 0.06 | 20 |
| Jharkhand | 74 | 143.80 | 0.05 | 21 |
| Uttaranchal | 49 | 125.60 | 0.04 | 22 |
| Dadra and Nagar Haveli | 70 | 123.98 | 0.04 | 23 |
| Meghalaya | 5 | 52.96 | 0.02 | 24 |
| Daman and Dieu | 39 | 55.20 | 0.02 | 25 |
| Assam | 18 | 1.49 | negl. | 26 |

*(Contd.)*

TABLE 3.15 (*Contd.*)

| (1) | (2) | (3) | (4) | (5) |
|---|---|---|---|---|
| Jammu and Kashmir | 5 | 8.40 | negl. | 27 |
| Manipur | 1 | 3.20 | negl. | 28 |
| Nagaland | 2 | 3.68 | negl. | 29 |
| Tripura | 2 | 0.68 | negl. | 30 |
| Andaman and Nicobar | 8 | 13.70 | negl. | 31 |
| Arunachal Pradesh | 2 | 11.00 | negl. | 32 |
| Lakshadweep | 1 | 0.50 | negl. | 33 |
| Mizoram | 1 | 1.50 | negl. | 34 |
| States Not Indicated | 5822 | 75296.50 | 26.76 | — |
| Total | 22084 | 281333.60 | 100.00 | — |

*Source* : Kumar, *The Financial Express*, July 2010.

Notably, the foreign capital inflows seems to have only benefited a handful of developed states, which have a well, developed physical infrastructure and are traditionally forward-looking. For instance, the top five states—Maharashtra, Delhi, Tamil Nadu, Karnataka and Gujarat—together account for 52 per cent of total FDI approvals since 1991, while the rest is spread thinly among the remaining states. At least 22 states, including Punjab and Karala (which incidentally have well developed social infrastructure), account for less than 1 per cent share in the total FDI approvals.

One implication of this could be the widening of regional disparity among the states leading to interregional imbalances as well as large-scale migration. However, the tide seems to have been turning of late with the governments of the lag-guard states stepping up their efforts to attract foreign capital. Many states also are in the process of formulating their own FDI policy, which is well within the rule of the land, to attract the foreign capital (Table 3.16).

## III.VI. OUTWARD FLOWS OF FDI FROM INDIA

We divide India's outward FDI flows in four sub-periods:

TABLE 3.16

**Foreign Direct Investment Approved (State-wise)**
**(Post-Policy Period from August 1991 to June 2010)**

*(Amount in Rs. million)*

| Sl. No. | State | No. of Approvals | | | Amount of FDI Approved | Percentage with Total FDI Approved |
|---|---|---|---|---|---|---|
| | | Total | Tech. | Fin. | | |
| | (1) | (2) | (3) | (4) | (5) | (6) |
| 1. | Andhra Pradesh | 933 | 231 | 702 | 126153.83 | 4.61 |
| 2. | Assam | 17 | 13 | 4 | 14.95 | negl. |
| 3. | Bihar | 46 | 22 | 24 | 7395.28 | 0.27 |
| 4. | Gujarat | 1019 | 498 | 521 | 173655.11 | 6.35 |
| 5. | Haryana | 751 | 281 | 470 | 32041.12 | 1.17 |
| 6. | Himachal Pradesh | 93 | 55 | 38 | 3630.90 | 0.13 |
| 7. | J & K | 5 | 3 | 2 | 84.10 | Negl. |
| 8. | Karnataka | 1797 | 432 | 1365 | 212208.81 | 7.76 |
| 9. | Kerala | 243 | 61 | 182 | 14807.82 | 0.54 |
| 10. | MP | 222 | 70 | 152 | 91607.06 | 3.35 |
| 11. | Maharashtra | 3689 | 1117 | 2572 | 474913.79 | 17.36 |

*(Contd.)*

TABLE 3.16 (*Contd.*)

| (1) | (2) | (3) | (4) | (5) | (6) |
|---|---|---|---|---|---|
| 12. Manipur | 1 | 0 | 1 | 31.85 | Negl. |
| 13. Meghalaya | 4 | 0 | 4 | 529.60 | 0.02 |
| 14. Nagaland | 2 | 1 | 1 | 36.80 | Negl. |
| 15. Orissa | 136 | 49 | 87 | 82290.03 | 3.01 |
| 16. Punjab | 178 | 54 | 124 | 19683.79 | 0.72 |
| 17. Rajasthan | 311 | 99 | 212 | 26469.91 | 0.97 |
| 18. TN | 2014 | 520 | 1494 | 227726.10 | 8.32 |
| 19. Tripura | 2 | 1 | 1 | 6.80 | Negl. |
| 20. UP | 722 | 260 | 462 | 46403.99 | 1.70 |
| 21. WB | 571 | 190 | 381 | 87012.93 | 3.18 |
| 22. Chattisgarh | 44 | 29 | 15 | 6327.41 | 0.23 |
| 23. Jharkhand | 72 | 48 | 24 | 1438.15 | 0.05 |
| 24. Uttaranchal | 48 | 22 | 26 | 1256.49 | 0.05 |
| 25. A & N Island | 8 | 0 | 8 | 137.87 | 0.01 |
| 26. Arunachal Pradesh | 2 | 0 | 2 | 110.60 | Negl. |
| 27. Chandigarh | 43 | 9 | 34 | 1469.60 | 0.05 |
| 28. D & N Haveli | 70 | 46 | 24 | 1239.80 | 0.05 |

| | | | | | | |
|---|---|---|---|---|---|---|
| 29. | Delhi | 1750 | 200 | 1550 | 332055.60 | 12.14 |
| 30. | Goa | 165 | 56 | 109 | 8795.88 | 0.32 |
| 31. | Lakshadweep | 1 | 0 | 1 | 5.00 | Negl. |
| 32. | Mizoram | 1 | 0 | 1 | 15.22 | Negl. |
| 33. | Pandicherry | 109 | 39 | 70 | 12409.55 | 0.45 |
| 34. | Daman & Dieu | 39 | 14 | 25 | 552.20 | 0.02 |
| 35. | Other (States Not Indicated) | 5760 | 2501 | 3259 | 743254.06 | 27.17 |
| | Grand Total | 20,868 | 6,921 | 13,947 | 2735772.01 | 100.00 |

*Note* : Increase/Decrease in FDI approvals on account of change in location.
*Source* : *SIA Newsletter*, 2002 and 2010, Government of India, New Delhi.

(a) 1948-1967, (b) 1968-1979, (c) 1980s, and (d) 1990s. We shall discuss them one by one in the following.

### (a) 1948-67 : Creating Locational Advantages with Import Protection

In this period the bulk of the FDI stock was of natural resource seeking and of trading type and had concentrated in raw materials, extractive, or survice sectors. Tea plantations and jute accounted for a little over a quarter of total FDI which together contributed half of India's exports; about 32 per cent was in trading and other services, 9 per cent in petroleum and only about 20 per cent in manufacturing other than jute. Creation of vocational advantages led to a sharp jump in the share of manufacturing in the FDI stock to over 40 per cent from around 20 per cent at the time of independence (*Kidron*, 1965).

### (b) 1968-79 : Protecting the Domestic Base of 'Created' Assets

The import substituting industrialization followed by India had created a reasonably diversified industrial base in the country with substantial machinery capability by early 1970s. Considerable learning and technological capability accumulation had taken place in Indian enterprises as protection policies restricted technology imports. Indian enterprises learnt to do trouble shooting, adapt the processes and products imported originally from their Western counterparts to Indian conditions, substitute imported raw materials by locally available ones, and made them more rugged to with-stand frequent power failures.

The share of chemical and engineering goods in India's total exports nearly doubled from 7.9 per cent to 15.5 per cent over 1969-70 to 1980-81 (*Kumar*, 1987). The number and magnitude of investments made by Indian enterprises in their wholly owned subsidiaries and joint ventures made by the year of government approval on the basis of firm wise unpublished data collected from the Indian Ministry of Commerce. In a five year period 64 new investments were made with a total Indian investment of Rs. 581 million in contrast to just 36 ventures existing in 1975 with a cumulative investment of Rs. 442 million.

It is also believe that bulk of Indian FDI (80 per cent in number and 95 per cent in terms of value) made in the 1970s gone to other developing countries. In fact, much of Indian FDI was concentrated in Malaysia, Indonesia, Singapore, Kenya, Sri Lanka and Nepal.

### (c) 1980s : 'Halting Reforms' for Improving International Competitiveness

Towards the end of the 1970s India's failure to step us significantly the volume and proportion of her manufactured exports in the background of the second oil price shock began to worry the policy-makers. The initial enthusiasm shown by Indian enterprises in international operations in the late 1970s wanted slightly in the early 1980s when the magnitude of FDI declined to 338 million from 581 million in the previous period although an equal number of investments were made (Table 3.17). In the second half of the 1980s, the overseas investment activity picked up again to 91 ventures abroad with a total Indian investment of Rs. 2030 million. Around the mid-1980s in geographical pattern of Indian FDI abroad had also registered a shift coinciding the increase in the magnitudes that took place.

Till the mid-1980s India's FDI tended to concentrate in developing countries. Since then, however, the share of industrialised countries has gone up steadily. In the second half of 1980s, industrialised countries hosted 27 of the 91 Indian ventures with 21.6 per cent of investments. In the late-1980s, the Eastern and Central European countries, which had been important markets for Indian exports, emerged as important hosts of Indian FDI with 14 ventures accounting for 32.6 per cent of Indian FDI in the period. The Southeast Asian countries hosted another 23 per cent of FDI of the period in 27 ventures.

The shift in terms of sectoral composition also came about in the mid-1980s since when the share of manufacturing in total FDI outflow declined from nearly 75 per cent in the early 1980s to about 55 per cent in the late 1980s. The fact that bulk (nearly 70 per cent) of FDI outflows to industrialised countries are in services and not in manufacturing is clear from Table 3.17 which shows the sectoral break-up of Indian FDI hosted by different regions. The share of services is also considerable in Southeast

TABLE 3.17

**Investments of Indian Enterprises in Overseas (by Year)**

*(Values in Millions Rupees)*

| *Region* | *<1970* | | *1970-85* | | *1866-95* | |
|---|---|---|---|---|---|---|
| | *No.* | *Indian Equity* | *No.* | *Indian Equity* | *No.* | *Indian Equity* |
| (1) | (2) | (3) | (4) | (5) | (6) | (7) |
| **South-east and East Asia** | 3 | 62.319 | 13 | 57.972 | 27 | 323.17 |
| Singapore | | | | | 9 | 25.147 |
| Malaysia | 2 | 59.884 | 5 | 14.173 | 5 | 60.702 |
| Thailand | 1 | 2.435 | 2 | 12.072 | 4 | 120.841 |
| Hong Kong | | | 1 | 0.28 | 2 | 0.307 |
| Others | | | 5 | 31.482 | 8 | 116.173 |
| **South Asia** | 1 | 0.23 | 1 | 0.699 | 7 | 95.143 |
| Sri Lanka | 1 | 0.23 | 1 | 0.899 | 3 | 52.303 |
| Nepal | | | | | 4 | 42.84 |
| Bangladesh | | | | | | |
| Maldives | | | | | | |
| Pacific Islands | | | | | 1 | 1.403 |
| Fiji | | | | | | |
| Solomon Island | | | | | 1 | 1.403 |
| Tongo | | | | | | |

| | | | | | | |
|---|---|---|---|---|---|---|
| Vanuatu | | | | | | |
| Africa | 3 | 77.997 | 2 | 186.61 | 10 | 94.317 |
| Mauritius | | | | | | |
| Kenya | 1 | 55.545 | 1 | 186.198 | 4 | 31.459 |
| Senegal | | | | | | |
| Egypt | | | | | | |
| Others | 2 | 22.452 | 1 | 0.414 | 6 | 62.788 |
| **Middle East** | | | 3 | 2.9 | 5 | 9.65 |
| UAE | | | 2 | 0.9 | 4 | 6.657 |
| Israel | | | | | | |
| Saudi Arabia | | | 1 | 2.0 | 1 | 2.993 |
| Jordan | | | | | | |
| Others | | | | | | |
| **E. & C. Europe** | | | | | 1 | 19.4 |
| Russia | | | | | | |
| Kazakhastan | | | | | | |
| Uzbekistan | | | | | | |
| Turkmenistan | | | | | | |
| Others | | | | | 1 | 19.4 |
| **Latin America** | | | | | | |
| Mexico | | | | | | |

*(Contd.)*

TABLE 3.17 (*Contd.*)

| *(1)* | *(2)* | *(3)* | *(4)* | *(5)* | *(6)* | *(7)* |
|---|---|---|---|---|---|---|
| Panama | | | | | | |
| **Developing Countries** | 7 | 140.546 | 19 | 248.181 | 51 | 543.083 |
| Western Europe | 7 | 52.609 | 1 | 0.359 | 11 | 33.439 |
| UK | 1 | 0.033 | 1 | 0.359 | 11 | 33.439 |
| Ireland | | | | | | |
| Netherlands | | | | | | |
| Germany | 3 | 10.403 | | | | |
| Switzerland | 3 | 42.173 | | | | |
| Others | | | | | | |
| **North America** | | | 1 | 0.037 | 3 | 4.426 |
| USA | | | 1 | 0.037 | 3 | 4.426 |
| Canada | | | | | | |
| Japan and Australia | | | 1 | 0.72 | | |
| Japan | | | | | | |
| Australia | | | 1 | 0.72 | | |
| Industrialised Countries | 7 | 52.609 | 3 | 1.116 | 14 | 37..865 |
| Grand Total | 14 | 193.155 | 22 | 249.297 | 65 | 580.948 |

(*Contd.*)

TABLE 3.17 (*Contd.*)

(*Values in Millions Rupees*)

| *Region* | *1996-2001* | | *2002-06* | | *2007-11* | | *Total* | |
|---|---|---|---|---|---|---|---|---|
| | *No.* | *Indian Equity* | *No.* | *Indian Equity* | *No.* | *Indian Equity* | *No.* | *Indian Equity* |
| *(1)* | *(8)* | *(9)* | *(10)* | *(11)* | *(12)* | *(13)* | *(14)* | *(15)* |
| **South-east and East Asia** | 8 | 32.616 | 27 | 466.504 | 87 | 1635.949 | 145 | 2578.53 |
| Singapore | 4 | 20.406 | 6 | 274.884 | 32 | 689.711 | 51 | 101.1488 |
| Malaysia | 3 | 6.21 | 8 | 90.113 | 17 | 466.358 | 40 | 707.44 |
| Thailand | | | 8 | 92.252 | 6 | 25.822 | 21 | 253.422 |
| Hong Kong | | | 4 | 9.046 | 9 | 80.289 | 17 | 99.902 |
| Others | 1 | 6.0 | 1 | 0.209 | 3 | 263.769 | 18 | 417.618 |
| **South Asia** | 14 | 31.141 | 8 | 96.884 | 29 | 845.813 | 60 | 1069.91 |
| Sri Lanka | 8 | 12.243 | 4 | 35.658 | 12 | 675.921 | 29 | 776.054 |
| Nepal | 6 | 19.898 | 3 | 31.146 | 9 | 137.555 | 22 | 231.439 |
| Bangladesh | | | 1 | 30.08 | 7 | 16.837 | 8 | 46.917 |
| Maldives | | | | | 1 | 15.5 | 1 | 15.5 |
| Pacific Islands | 2 | 0.728 | | | 1 | 1.398 | 4 | 3.529 |
| Fiji | | | | | | | 1 | 1.403 |
| Solomon 1st | | | | | | | 1 | 0.529 |

(*Contd.*)

TABLE 3.17 (*Contd.*)

| (1) | (8) | (9) | (10) | (11) | (12) | (13) | (14) | (15) |
|---|---|---|---|---|---|---|---|---|
| Tongo | 1 | 0.529 | | | | | 1 | 0.199 |
| Vanuatu | 1 | 0.199 | | | 1 | 1.398 | 1 | 1.398 |
| Africa | 13 | 210.61 | 7 | 16.506 | 27 | 916.874 | 62 | 1502.914 |
| Mauritius | | | 2 | 7.089 | 12 | 782.711 | 14 | 789.8 |
| Kenya | 2 | 4.123 | 1 | 1.404 | 3 | 6.954 | 12 | 285.771 |
| Senegal | 1 | 142.18 | | | | | 1 | 142.18 |
| Egypt | 3 | 13.523 | | | 3 | 68.292 | 6 | 81.815 |
| Others | 7 | 50.784 | 4 | 8.013 | 9 | 58.917 | 29 | 203.348 |
| **Middle East** | 7 | 21.574 | 6 | 345.85 | 31 | 4556.043 | 52 | 4836.017 |
| UAE | 2 | 12.639 | 2 | 1.75 | 22 | 3263.028 | 32 | 3284.974 |
| Israel | | | | | 1 | 677.184 | 1 | 877.164 |
| Saudi Arabia | 2 | 5.538 | | | 3 | 590.85 | 7 | 801.181 |
| Jordan | | | 2 | 265.07 | | | 2 | 285.070 |
| Others | 3 | 3.397 | 2 | 79.03 | 5 | 25.201 | 10 | 107.828 |
| **E. & C. Europe** | | | 14 | 662.521 | 53 | 794.036 | 68 | 1475.947 |
| Russia | | | 8 | 94.942 | 25 | 466.257 | 33 | 561.199 |
| Kazakhastan | | | 2 | 523.500 | 1 | 5.013 | 3 | 528.513 |
| Uzbekistan | | | 1 | 12.000 | 9 | 152.452 | 10 | 164.452 |

| | | | | | | | | |
|---|---|---|---|---|---|---|---|---|
| Turkmenistan | | | 2 | 3.479 | 15 | 162.47 | 18 | 185.339 |
| **Latin America** | | | 2 | 2.701 | 4 | 230.75 | 6 | 233.451 |
| Mexico | | | | | 2 | 162.278 | 2 | 162.278 |
| Panama | | | 2 | 2.701 | 2 | 68.472 | 4 | 71.173 |
| **Developing Countries** | 44 | 296.669 | 64 | 1590.966 | 212 | 8980.863 | 397 | 11800.398 |
| Western Europe | 13 | 10.698 | 14 | 248.135 | 73 | 1547.686 | 119 | 1892.926 |
| UK | 10 | 7.664 | 8 | 240.682 | 36 | 698.882 | 67 | 981.059 |
| Ireland | | | | | 2 | 172.35 | 2 | 172.35 |
| Netherlands | | | 2 | 2.654 | 6 | 147.588 | 8 | 150.242 |
| Germany | 1 | 0.35 | 1 | 2.3 | 8 | 109.06 | 13 | 122.113 |
| Switzerland | 1 | 2.522 | 3 | 2.499 | 19 | 341.486 | 23 | 346.507 |
| Others | | | | | | | | |
| **North America** | 7 | 31.086 | 13 | 190.647 | 55 | 915.688 | 79 | 1141.884 |
| USA | 7 | 31.086 | 13 | 190.647 | 53 | 876.079 | 77 | 1102.275 |
| Canada | | | | | 2 | 39.609 | 2 | 39.609 |
| Japan & Australia | | | | | 4 | 206.337 | 5 | 207.047 |
| Japan | | | | | 2 | 201.027 | 2 | 201.01 |
| Australia | | | | | 2 | 5.310 | 3 | 6.037 |
| Industrialised Countries | 20 | 41..784 | 27 | 438..782 | 133 | 2669.701 | 203 | 3241.857 |
| Grand Total | 64 | 338.453 | 91 | 2029.748 | 344 | 11650.564 | 600 | 15042.165 |

*Source* : Own computations on the basis of unpublished data from Ministry of Commerce, Government of India.

TABLE 3.18(a)
**Investments of Indian Enterprises in Overseas (by Industry)**

*(Values in Millions Rupees)*

| *Industry* | *<1970* | | *1970-85* | | *1996-95* | |
|---|---|---|---|---|---|---|
| | *No.* | *Indian Equity* | *No.* | *Indian Equity* | *No.* | *Indian Equity* |
| (1) | (2) | (3) | (4) | (5) | (6) | (7) |
| Extractive | | | 1 | 0.8 | 2 | 33.835 |
| Light Eengineering | 4 | 31.765 | 4 | 7.816 | 13 | 162.155 |
| Textiles | 3 | 64.995 | 5 | 39.137 | 5 | 61.545 |
| Chemicals and Pharmaceuticals | | | | | 5 | 31.254 |
| Food Products | | | | | 1 | 0.573 |
| Leather and Rubber | | | 1 | 2.0 | 1 | 0.7 |
| Others | 1 | 46.786 | 6 | 197.754 | 4 | 104.127 |
| Manufacturing Total | 8 | 143.546 | 16 | 246.707 | 29 | 360.444 |
| Hotels and Restaurants | | | 2 | 7.57 | 7 | 84.096 |
| Engineering Services | | | 1 | 0.26 | 1 | 2.6 |
| Trading | 1 | 5.1 | 1 | 0.359 | 10 | 11.239 |
| Consultancy | 1 | 0.403 | 1 | 0.414 | 4 | 29.153 |
| Others | 4 | 44.106 | | | 12 | 59.581 |
| Services Total | 6 | 49.609 | 5 | 1.79 | 34 | 186.669 |
| Grand Total | 14 | 193.155 | 22 | 249.297 | 65 | 580.948 |

TABLE 3.18(a) (Contd.)

*(Values in Millions Rupees)*

| Industry | 1996-2001 | | 2002-06 | | 2007-11 | | Total | |
|---|---|---|---|---|---|---|---|---|
| | No. | Indian Equity | No. | Indian Equity | No. | Indian Equity | No. | Indian Equity |
| (1) | (8) | (9) | (10) | (11) | (12) | (13) | (14) | (15) |
| Extractive | 1 | 0.313 | | | 1 | 3117.6 | 5 | 3152.548 |
| Light Engineering | 7 | 32.882 | 7 | 59.915 | 30 | 1189.852 | 65 | 1484.385 |
| Textiles | | | 3 | 30.038 | 11 | 214.261 | 27 | 409.976 |
| Chemicals and Pharmaceuticals | 11 | 162.093 | 13 | 463.851 | 34 | 1848.427 | 63 | 2505.625 |
| Food Products | 5 | 13.448 | 3 | 21.269 | 6 | 68.575 | 15 | 103.865 |
| Leather and Rubber | 2 | 11.591 | 7 | 488.166 | 6 | 514.161 | 17 | 1016.618 |
| Others | 5 | 32.216 | 4 | 44.948 | 32 | 1284.037 | 52 | 1709.958 |
| Manufacturing Total | 30 | 252.23 | 37 | 1108.187 | 119 | 5119.31 | 239 | 7230.427 |
| Hotels and Restaurants | 4 | 29.71 | 10 | 144.578 | 11 | 104.804 | 34 | 363.945 |
| Engineering Services | 1 | 0.59 | 2 | 69.302 | 18 | 212.695 | 23 | 285.447 |
| Trading | 4 | 23.752 | 12 | 103.717 | 78 | 992.262 | 106 | 1136.429 |
| Consultancy | 6 | 2.505 | 7 | 138.326 | 9 | 121.208 | 28 | 292.009 |
| Others | 18 | 29.353 | 23 | 465.638 | 108 | 1982.683 | 165 | 2581.36 |
| Services Total | 33 | 85.910 | 54 | 921.561 | 224 | 3413.652 | 356 | 4659.105 |
| Grand Total | 64 | 338.453 | 91 | 2029.748 | 344 | 11650.564 | 600 | 15042.165 |

*Source* : Own computations on the basis of unpublished data from Ministry of Commerce, Government of India.

TABLE 3.18(b)
**Indian Outward FDI by Region and Sector**

**(1970-2011)**

*(Values in Million of Rupees)*

| Region of Destination | Extractive | Manufacturing | | | | | | |
|---|---|---|---|---|---|---|---|---|
| | Total | Light Engineering | Textiles | Chemicals and Pharmaceuticals | Food Products | Leather and Rubber | Other | Manufacturing Sub-total |
| (1) | (2) | (3) | (4) | (5) | (6) | (7) | (8) | (9) |
| South-east and East Asia | | 712.757 (27.6) | 169.036 (6.56) | 228.666 (8.87) | | 17.632 (0.68) | 260.893 (10.1) | 1388.984 (53.87) |
| South Asia | 33.835 (3.16) | 7.595 (0.71) | 29.51 (2.76) | 101.928 (9.53) | 30.364 (2.8) | 8.491 (0.79) | 709.721 (66.3) | 887.609 (82.96) |
| Pacific Island | | | | 3.529 (100) | | | | 3.529 (100) |
| Africa | | 65.062 (4.3) | 123.398 (8.21) | 150.348 (10.0) | 3.203 (0.21) | 488.569 (32.5) | 229.547 (15.3) | 1060.127 (70.54) |
| Middle East | 3118.4 (63.18) | 33.186 (0.67) | 45.396 (0.92) | 1511.844 (30.6) | 13.918 (0.28) | 2.0 (0.04) | 31.563 (0.11) | 1637.907 (33.18) |

| | | | | | | | | |
|---|---|---|---|---|---|---|---|---|
| Eastern and Central Europe | | 219.192 (14.9) | | 46.99 (3.18) | 23.418 (1.59) | 497.6 (33.7) | 241.753 (16.38) | 1028.953 (69.71) |
| Latin America | | 1.773 (0.76) | | | | | 160.0 (68.54) | 161.773 (69.3) |
| Developing Countries Total | 3152.24 (26.71) | 1039.565 (8.81) | 367.34 (3.11) | 2.43.305 (17.32) | 70.903 (0.60) | 1014.29 (8.60) | 1631.68 (13.83) | 6168.882 (52.28) |
| Western Europe | 0.313 (0.02) | 332.489 (17.6) | 23.371 (1.23) | 229.467 (12.1) | 32.662 (1.72) | 2.3 (0.12) | 69.399 (3.67) | 689.688 (36.43) |
| North America | | 112.331 (9.84) | 19.265 (1.69) | 227.566 (19.93) | 0.3 (0.03) | | 7.082- (0.62) | 366.544 (32.10) |
| Japan and Australia | | | | 5.317 (2.57) | | | | 5.317 (2.57) |
| Industrialised Countries Total | 0.313 | 444.82 (0.01) | 42.636 (13.72) | 462.35 (1.32) | 32.962 (14.26) | 2.3 (1.02) | 76.481 (0.07) | 1061.549 (2.35) |
| Grand Total | 3152.55 (20.96) | 1484.385 (9.86) | 409.976 (2.72) | 2505.63 (16.7) | 103.865 (0.69) | 1016.6 (6.76) | 1709.96 (11.37) | 7230.416 (48.1) |

(*Contd.*)

TABLE 3.18(b) (Contd.)

(Values in Million of Rupees)

| Region of Destination | Services | | | | | | |
|---|---|---|---|---|---|---|---|
| | Hotels and restaurants | Engineering Services | Trading | Cansul-tancy | Financial and others | Services sub-total | Total |
| (1) | (10) | (11) | (12) | (13) | (14) | (15) | (16) |
| South-east and East Asia | 10.974<br>(0.43) | 0.26<br>(0.01) | 404.225<br>(15.7) | 52.924<br>(2.05) | 721.163<br>(28.0) | 1189.546<br>(46.13) | 2578.53<br>(100) |
| South Asia | 61.267<br>(5.72) | 0.59<br>(0.06) | 4.575<br>(0.43) | | 82.034<br>(7.67) | 148.466<br>(13.88) | 1069.91<br>(100) |
| Pacific Island | | | | | | | 3.529<br>(100) |
| Africa | 34.055<br>(2.27) | 2.726<br>(0.18) | 39.747<br>(2.64) | 29.926<br>(1.99) | 336.33<br>(22.4) | 442.787<br>(29.46) | 1502.91<br>(100) |
| Middle East | 20.993<br>(1.65) | 5.194<br>(0.11) | 5.483<br>(0.11) | 81.317<br>(1.65) | 84.723<br>(1.72) | 179.71<br>(3.64) | 4936.02<br>(100) |
| Eastern and Central Europe | 206.01<br>(13.6) | | 125.8<br>(8.52) | 10.588<br>(0.72) | 104.61<br>(7.1) | 447.008<br>(30.29) | 1475.95<br>(100) |
| Latin America | | | 2.278<br>(0.98) | | 69.4<br>(29.73) | 71.678<br>(30.70) | 233.451<br>(100) |
| Developing Countries Total | 315.299<br>(2.67) | 8.77<br>(0.07) | 582.108<br>(4.93) | 174.755<br>(1.48) | 398253<br>(11.85) | 2479.195<br>(21.01) | 11800.3<br>(100) |

| | | | | | | | |
|---|---|---|---|---|---|---|---|
| Western Europe | 7.735<br>(0.4) | 64.652<br>(3.42) | 406.8<br>(21.5) | 25.946<br>(1.37) | 697.792<br>(36.86) | 1202.925<br>(63.55) | 1892.93<br>(100) |
| North America | 37.091<br>(3.25) | 212.205<br>(18.57) | 147.521<br>(12.92) | 91.308<br>(8.00) | 287.395<br>(25.17) | 775.34<br>(67.9) | 1375.34<br>(100) |
| Japan and Australia | 3.82<br>(1.84) | | | | 197.91<br>(95.59) | 201.73<br>(97.43) | 207.047<br>(100) |
| Industrialised Countries Total | 48.646<br>(1.50) | 276.677<br>(8.53) | 554.321<br>(17.10) | 117.254<br>(3.62) | 183.097<br>(36.49) | 2179.995<br>(67.25) | 3241.86<br>(100 |
| Grand Total | 363.945<br>(2.42) | 285.447<br>(1.90) | 1136.43<br>(7.56) | 292.009<br>(1.94) | 2381.36<br>(15.8) | 4659.19<br>(29.6) | 15042.2<br>(100) |

*Source* : Own computations on the basis of unpublished data from Ministry of Commerce, Government of India.

TABLE 3.19

**Foreign Direct Investment Approved in West Bengal (1991-2010)**

| *Country Name* | *Status and Number of Projects* | | | | | | | | | | |
|---|---|---|---|---|---|---|---|---|---|---|---|
| | *Implemented* | *Adv. Stage of Implemented* | *Under Implemented* | *Dropped* | *No Progress* | *No. Response about pro.* | *Name not available* | *Not in W.B.* | *F.C. amended* | *No. FDI Approval* | *Investment (Rs. in lakh)* |
| *(1)* | *(2)* | *(3)* | *(4)* | *(5)* | *(6)* | *(7)* | *(8)* | *(9)* | *(10)* | *(11)* | *(12)* |
| Australia | 3 | 0 | 1 | 1 | 1 | 15 | 0 | 0 | 0 | 0 | 12695.71 |
| Armenia | 1 | 0 | 0 | 0 | 0 | 0 | 0 | 0 | 0 | 0 | 193.00 |
| Austria | 2 | 0 | 0 | 0 | 0 | 3 | 0 | 0 | 0 | 0 | 3984.10 |
| Bangladesh | 0 | 0 | 0 | 0 | 0 | 1 | 0 | 0 | 0 | 0 | 52.80 |
| Belgium | 1 | 0 | 0 | 0 | 0 | 2 | 0 | 0 | 0 | 0 | 71.00 |
| Cayman Island | 0 | 0 | 0 | 0 | 0 | 0 | 0 | 1 | 0 | 0 | 1600.00 |
| China | 1 | 0 | 0 | 2 | 0 | 0 | 0 | 0 | 0 | 0 | 200.64 |
| Finland | 1 | 0 | 0 | 1 | 1 | 0 | 0 | 0 | 0 | 0 | 836.75 |
| France | 7 | 0 | 0 | 0 | 0 | 1 | 0 | 0 | 0 | 0 | 463.86 |
| Germany | 17 | 6 | 7 | 5 | 3 | 30 | 0 | 2 | 0 | 0 | 30690.81 |
| Hong Kong | 1 | 0 | 1 | 1 | 0 | 2 | 0 | 0 | 0 | 0 | 33118.48 |
| Iceland | 0 | 0 | 0 | 1 | 0 | 1 | 0 | 0 | 0 | 0 | 148.10 |
| Italy | 1 | 0 | 0 | 2 | 1 | 4 | 0 | 0 | 0 | 0 | 841.15 |

| | | | | | | | | | | | |
|---|---|---|---|---|---|---|---|---|---|---|---|
| Japan | 4 | 1 | 2 | 1 | 1 | 1 | 0 | 2 | 0 | 1 | 109977.8 |
| Korea (S) | 0 | 1 | 0 | 2 | 0 | 1 | 0 | 0 | 0 | 0 | 10704.13 |
| Kuwait | 0 | 0 | 0 | 1 | 0 | 0 | 0 | 0 | 0 | 0 | 13875.00 |
| Malaysia | 1 | 1 | 1 | 1 | 0 | 0 | 0 | 1 | 0 | 0 | 7548.00 |
| Mauritius | 5 | 0 | 7 | 1 | 2 | 1 | 0 | 0 | 0 | 0 | 167999.00 |
| NRI | 5 | 1 | 2 | 3 | 2 | 12 | 0 | 0 | 0 | 1 | 13319.25 |
| Nepal | 0 | 0 | 1 | 0 | 0 | 0 | 0 | 0 | 0 | 0 | 300.00 |
| Netherland | 3 | 2 | 4 | 1 | 0 | 2 | 0 | 1 | 0 | 0 | 4178.99 |
| Russia | 0 | 0 | 1 | 0 | 0 | 0 | 0 | 0 | 0 | 0 | 12.00 |
| Saudi Arabia | 0 | 0 | 0 | 0 | 0 | 4 | 0 | 0 | 0 | 0 | 3956.80 |
| Singapore | 5 | 0 | 0 | 0 | 1 | 2 | 0 | 0 | 0 | 0 | 2261.08 |
| South Africa | 0 | 0 | 0 | 1 | 0 | 0 | 0 | 0 | 0 | 0 | 25.00 |
| Spain | 0 | 0 | 0 | 0 | 0 | 1 | 0 | 0 | 0 | 0 | 41.65 |
| Sweden | 1 | 0 | 0 | 0 | 0 | 0 | 0 | 0 | 0 | 0 | 32.75 |
| Switzerland | 9 | 1 | 2 | 0 | 0 | 1 | 0 | 0 | 0 | 0 | 11822.31 |
| U.K. | 17 | 0 | 4 | 3 | 0 | 75 | 10 | 1 | 0 | 1 | 14050.91 |
| U.S.A. | 15 | 3 | 12 | 4 | 0 | 122 | 40 | 0 | 0 | 3 | 288245.1 |
| Euro Issue | 1 | 1 | 0 | 4 | 0 | 1 | 0 | 0 | 0 | 0 | 157890.3 |
| British Virginia | 1 | 0 | 0 | 2 | 0 | 0 | 0 | 0 | 0 | 0 | 175.50 |
| West Indies | 0 | 0 | 0 | 0 | 1 | 0 | 0 | 0 | 0 | 0 | 100.00 |
| Unindicated Countries | 0 | 0 | 0 | 0 | 0 | 11 | 0 | 0 | 0 | 0 | 0.00 |
| Total | 102 | 17 | 45 | 37 | 13 | 293 | 50 | 8 | 0 | 6 | 891411.97 |

*Source* : Ministry of Industry, Government of India, New Delhi, 2011.

and East Asian countries (46.13 per cent) a region constituting countries at a higher place in IDP than India. This is because the ownership advantages of Indian enterprises for overseas production which usually comprised the process or product adaptations, managerial and technical manpower, and equipment fabrication facilities, etc. which have been effective in countries at a lower stage of development fade before the ownership advantages of enterprises in industrial countries and increasingly in the Southeast and East Asian countries.

### (d) 1990-2011: Two Decades of Structural Adjustment and Globalisation

In the financial year 1990-91, India entered a period of severe balance of payments crisis and political uncertainty. A rapid increase in India's external debt coupled with the political uncertainty-led international credit rating agencies to lower India's rating both for short and long-term borrowing. This made borrowing in international commercial markets difficult and also led to a outflow of foreign currency deposits kept in India by non-resident Indians.

The 1991-2011 periods has also witnessed the liberalisation of restrictions to remit cash abroad for making outward FDI. The removal of these restrictions as well as improved transparency of policy regime perhaps explains a record 345 outward investments being approved with a projected Indian equity of Rs. 11.65 billion. Thus, 57.3 per cent of 600 ventures abroad at the end of 2011 accounting for 77.5 per cent of total Indian outward FDI have been committed between 1991 and 2011 (Table 3.17).

Middle-East accounts for a big chunk (39 per cent) of India's FDI in the period. However, bulk (26 per cent) of it is on account of a single large natural resource (Petroleum exploration) seeking project in UAE. The Southeast Asia hosts 67 ventures with a 14 per cent share of all FDI abroad. African countries hosted 27 projects with 7.86 per cent of FDI. India's centiguous neighbours in South Asia which had been trailing behind Southeast Asia and Africa in terms of their importance as host of Indian FDI attracted 29 ventures with a 7.2 per cent of total investments. Indian investments in this region had been restricted to Nepal and Sri Lanka. Since mid-1980s, Bangladesh and more recently, Maldives have played hosts to Indian enterprises [Table 3.18(a)-(b)].

## III.VII. FDI FLOWS IN WEST BENGAL

West Bengal, one of the India's most important states, was following the socialist theory of states in the early periods of economic reforms taken by Indian Government in 1991. At the end of 1994, West Bengal Government realized that to face up the internal challenge from other Indian states and competition from abroad, the state also need some kind of sources to rebuild its seek industries and to build up new projects.

The state government has due importance to the monitoring of foreign direct investment proposals. A considerable number of foreign direct investments approvals have been received for setting up new projects and to bring smoothness in the trading process of local products since 1991 in West Bengal. During the period from August 1991 to June 2010, 571 approvals have been received for units in West Bengal, involving foreign equity participation of Rs. 8914.12 crore. Of these, 102 FDI approvals involving foreign equity participation of Rs. 3146.30 crore have already been implemented and 17 projects involving foreign equity participation of Rs. 2393.86 crore are under different stages of implementation (Table 3.19).

A review of the FDI proposals received in West Bengal during the last 10 years indicates a major change in industrial structure of the state. Out of 571 approvals, the state has already implemented 102 projects, 17 projects are in advance stages of implementation, 45 projects are under implementation, 37 projects are dropped, 13 have no progress and 293 have no response about progress. Out of other 64 projects, 8 projects are not implemented in West Bengal, 6 projects have no FDI approvals and for remaining 50 projects, name of the project are still not available.

## III.VIII. SUMMARY AND CONCLUSION

Throughout this chapter, we have highlighted the nature and magnitude of foreign direct investment flows (both inflows and outflows) in India. For this we have also concentrated on the evaluation of Indian government's policy to attract more inflows into the country. This chapter gives us the idea of the inclusion of FDI into different sectors, different regions and various fields of India. The whole view of FDI inflows and outflows into and from the country during the first 20 years of economic reforms has been analyzed here.

For Indian economy, how helpful the FDI is to answer this question are now concentrate the impacts of FDI into Indian economy in the next chapter.

## References


Dutta, R. and K.P. Sundaram (2010), *Indian Economics*, New Delhi, p. 320.

Govt. of W.B. (2001), *A Review of the Industrial Scene in West Bengal : Annual Report, 2000-01*, Commerce and Industries Department, Kolkata.

Govt. of India (2000), *Economic Survey, 1999-2000*, Ministry of Finance, New Delhi.

———, (2002), *Economic Survey, 2001-02*, Ministry of Finance, New Delhi.

———, (2010), *Economic Survey, 2009-10*, Ministry of Finance, New Delhi.

———, (2012), *Economic Survey, 2011-12*, Ministry of Finance, New Delhi.

———, (2000), *SIA Newsletter*, Vol. X, No. 9, New Delhi.

———, (2002), *SIA Newsletter*, Vol. XII, No. 9, New Delhi.

———, (2010), *SIA Newsletter*, Vol. XX, No. 9, New Delhi.

———, (2009), *Economic and Commerce Bulletin*; Ministry of Commerce, New Delhi.

Kidron, Michal (1965), *Foreign Investments in India*, London: Oxford University Press.

Kumar, Nagesh (1987), 'Foreign Investment and Export Orientation: The Case of India', in Seiji Naya *et. al.* (eds.), *Direct Foreign Investment and Export Promotion : Policies and Experiences in Asia*, Honolulu, Howai : East West Center.

Kumar, N. (1998), "Liberalisation and Changing Patterns of FDIs : Has India's Relative Attractiveness as a Host of FDI Improved?" *Economic and Political Weekly*, Vol. XXXIII, No. 22, May 30.

Pan, S. and R.K. Sen (2007), *Foreign Direct Investment and Trade in India*, Deep & Deep Publications Pvt. Ltd., New Delhi.

RBI (2000), *Hand Book of Statistics of the Indian Economy*, RBI Publication, New Delhi.

RBI (2009), *Report on Currency and Finance*, RBI Publications, Mumbai.

UNCTAD (2001), *World Investment Report: Promoting Linkages*, United Nations, Bookwell Publication, Delhi.

World Bank (1999), *World Development Indicators*, Geneva.

CHAPTER

# 4

# *Impacts of Foreign Direct Investment on Indian Economy*

## IV.I. INTRODUCTION

*Foreign direct investment describes a category of international investment made by a resident entity in one economy (direct investor) with the objective of establishing a lasting interest in an enterprise resident in an economy other than that of the investor (direct investment enterprise).* 'Lasting interest' implies the existence of a long-term relationship between the direct investor and the enterprise and a significant degree of influence by the direct investor on the management of the direct investment enterprise. Direct investment involves both the initial transacting between the two entities and all subsequent capital transactions between them and among affiliated enterprises, both incorporated and unincorporated.

Today, foreign direct investment is seen as an instrument to facilitate and support domestic investment for achieving a higher level of economic development, since it benefits both the domestic industry as well as the consumer, by providing opportunities for technological up-gradation, access to global managerial skills and practices, optimal utilization of human and natural resource, making industry internationally competitive, opening up export markets, providing backward and forward linkages and access to international quality goods and services. In the wake of current era of globalization a transnational economic region has emerged. With the establishment of a global economic order in the form of World Trade Organization (WTO), the nations of the world have moved towards integration their economies. The economic activities in any country need substantial investments and the FDI tends to bridge the investment-saving gap to achieve sustained growth. Besides the long-term additional capital that it brings in, FDI also tends to facilitate up-gradation and transfer of technology and introduction of modern production and management practices.

It has been observed that liberalization of the economic policy and changes in the structure of the economy has not translated fully into attracting greater investments due to a variety of reasons. Existing procedures of project formulation, appraisal approval particularly for government projects, inadequacies in the existing management system and inadequate skills in project formulation, appraisal and management are some of the major reasons behind delays in the investment approvals and implementation of projects.

Various studies have shown that complexities in the approvals required for primary resources, like land, power, etc. multiplicity of approvals, disproportionate level of details sought with applications are among the major difficulties in the implementation of projects. Many approvals also do not seem to serve any public interest. Recent studies have shown that, which handling of approvals at central level has registered or marked improvement, state level handling of approvals and reducing ground level hassles have emerged as important issues.

There is also a need to align the FDI reporting system with the international reporting practices so as to facilitate proper international comparisons in respect of FDI flows.

With this background, this chapter approaches to assessing the impacts of foreign direct investment on Indian economy. Throughout the chapter, we shall try to analyze the impacts of FDI on GDP Growth; on saving-investment gap; on production, productivity and efficiency; on employment and wage; on trade and balance of payment and on inequality. Then we shall try to produce elasticity of FDI with respect to its determinants.

## IV.II. IMPACTS OF FOREIGN DIRECT INVESTMENT IN INDIA

Through several types of reforms were undertaken in the nineties, external sector reforms have been the most successful one of that. They have confounded all the fears of Indian critics and the skeptics that imports would go through the roof and current account deficits would balloon. They confirmed the faith of the reformers that a well-regulated market-based foreign trade and payments system would be more efficient and equally stable. Both the trade and invisibles account are now much more resilient that they were in the eighties.

Capital flows are now much more diversified and therefore, much less risky for the country. Both FDI and portfolio inflows increased rapidly through the mid-nineties. The strength of the external account rests substantially on the flexibility of the 'managed float', in response to changes in demand-supply conditions in the exchange market. Difficulties and temporary weaknesses have emerged and will arise in the future if and only if considerations other than marked supply-demand determine the management of the floating exchange rate.

Foreign direct investment has some great importance throughout the years especially after 1990 when reforms were taken for Indian economy. Since 1990 a huge amount of FDI inflows came into India. With this it becomes a growing source of finance and has some positive impact on productivity of Indian firms. It also helps Indian economy to fill up the savings investment gaps throughout the years. In the next few sub-sections we shall try to find out the real position of FDI in Indian economy.

### IV.II.I. Impact of FDI on GDP Growth

#### *The Model*

The role of FDI in economic growth might be analyzed in the framework of a production function model that treats FDI as an additional production input. One can then specify an aggregate production function fairly simply as :

$$Y = f(L, K_D, K_F) \tag{4.1.1}$$

where Y is aggregate real output, L is the labour input, $K_D$ is the stocks of domestic capital and $K_F$ represents the stocks of foreign capital (here $K_F$ is for FDI flows). Taking the total derivative in equation (4.1.1), dividing throughout by Y, and slightly manipulating items in the right hand side yield,

$$dY = \frac{\partial Y}{\partial L}.dL + \frac{\partial Y}{\partial K_D}.dK_D + \frac{\partial Y}{\partial K_F}.dK_F$$

$$\frac{dY}{Y} = \frac{\partial Y/Y}{\partial L/L}.\frac{dL}{L} + \frac{\partial Y/Y}{\partial K_D/K_D}.\frac{dK_D}{K_D} + \frac{\partial Y/Y}{\partial K_F/K_F}.\frac{dK_F}{K_F} \tag{4.1.2}$$

Let $\beta_1$, $\beta_2$ and $\beta_3$ be the output elasticity's of L, $K_D$ and $K_F$. With the addition of a constant term ($\beta_0$) and a stochastic component ($\mu$), we obtain the familier expression.

$$\dot{Y} = \beta_0 + \beta_1 \dot{L} + \beta_2 \dot{K}_D + \beta_3 \dot{K}_F + \mu \tag{4.1.3}$$

where a dot over a variable indicates its rate of growth. Since growth rates of $K_D$ and $K_F$ are usually not known, equation (4.1.3) can be reformulated from equation (4.1.2) by replacing $\dot{K}_D$ and $\dot{K}_F$ by the more tractable variables $\frac{dK_D}{Y}$ and $\frac{dK_F}{Y}$ which approximate ratios of domestic and foreign investment to output, as follows:

$$\dot{Y} = \beta_0 + \beta_1 \dot{L} + \frac{\partial Y}{\partial K_D}.\frac{dK_D}{Y} + \frac{\partial Y}{\partial K_F}.\frac{dK_F}{Y} + \mu \tag{4.1.4}$$

or replacing $dK_D$ and $dK_F$ (changes in domestic and foreign capital stock, respectively) by $I_D$ and $I_F$ (domestic and foreign investment, respectively)

$$\dot{Y} = \beta_0 + \beta_1 \dot{L} + \alpha_2 \frac{I_D}{Y} + \alpha_3 \frac{I_F}{Y} + \mu \tag{4.1.5}$$

where $\alpha_2 (\equiv \partial Y/\partial K_D)$ and $\alpha_3 (\equiv \partial Y/\partial K_F)$ marginal physical product of domestic and foreign capitals, respectively. In the following analysis, the estimated coefficient of $\frac{I_F}{Y}$ ($\alpha_3$) is of particular interest because it will indicate the direction and magnitude of the impact of inward FDI flows on economic performance.

### *The Data Set*

Equation (4.1.5) constitutes the basis for our cross section and panel analysis of the impact of FDI on economic growth in 1980-2010. The empirical specifications may be modified slightly based on some stylized facts about patterns of inward FDI and economic growth in India, as shown in Table 4.1. First, the most impressive character of the time trend is the sharp FDI boom since 1991 in contrast with steady but small amount of inflows in the 1980s. In fact, the twenty-year (1991-2010) inflows amounted to Rs. 281333.60 crore. Moreover, the bottom line of Table 4.1 indicates that at the same time as the FDI boom, India's average growth rate of GDP in 1991-2010 (5.9%) is

TABLE 4.1

**FDI Flows and GDP Growth Rates in India (1980-2010)**

*(Rs. in crore in current prices and percentage)*

| *Provinces* | *Average Growth Rate of GDP (per cent)* | | *FDI Flows and Their Shares in Total 1991-2010* | |
|---|---|---|---|---|
| | *1980-90* | *1991-2010* | *Flows (Rs.)* | *Share (%)* |
| *(1)* | *(2)* | *(3)* | *(4)* | *(5)* |
| Maharashtra | 4.55 | 7.87 | 48722.40 | 17.32 |
| Delhi | 12.76 | — | 33806.58 | 12.02 |
| Tamil Nadu | 4.67 | 8.48 | 23470.30 | 8.34 |
| Karnataka | 3.98 | 8.13 | 21945.00 | 7.80 |
| Gujarat | 3.43 | 7.75 | 18453.20 | 6.56 |
| Andhra Pradesh | 3.76 | 6.25 | 13092.24 | 4.65 |
| Madhya Pradesh | 1.79 | 6.66 | 9227.30 | 3.28 |
| West Bengal | 2.90 | 9.72 | 8808.30 | 3.13 |
| Orissa | 1.58 | 5.96 | 8229.00 | 2.92 |
| Uttar Pradesh | 2.50 | 4.85 | 4795.00 | 1.70 |

*(Contd.)*

TABLE 4.1 (*Contd.*)

| *(1)* | *(2)* | *(3)* | *(4)* | *(5)* |
|---|---|---|---|---|
| Haryana | 4.34 | 5.74 | 3519.40 | 1.25 |
| Rajastan | 4.95 | 5.39 | 3004.70 | 1.07 |
| Punjab | 3.61 | 7.02 | 1968.40 | 0.70 |
| Kerala | 2.49 | 8.53 | 1527.80 | 0.54 |
| Pondicherry | 0.94 | — | 1242.29 | 0.44 |
| Himachal Pradesh | 3.05 | — | 1173.90 | 0.42 |
| Goa | 6.17 | — | 970.62 | 0.35 |
| Bihar | 1.85 | 3.05 | 739.50 | 0.26 |
| Chhattisgarh | — | — | 632.70 | 0.22 |
| Chandigarh | — | — | 161.97 | 0.06 |
| Jharkhand | — | — | 143.80 | 0.05 |
| Uttaranchal | — | — | 125.60 | 0.04 |
| D and N Haveli | — | — | 123.98 | 0.04 |
| Meghalaya | 2.47 | — | 52.96 | 0.02 |
| Daman and Diu | — | — | 55.20 | 0.02 |
| Assam | 2.51 | 5.12 | 1.49 | negl. |
| Jammu and Kashmir | 0.08 | — | 8.40 | negl. |
| Manipur | 2.60 | — | 3.20 | negl. |
| Nagaland | 3.21 | — | 3.68 | negl. |
| Tripura | 2.68 | — | 0.68 | negl. |
| A and N Islands | 0.29 | — | 13.70 | negl. |
| Arunachal Pradesh | 7.12 | — | 11.00 | negl. |
| Lakshadweep | — | — | 0.50 | negl. |
| Mizoram | — | — | 1.50 | negl. |
| States not indicated | — | — | 75296.50 | 26.76 |
| Total | 5.8 | 5.9 | 281333.60 | 100.00 |

*Sources*: (i) Calculated from *National Human Development Report*, 2010, Planning Commission, Government of India, New Delhi.
(ii) *Currency and Finance*, RBI.

slightly higher than that in 1980-90 (5.8%) by 0.1 percentages. To bring out any possible structural variations between the 1990's separate cross-section estimations are to be conducted for two sub-periods: 1980-90 and 1991-2010.

### *The Results*

From Table 4.1, it is clear that average growth rate of GDP has increased for more or less to all the states of India. During this period, inflows of FDI also have increased. In this case share of FDI is maximum for the states like Maharashtra (17.32), Delhi (12.02), Tamil Nadu (8.34), Karnataka (7.80) and Gujarat (6.56). The influence of FDI inflow to GDP is negligible for the North-Eastern states like Assam, Manipur, Nagaland, Tripura and Mizoram. Inflows of FDI also have negligible impact on GDP for some of the union territories like Andaman and Nicobar Islands, Lakshadweep, and Daman and Diu. So from the above result, it is found that inflows of FDI affect a little for some parts of India and in some other cases, it has marginal impacts.

### IV.II.II. FDI and Savings-Investment Gap

The gross domestic savings rate has continued to rise after liberalisation. It rose from above 20 per cent of GDP in the late 1980s to above 25 percent in recent years 2010-11, though it has declined in 1997-98 to 23 percent. The household sector continues to account for about three-quarters of the total savings in India. This increase is primarily due to increase in bank deposits and contractual savings mobilized from households. On the other hand, financial savings in the form of shares and debentures held by households declined, reflecting industrial declaration. Though private savings increased, public sector savings have failed to increase in recent years despite pronouncements by the government to raise it. After liberalization, gross domestic capital formation has remained higher than gross domestic savings by 1-2 percent of GDP. Foreign savings most of which came as FDI bridged this investment-savings gap.

The growth rate of around 6 percent per year in the post-reform period was achieved with an average investment rate of around 23 percent of GDP. Accelerating to 8 percent growth will require a commensurate increase in investment. Growth rates of this magnitude in East Asia were associated with investment rates ranging from 36 to 38 per cent of GDP. From which it can be argued that there was over investment in East Asia, especially in recent years, it is unlikely that India can accelerate to 8 percent growth unless it can raise the rate of investment to around 29-30 percent of GDP. This can be financed by increasing foreign direct investment, but even if FDI increases from the present level of 0.91 percent of GDP to 2.0 percent—an optimistic but not impossible target domestic savings would still have to increase by at least 5 percentage points of GDP. (Pan and Sen, 2007).

The saving and investment rates in India are high as judged by the country's level of economic development. Gross domestic savings improved marginally from 23.1 percent of GDP in 1999-2000 to 23.4 percent of GDP in 2010 as a result of better performance by household savings and private corporate savings. However, there was a steep fall in public sector savings due to an increase in the dis-saving of government administrative departments. In fact, public sector savings were negative in 1998-99, 1999-2000 and 2001. As a percentage of GDP, public sector savings declined from (–) 0.9 percent in 1999-2000 to (–) 1.7 percent in 2010. GOI, 2012.

Gross domestic investment at current prices declined marginally from 23.2 percent of GDP in 1999-2000 to 22.9 percent of GDP in 2010 mainly due to a fall in private sector investment. The rate of gross capital formation in real terms also declined from 18.7 percent of NDP in 1990-91 to 16.4 percent of NDP in 2001 due to deceleration in the growth rates of net domestic capital formation in both public and private sectors.

From Table 4.2 it is found that India's private savings rate (comprising household and private corporate savings) is more or less comparable to those achieved by the high performing East Asian economies. However, its public savings is very low and is a major constraint on domestic resource mobilization. Government is restructuring public expenditure to foster domestic savings, release resources for physical and social infrastructure development and to reduce crowding out effect on private investment. When there is dearth of savings, FDI could plays a positive role to fill up the saving-investment gap.

Saving-investment gap shows an ups-and-down

TABLE 4.2

**Sarving-Investment Gap and FDI**

*(Per cent of GDP)*

| *Year* | *Combined Fiscal Deficit of Central and State Govts. (% of GDP)* | *Gross Domestic Saving* | | *Gross Domestic Capital Formation* | | *Net Domestic Saving (as % of NDP)* | *Net Domestic Capital Formation (as % of NDP)* | *Saving-Investment Gap* | *Net Inflow of Foreign Capital (as % of NDP)* | *Net FDI INflows (% of GDP)* |
|---|---|---|---|---|---|---|---|---|---|---|
| | | *Private Sector* | *Public Sector* | *Private Sector* | *Public Sector* | | | | | |
| *(1)* | *(2)* | *(3)* | *(4)* | *(5)* | *(6)* | *(7)* | *(8)* | *(9)* | *(10)* | *(11)* |
| 1990-91 | 9.4 | 22.0 | 1.1 | 14.7 | 9.3 | 15.1 | 18.7 | -0.9 | 3.6 | 0.03 |
| 1991-92 | 7.0 | 20.1 | 2.0 | 13.1 | 8.8 | 14.0 | 14.6 | 0.2 | 0.6 | 0.11 |
| 1992-93 | 7.0 | 20.2 | 1.6 | 15.2 | 8.6 | 12.1 | 14.3 | -2.0 | 2.2 | 0.20 |
| 1993-94 | 8.3 | 21.9 | 0.6 | 13.0 | 8.2 | 14.2 | 14.8 | 1.3 | 0.6 | 0.29 |
| 1994-95 | 7.1 | 23.2 | 1.7 | 14.7 | 8.7 | 16.4 | 15.0 | 1.5 | -1.4 | 0.59 |
| 1995-96 | 6.5 | 23.1 | 2.0 | 18.9 | 7.7 | 16.3 | 17.9 | -1.5 | 1.6 | 0.61 |
| 1996-97 | 6.4 | 21.5 | 1.7 | 14.7 | 7.0 | 16.7 | 16.1 | 1.5 | 1.4 | 0.85 |
| 1997-98 | 7.3 | 21.8 | 1.3 | 16;0 | 6.6 | 14.6 | 16.2 | 0.5 | 1.6 | 0.61 |
| 1998-99 | 8.9 | 22.6 | -1.0 | 14.8 | 6.6 | 13.3 | 14.5 | 0.2 | 1.2 | 0.53 |
| 1999-2000 | 9.4 | 24.0 | -0.9 | 16.1 | 7.1 | 15.2 | 16.4 | -0.1 | 1.2 | 0.54 |
| 2000-01 | 9.6 | 25.1 | -1.7 | 15.8 | 7.1 | 15.3 | 16.0 | 0.5 | 0.7 | 0.91 |

*Note* : Gross/Net domestic product at current market prices.

*Sources* : (i) Central Statistical Organisation. (ii) World Bank Indicators Database. (iii) Statistical Outline of India, various years.

movement throughout the first two decades of so-called economic reforms. In 1990-91, 1992-93, 1995-96 and in 1999-2000 saving-investment gaps were negative means domestic savings rate is slightly higher than domestic investment rate. Excepting these four years, most of the years show a huge saving-investment gap. This gap increased from 0.2 percent in 1991-92 to 1.5 percent in 1994-95 and 1996-97. Since then this gap is reduced due to a huge FDI inflows came to India. Net FDI inflows increased from 0.03 percent of GDP in 1990-91 to 0.85 percent of GDP in 1996-97 and then decreased for three consecutive years and then again increased to 0.91 percent of GDP in 2001. (RBI, 2012).

Private savings have been buoyant in the post-reform period, but public savings have declined steadily. This trend needs to be reversed. An increase in public savings will have some negative effect on private savings as, for example, when higher tax revenues lead to a reduction in disposable income in the private sector, which in turn reduces private savings, but the net effect well still is positive. Both the central government and the state governments would have to take a number of hard decisions to bring about improvements in their respective spheres.

The fiscal failures of both the central and the state governments have squeezed the capacity of both the center and the states to undertake essential public investment. High levels of government borrowing have also crowded out private investment unless this problem is addressed, the potential benefits from reforms in other areas will be eroded, and it may be difficult even to maintain the average growth rate of 6 percent experienced in the first ten years after the reforms, let alone accelerate to 8 percent. And to achieve that target a huge investment is needed a part of which should come in the form of FDI. Thus, FDI playing a supplementary role to the domestic investment particularly when there is dearth of domestic saving.

### IV.II.III. Impact of FDI on Production, Productivity and Efficiency

It is widely believed that the acquisition of technology by firms plays an instrumental role in improving their productivity and driving overall economic growth. As a result, economists have attached considerable importance by understanding the various mechanisms through which firms acquire technology and assessing their impact on productivity. Government also promote inward foreign direct investment to encourage technology 'spillovers' from foreign to domestic firms.

If foreign firms introduce new products or processes to the domestic market, domestic firms may benefit from the accelerated diffusion of new technology. In some cases, domestic firms may increase productivity simply by observing nearly foreign firms. In other cases, diffusion may occur from labour turnover as domestic employees move from foreign to domestic firms.

### *Methodology*

To find out the impact of FDI on productivity, we use annual *Census data on over 4,000 Indian firms.* Here we find, (i) a positive relationship between increased foreign equity participation and plant performance, suggesting that individual plants do benefit from foreign investment. However, the positive own plant effect is only robust for smaller plants, defined as plants with less than 50 employees. For large enterprises, the positive effects of foreign investment disappear when plant-specific differences are takes into account. This suggests that foreign investors are investing in the more productive plants. (ii) Productivity in domestically owned plants declines when foreign investment increases. This suggests a negative spillover from foreign to domestic enterprises, which we interpret as a market stealing effect. If we add up the positive own-plant effect and the negative spillovers, on balance the impact of foreign investment on domestic plant productivity is quite small.

### The Framework

We estimate a log-linear production function at the plant level to answer two basic questions : (a) whether FDI (foreign equity participation) is associated with an increase in the plant's productivity, and (b) whether foreign ownership in an industry affects the productivity of domestically owned firms in the same industry i.e., whether there are positive or negative 'spillovers' to domestic enterprises. Both hypotheses (a) and (b) can be nested in the same general specification:

$$Y_{ijt} = C + \beta_1 FDI\_Plant_{ijt} + \beta_2 FDI\_Setor_{jt}$$
$$+\beta_3 (FDI\_Plant_{ijt})(FDI\_Sector_{jt}) + (\beta_4 X_{ijt} + e_{ijt}) \qquad (4.3.1)$$

where, $Y_{ijt}$ ⇒ Output for Plant i in Sector j at time t

$FDI\_Plant_{ijt}$ ⇒ Share of FDI at the plant level (0-100%)

$FDI\_Sector_{jt}$ ⇒ measure of the presence of foreign ownership in the industry

$(FDI\_Plant_{ijt})$ $(FDI\_Sector_{jt})$ ⇒ coefficient on the interaction between plant level and sector_level FDI

$X_{ijt}$ ⇒ input vector for plant i in sector j at time t.

(i) If foreign ownership in a plant increases that plant's productivity, we should observe a positive coefficient on $FDI\_Plant_{ijt}$.

(ii) To the extent that the productivity advantages of foreign firms spillover to domestic firms, the coefficient on $FDI\_Sector_{jt}$ should be positive.

(iii) $(FDI\_Plant_{ijt})$ $(FDI\_Sector_{jt})$ allows us to determine the interaction between plant_level and sector_level FDI if the effects of foreign presence on other foreign firms differ from the effects on domestic firms. To the extent that plants with FDI benefit from the presence of other foreign plants, the coefficient should be positive. Its joint ventures are negatively affected by the activities of other foreign plants, the coefficient should be negative.

### The Data Set

A firm_level dataset is compiled from the *Prowess database,*[1] which contains information primarily from the income statements and balance sheets of listed companies, comprises more than 70 percent of the economic activity in the organized industrial sector of India. The size of the dataset varies by year covers the period 1989-2010. Since overall exit rates are very low, we use an unbalanced panel of companies for estimation purposes. Because firms are under no legal obligation to report balance sheet data, a small percentage of firms exit and re-enter the database. These firms are excluded from the analysis. For this reason, we verify the robustness of our results by conducting our analysis using only the subset of companies whose information is available for all years. The dataset contains information on about 4,100 individual manufacturing companies.

The dataset contains information on foreign ownership; assets output employment, input costs, location and product destination. FDI_Plant is defined as the percentage of subscribed capital (equity) owned by foreign investors. FDI_Sector is defined as foreign equity participation averaged over all plants in the sector, weighted by each plants share in sectoral employment. In particular, foreign investment at the sectoral level is defined as:

$$FS_{jt} = \frac{\sum_i FS_{ijt}(Emp_{ijt})}{\sum_i Employment_{ijt}} \tag{4.3.2}$$

Since foreign firms tend to be more capital-intensive than domestic firms, the share of foreign firms is significantly higher if weighted by physical capital outputs defined as total output at the plant level, deflated by an annual producer price deflator which varies across four digit industries. Skilled and unskilled labour is defined in terms of members of workers, rather than worker hours, which were not available over the entire sample.

### *The Impact*

The dependent variable the log of real output for plant *i* in sector *j* at time *t*, is regressed on its inputs and on foreign equity participation. Plant_level inputs (expressed in logarithms) include unskilled labour, skilled labour, materials and capital. In addition to a random component, which varies across plants $e_{it}$, we allow for a time varying component $D_t$ and control for productivity differences across industries by including dummies. All reported estimates include corrections for heteroscedasticity. From Table 4.3 it is found that the coefficient on foreign ownership within the plant (Plant_FDI) is positive and statistically significant, suggesting that there are large productivity gains associated with foreign equity participation (column 1). The point estimate, 0.105 suggests that output in plants, which increased foreign equity participation from zero to

TABLE 4.3

**Impact of Foreign Ownership on Total Factor Productivity**

| | *Impact of FDI on Productivity* | | *Impact of FDI on Output* | | *Impact of FDI on Change in Productivity* | | | |
|---|---|---|---|---|---|---|---|---|
| | *OLS with industry dummies* | *OLS without industry dummies* | *Weighted least squares* | *OLS with industry dummies and no factor inputs* | *First differences* $(Y_t - Y_{t-1})$ | *Second differences* $(Y_t - Y_{t-2})$ | *Third differences* $(Y_t - Y_{t-3})$ | *Fourth differences* $(Y_t - Y_{t-4})$ |
| *(1)* | *(2)* | *(3)* | *(4)* | *(5)* | *(6)* | *(7)* | *(8)* | *(9)* |
| Foreign ownership in the plant (Plant_FDI) | 0.105 (0.027) | 0.158 (0.028) | 0.142 (0.039) | 2.176 (0.124) | .0.003 (0.037) | 0.018 (0.039) | 0.042 (0.043) | -0.011 (0.049) |
| Foreign ownership in the sector (Sector_FDI) | -0.267 (0.061) | 0.058 (0.030) | -0.206 (0.155) | -1.258 (0.232) | -0.238 (0.067) | -0.302 (0.065) | -0.248 (0.071) | -0.320 (0.083) |
| (Plant_FDI) (Sector_FDI) | ·0.356 (0.181) | -0.212 (0.189) | 0.314 (0.226) | 5.003 (0.810) | 0.262 (0.223) | 0.420 (0.246) | 0.384 (0.252) | 0.658 (0.288) |
| Number of plants | 10257 | 10257 | 10257 | 10372 | 9489 | 7158 | 5132 | 3607 |
| Number of observations | 43010 | 43010 | 43010 | 46947 | 32521 | 23136 | 16100 | 11045 |
| Husman test ($\chi^2$) | 38.4 | — | 82.9 | — | — | — | — | — |
| $R^2$ | 0.96 | 0.95 | 0.96 | 0.32 | 0.53 | 0.60 | 0.64 | 0.65 |

*Note* : All standard errors (denoted in parentheses) are corrected for heteroscedasticity.

100 percent, would be 10.5 percentage points higher than for comparable domestic plants. Since we already control for differences in inputs, this 10.5 percent increment is a pure total factor productivity gain.[2]

In contrast, we find that domestic plants in sectors with more foreign ownership are significantly less productive that those in sectors with a smaller foreign presence. The point estimate for Sector_FDI in the second row of Table 4.3 is large in magnitude significant, and negative. The results imply that an increase in the share of FDI from 0 to 10 percent leads to as much as a 2.67 percentage point decline in domestic productivity.[3]

The coefficient on the interaction term; (Plant_FDI) (Sector_FDI) is positive and statistically significant. The positive coefficient suggests that for plants with foreign equity participation, there is positive spillover from foreign investment (FDI)—in contrast to domestic firms. Joint ventures benefit from FDI in the plant as well as from FDI in other plants within the same sector.

So, the above analyses suggest that if productivity is pro-cyclical, we would wrongly infer that FDI has a negative impact on domestic productivity. Using a panel of more than 4,000 Indian plants between 1989 and 2010, we identify two effects of FDI on domestic enterprises—

(a) Increases in foreign equity participation are correlated with increases in productivity for recipient plants with less than 50 employees, suggesting that these plants benefit from the productive advantages of foreign owners.

(b) Increases in foreign ownership negatively affect the productivity of wholly domestically owned firms in the same industry.

### IV.II.IV. Impact of FDI on Employment

There is always a fear with India's policy-makers' mind that FDI inflows may decrease employment in the country. The labour market in the country is affected badly by FDI. Sometimes it is heard from managers of firms that investment will be to the advantage of workers because the lower wage costs in the country make the firm more competitive.

To find out the relationship between FDI and employment, we set-up a simple model with one firm, which at the labour market in the country faces a trade union. These two parties bargain over the wage rate in the home country. The firm has to bargain over the wage rate with a local trade union. If there is a big degree of complementarity between activities moved abroad and activities remaining in the home country, it is likely that the firm and the home country workers agree whether it is preferable to undertake FDI. But if there is a big degree of substitutability between activities in foreign affiliates and activities in the home country, it is likely that the firm gains but the workers lose from FDI.

We consider the following cases for supporting the model:

(a) The firm decides whether to move activities to the host country and by this splitting the workers into two groups.
(b) A share of the employment is 'given away' to the workers in the host country.
(c) Employment is determined after the firm has decided whether to move activities abroad and after the wage bargaining has taken place.
(d) There are no transportation costs or other costs of international trade.

### *The Model*

Here we consider a two country partial equilibrium model where a single monopolistic firm faces the following inverse demand function:

$$P = CQ^{-b},\ O<b<1,\ C>O \qquad (4.4.1)$$

where P is the price and Q is total world demand. We assume that there are two activities of production process (namely, activity 1 and activity 2) in which two intermediate goods are being produced. These two activities need the same kind of labour as input. The intermediate goods combine into final production as captured by the following constant returns to scale CES production function:

$$\left.\begin{array}{l} q = [y_1^{\rho} + y_2^{\rho}]^{1/\rho},\quad \rho \in [-\alpha, 1] \\ y_i = l_i,\quad i = 1,\ 2\ \ldots\ldots\ldots\ldots\ldots \end{array}\right\} \qquad (4.4.2)$$

where $y_i$ = production of the intermediate good i, $l_i$ is labour input in activity i, and q is final output.

From (4.4.2) we get the following variable cost function :

$$C(\varpi_1, \varpi_2, q) = [\varpi_1^r + \varpi_2^r]^{1/r} q, \quad r = \rho / (\rho - 1). \qquad (4.4.3)$$

where $\varpi_i$ = the wage paid to workers employed in activity i.

Let,
(i) Activity 1 $\Rightarrow$ firm's part of production in the home country, Activity 2 $\Rightarrow$ firm chooses to move a part of production abroad
(ii) Activity 1 incurs the cost G which could be a cost to research and development
(iii) Plant–specific fixed costs associated with activity 2 are the same in the home and in the host country (and included in G)
(iv) When activity 2 is taking place in both countries the extra fixed costs are sufficiently high that the firm will never choose to split up activity 2 (i.e. the firm will only produce intermediate good 2 at one location).

Therefore, the maximized profit of firm:

$$\pi = K_2[\varpi_1^r + \varpi_2^r]^{(b-1)/rb} - G, \quad K_2 = CK_1^{1-b} - K_1$$

$$K_1 = [(1-b)C]^{1/b} \qquad (4.4.4)$$

The workers in the home country as well as in the host country are organized in trade unions, which seek to maximize the objective function of the form:

$$U_i = L_i(\varpi_i - \overline{\varpi}_i), \quad i = f, h, \ldots\ldots \qquad (4.4.5)$$

where f and h denote foreign (host) and home country, respectively. $\overline{\varpi}_i$ is the competitive wage in country i, and it is implicitly assumed that trade union members who do not get a job in the firm, get the competitive wage in some alternative job. $L_i$ is total employment in the firm in country i. Hence, we assume that workers in the two activities, in same country, get the same wage.

Wages are determined in negotiations between the firm and the trade unions and the outcome is assumed to be given by the Nash bargaining solution. The outcome of the bargaining in country i is given as:

$$\varpi_i = \text{barg max } U_i(\pi - \bar{\pi}_i), \qquad i = h, \; f. \tag{4.4.6}$$

Now, if the firm is local, $\bar{\pi}_h = -G$

If the firm is multinational, $\bar{\pi}_i = -G, \text{if } \delta \le 1, \; i = h, f$ (4.4.7)

$$\bar{\pi}_i = K_2 \varpi_j^{(b-1)/b} - G, \text{ if } \delta > 1, \; i, j = h, \; f, \; i \ne j \tag{4.4.8}$$

where $\delta$ is the elasticity of substitution between the two intermediate goods in production of final output and $\delta = 1/(1-\rho) \in [0, \alpha]$.

***(a) Without FDI***

Without any FDI, the firm remains local implying that $\varpi_1 = \varpi_2 = \varpi_h$. The profit

$$\pi = \tilde{K}_2 \varpi_h^{(b-1)/b} - G, \; \tilde{K}_2 = K_2 2^{(b-1)/rb} \tag{4.4.9}$$

Since the home trade union suppliers' works to both activities in the firm, total employment is

$$L_h = l_1 + l_2 = \tilde{K}_1 \varpi_h^{-1/b}, \; \tilde{K}_1 = K_1 2^{(b-1)/rb} \tag{4.4.10}$$

This leads to the following payoff function:

$$U_h = \tilde{K}_1 \varpi_h^{-1/b} (\varpi_h - \bar{\varpi}_h) \tag{4.4.11}$$

By inserting (4.4.9) and (4.4.11) in (4.4.6), the first order condition to the maximization problem implies

$$\varpi_h = \frac{1}{2} \varpi_h \left( \frac{2-b}{1-b} \right) \tag{4.4.12}$$

We have get the intuitive result that the wage in increasing in the alternative wages of trade union members (i.e. $\bar{\varpi}_a$).

***(b) With FDI***

Now, if we take FDI, i.e. the firm chooses to move activity 2 to the host country, the firm's profit is given by (4.4.4) where $\varpi_1 = \varpi_h$ and $\varpi_2 = \varpi_f$.

The payoff to the unions is:

$$U_i = K_i \varpi_i^{r-1}[\varpi_i^r + \varpi_j^r]^{[b(1-r)-1]/rb}(\varpi_i - \overline{\varpi}_i),\ i, j = h, f, i \neq j \tag{4.4.13}$$

By using (4.4.6), we get the first order condition to the maximization problem with respect to $\varpi_h$:

$$[r-(r-1)\varpi_h^{-1}\overline{\varpi}_h + \frac{b(1-r)-1}{b}\varpi_h^{r-1}][\varpi_h^r + \varpi_f^r]^{-1}(\varpi_h - \overline{\varpi}_h)$$

$$+ \frac{K_2 \frac{b-1}{b}\left[\varpi_h^{r-1}(\varpi_h^r + \varpi_f^r)^{[b(1-r)-1]/rb}(\varpi_h - \overline{\varpi}_h)\right]}{[K_2(\varpi_h^r + \varpi_f^r)^{(b-1)/rh} - (\overline{\pi}_h + G)]} = 0 \tag{4.4.14}$$

For the host county an equivalent expression can be obtained. We can now, in principle, solve for the Nash equilibrium in $\varpi_h$ and $\varpi_f$, but the complexity of the two first-order conditions implies that we cannot get closed from solutions.

Here, we consider some special cases:

*(i) The Leontief Case*

If, $\delta \to 0 (\rho \to -\alpha$ and $r \to 1)$, we have the Leontief production function. Now, if the firm is multinational, the domestic wage becomes

$$\varpi_h = \frac{2-b}{4(1-b)^2 - b^2}[\overline{\varpi}_h 2(1-b) + b\overline{\varpi}_f] \tag{4.4.15}$$

There is a similar expression for the foreign wage. By comparing (4.4.12) and (4.4.15), it is easily seen that

$$\varpi_h \Big|_{\text{with FDI}} > \varpi_h \Big|_{\text{without FDI}} \tag{4.4.16}$$

The cost associated with production in the home country is, therefore, less important for the firm when it is multinational than when it is local. The trade union exploits that to get a higher wage when the firm is multinational.

Let us turn to employment. As we know that the firm prefers to be multinational if

$$\frac{\overline{\varpi}_h}{\overline{\varpi}_h + \overline{\varpi}_r} > \frac{(2-b)(1-b)}{4(1-b)^2 - b^2} \tag{4.4.17}$$

So, home employment is higher with FDI than without FDI if

$$\frac{\overline{\varpi}_h}{\overline{\varpi}_h + \overline{\varpi}_f} > 2^b \frac{(2-b)(1-b)}{4(1-b)^2 - b^2} \tag{4.4.18}$$

So, domestic employment increases if the firm becomes multinational, but the advantage for the firm (and the union) of FDI has to be sufficiently large.

*(ii) The Cobb-Douglas Case*

If $\rho = 1$ $(\rho = r \rightarrow 0)$, we have the Cobb-Douglas production function. Without FDI, the home wage is given by (4.4.12). With FDI, the demand of labour for the two kinds of activities becomes:

$$l_i = K_i 2^{-1/b} \varpi_i^{[-(b+1)]/2b} \varpi_j^{(b-1)/2b}, \quad i, j = h, f, i \neq j \tag{4.4.19}$$

Hence, we see that labour demand in both activities is decreasing in $\varpi_h$ was well as in $\varpi_f$. By solving the bargaining problem we find that the wage became:

$$\varpi_i = \overline{\varpi}_i\left(\frac{1}{1-b}\right), \quad i = h, f \tag{4.4.20}$$

By comparing (4.4.12) to (4.4.20), we see that

$$\varpi_h \Big|_{\text{with FDI}} > \varpi_h \Big|_{\text{without FDI}} \tag{4.4.21}$$

The reason for this is that, when workers are split up in two groups, the size of the home wage becomes less important for the firm and the demand elasticity for home labour decreases. This, the home trade union exploits in the wage bargaining to get a higher wage.

In this situation, the firm chooses to become multinational if the profit as multinational is higher than the profit as local, i.e.

$$\left(\frac{\overline{\varpi}_h}{\overline{\varpi}_f}\right) > \left(1 - \frac{b}{2}\right)^{-2} \tag{4.4.22}$$

If, $\overline{\varpi}_h = \overline{\varpi}_f$, the above condition will not be satisfied. Hence, a necessary condition for FDI is that $\overline{\varpi}_f < \overline{\varpi}_h$.

The trade union prefers the firm to be multinational if

$$\left(\frac{\overline{\varpi}_h}{\overline{\varpi}_f}\right) > \left(1 - \frac{b}{2}\right)^{(-2)/(1-b)}$$

This wage effect may dominate the employment effect. Employment in the home country is decreasing in the wage in the host country (form 4.4.19). If $\overline{\varpi}_f$ is low, the employment loss for domestic workers, if the firm becomes multinational, is smaller. So, domestic employment is higher when the firm is multinational than when it is local if

$$\left(\frac{\overline{\varpi}_h}{\overline{\varpi}_f}\right) > \left(1 - \frac{b}{2}\right)^{(-2)/(1-b)} \left(1 - \frac{b}{2}\right)^{(-2)/(1-b)} \qquad (4.4.23)$$

So, FDI gives rise to higher domestic employment if $\overline{\varpi}_f$ is low relatively to $\overline{\varpi}_h$.

### *(iii) The Perfect Substitutes Case*

If, $\delta \to \alpha$ ($\rho \to 1$, $r \to -\alpha$) the two intermediate goods are perfect substitutes in production of the final good. To make this easier, we assume that the competitive wage in the host country is lower than the bargained wage in the home country when the firm is local, i.e.

$$\overline{\varpi}_i < \frac{1}{2}\overline{\varpi}_f\left(\frac{2-b}{1-b}\right), \ i, f = h, f, i \neq j \qquad (4.4.24)$$

This condition implies that the multinational firm will not simply behave as a local firm.

If the home trade union accepts a wage is an $\in$ lower than the foreign wage, all employment well be placed in the home country. Similar for the foreign trade union also. However, the home (foreign) trade union will never accept a wage below $\overline{\varpi}_h$ ($\overline{\varpi}_f$). The equilibrium with the highest possible wage can be described as:

if $\overline{\varpi}_i < \overline{\varpi}_j$, then $\varpi_i = \overline{\varpi}_j$ (4.4.25)

$$l_i = k_1^{-1/b} \quad (4.4.26)$$

$$l_j = 0 \quad (4.4.27)$$

if $\overline{\varpi}_f = \overline{\varpi}_h$, then $\varpi_h = \varpi_f = \overline{\varpi}_h$ (4.4.28)

$$l_h = l_f = \frac{1}{2} K_1 \overline{\varpi}_h^{-1/b} \quad (4.4.29)$$

If the competitive wage is the same in the two countries, we have assumed that employment is shared equally among the two countries.

By using (4.4.12) and (4.4.24), we find that

$$\varpi_h \Big|_{\text{without FDI}} \geq \varpi_h \Big|_{\text{with FDI}} \quad (4.4.30)$$

So, the firm and the trade union always disagree on whether FDI is preferable.

***The Results***

Thus from the above analyses, it is found that the injection of FDI into the economy generates employment in two stages. First, it creates 'primary' employment for workers engaged directly in new capital goods projects. Secondly, their spending gives rise to 'secondary' employment in the industries producing consumer goods on the one hand and intermediate goods required for the capital and consumer goods on the other. Thus, ultimately the indirect or secondary employment generated by the investment would be many times the volume of direct or primary employment initially created by it (Table 4.4). Judged from this angle, the long-run effect of FDI on employment in the host country like India should be considerable.

From Table 4.4 it is also cleared that during 1980-2010 period employment growth shows a fluctuating trend. For states like Assam, Bihar, Goa, Kerala, Punjab and Sikkim growth in employment has increased. But in some states like Andhra Pradesh, Haryana, Himachal Pradesh, Karnataka, Madhya Pradesh, Maharashtra and West Bengal growth in employment was decreased. So, though FDI inflows increase wages but it is rather less beneficial for employment generation.

TABLE 4.4
**Growth in Employment in Indian States (1980-2010)**

| States/UT's | 1980 to 1994-95 | | | 1995-96 to 2009-10 | | |
|---|---|---|---|---|---|---|
| | Male | Female | Persons | Male | Female | Persons |
| (1) | (2) | (3) | (4) | (5) | (6) | (7) |
| Andhra Pradesh | 2.1 | 2.7 | 2.4 | 1.6 | 0.3 | 1.1 |
| Arunachal Pradesh | — | — | — | 0.5 | –0.7 | 0.0 |
| Assam | 1.3 | 3.2 | 1.6 | 2.5 | 2.3 | 2.5 |
| Bihar | 1.8 | –1.7 | 0.9 | 2.3 | 3.0 | 2.5 |
| Goa | 1.7 | –3.0 | 0.1 | 2.6 | –4.1 | 0.8 |
| Gujarat | 2.4 | 1.6 | 2.1 | 2.1 | 2.2 | 2.1 |
| Haryana | 2.5 | 4.7 | 3.1 | 1.9 | –3.1 | 0.6 |
| Himachal Pradesh | 2.8 | 3.0 | 2.9 | 1.4 | 1.5 | 1.4 |
| Jammu and Kashmir | 1.7 | 5.9 | 2.9 | 2.2 | –1.2 | 1.1 |
| Karnataka | 2.2 | 2.4 | 2.3 | 2.0 | 0.8 | 1.6 |
| Kerala | 2.0 | –1.2 | 0.9 | 1.6 | 1.4 | 1.6 |
| Madhya Pradesh | 2.4 | 1.7 | 2.2 | 1.9 | 1.5 | 1.4 |
| Maharashtra | 2.1 | 2.4 | 2.3 | 1.8 | –0.2 | 1.0 |
| Manipur | 3.6 | 2.9 | 3.3 | 3.2 | –0.3 | 2.0 |
| Meghalaya | 3.1 | 4.0 | 3.5 | 2.3 | 3.0 | 2.6 |
| Mizoram | 3.1 | 20.5 | 6.3 | 2.9 | 5.9 | 4.0 |
| Nagaland | 19.7 | 34.5 | 22.4 | 4.6 | 15.9 | 8.6 |
| Orissa | 1.8 | 2.9 | 2.1 | 1.5 | 1.0 | 1.3 |
| Punjab | 1.8 | –1.4 | 1.0 | 1.5 | 6.1 | 2.6 |
| Rajasthan | 2.6 | 2.4 | 2.5 | 2.2 | 1.5 | 1.5 |
| Sikkim | 2.9 | 0.6 | 3.3 | 1.4 | 9.1 | 3.4 |
| Tamil Nadu | 1.6 | 2.0 | 1.8 | 1.4 | –0.3 | 0.8 |
| Tripura | 3.3 | 10.4 | 4.3 | 2.7 | –5.5 | 1.4 |
| Uttar Pradesh | 2.3 | 1.1 | 2.0 | 1.8 | 1.4 | 1.7 |
| West Bengal | 2.4 | 2.1 | 2.4 | 1.6 | –0.8 | 1.1 |
| Andaman & Nicobar Islands | 3.9 | 12.9 | 6.1 | 2.4 | –8.0 | –0.7 |
| Chandigarh | 3.7 | 5.0 | 3.9 | 2.5 | –1.1 | 1.8 |

(*Contd.*)

TABLE 4.4 (Contd.)

| (1) | (2) | (3) | (4) | (5) | (6) | (7) |
|---|---|---|---|---|---|---|
| Dadra & Nagar Haveli | 4.5 | 3.4 | 4.0 | 3.5 | –2.0 | 1.2 |
| Daman and Diu | 4.2 | –2.7 | 1.8 | 4.8 | 7.0 | 5.4 |
| Delhi | 4.1 | 3.2 | 3.9 | 2.7 | 4.2 | 2.9 |
| Lakshadweep | — | — | — | 3.8 | 11.0 | 5.2 |
| Pondicherry | 3.4 | 1.4 | 2.8 | 3.5 | 3.0 | 3.4 |
| All India | 2.2 | 1.7 | 2.1 | 1.9 | 0.9 | 1.6 |

*Notes* : (1) Growth in employment has been estimated as compound annual growth in the persons employed in the age group 15 years and above on the usual principal and subsidiary status.

(2) Work Force Participation Rates assumed to be the same for Goa and Daman & Dieu for 1980.

(3) 1980 NSSO survey excludes Arunachal Pradesh, Lakshadweep, Dadra & Nagar Haveli (Urban) and Nagaland (Rural).

*Sources* : (i) The 38th, 50th and the 55th *Rounds of the NSSO* on Employment and Unemployment Situation in India.

(ii) *Census of India*, 1981, 1991, 2001 and 2011 and Report of the Technical Group of Population Projections, RGI, 2006.

## IV.II.V. Impact of FDI on Trade and Balance of Payments

The liberalization of India's external sector during past two decades was extremely successful in meeting the Balance of Payments (BoP) crisis of 1990 and putting the BOP on a sustainable path. These reforms improved the openers of the Indian economy *vis-a-vis* other emerging economies. Still Indian economy is relatively closed compared to its *'peer competitors'* Further reduction of tariff protection and liberalization of capital flows specially FDI will enhance the efficiency of the economy and along with reform of domestic policies will stimulate investment, growth and trade performance.

External reforms were among the most successful reforms undertaken in India during the nineties. These reforms have opened up the economy, strengthened the external account, and made it much less vulnerable to shocks. India's trade share rose by 0.11 per cent of world trade during the nineties raising India's world ranking by six positions. India also became more open in terms of capital flows with its rank in terms of FDI inflows rising by nine positions. Equity inflows increased even more rapidly to raise India's rank among the emerging markets by eight positions during the nineties. In 1999 only 13 emerging markets received more FDI than India and only five received more equity inflows. Of these, China, South Korea, Thailand and Brazil had larger inflows of both FDI and foreign equity than India during this year. With the above information now we shall highlighted the role of FDI in India's balance of payments and foreign trade behaviour.

### (a) FDI and Balance of Payments

East Asian crisis has raised a fundamental question about the risks of capital account liberalization. A question that is often asked now is whether the capital account is more a source of economic difficulties and risk than benefit. *Bhagwati* (1998) is of the view that full capital mobility is not a necessary condition for free trade. He argues that governments should restrict the global flow of capital even while vigorously promoting free trade in goods and services. Even if one was to believe that capital flows are generally productive, there is still an important difference between embracing free portfolio capital mobility and a policy of attracting equity investment. *Krugman* (1998) advocates capital controls purely as a stop-gap measure on grounds that it allows crisis hit countries to adopt more expansionary monetary and fiscal policies and hence promote a faster recovery of the real economy. *Stiglitz* (1998) contends that the cost of disruption due to swings in expectations is invariably high for countries like India. Thus, there exists a case for more direct intervention in less sophisticated economies. *Fischer* (1998) pointed out that the benefits of liberalizing the capital account outweigh the potential costs. Currency controls will impose distortions on the economy, no matter how well executed, and the longer they are in place the more serious they tend to get.

The benefits of free capital flows are well known. If capital mobility can lead to better resource allocation, it becomes a contributory factor to improved output and trade. A country can not wish away capital flows in all forms other than FDI. What is needed is a clear identification of capital flows that can tend to be 'volatile' and use appropriate measures to discourage such flows.

The capital account of India's balance of payments underwent a significant change in the 90s. In the 80s the current account deficit was mainly financed by three sources— external assistance, commercial borrowing and NRI deposits. The 90s saw a marked increase in non-debt creating inflows. Net external assistance waned in importance with net inflows more than halving from US $ 2.1 billion (1990-95) to US $ 0.9 billion (1995-2000), as disbursements declined (from US $ 3.5 billion to US $ 2.9 billion) coupled with increased amortization (from US $ 1.4 billion to US $ 2.0 billion). Net external commercial borrowings during the second half of the 90s averaged US $ 2.6 billion per annum. Inflows under NRI deposits averaged US $ 1.8 billion during the second half of the 90s. All these three sources taken together accounted for a much lower share of the capital flows during the 90s and more particularly in the second half. The contribution of FDI inflows to total capital flows increased from an average of only 7 per cent during the first half of the 90s to around 33 per cent during 1995-2010. Portfolio inflows increased from 18 per cent to 28 per cent over the same period. Thus the share of the non-debt creating inflows comprising of FDI and FPI in the total capital inflows increased to 61 per cent during 1995-2010. So, in the balance of payments, FDI has shown a steady increase (Table 4.5).

### (b) FDI and Foreign Trade

In 1991, India made a decisive shift to a more open and liberal economy. External openers do provide significant opportunities for growth. It is undeniable that across the country, articulate people, especially those in the middle class, are responding positively to newly emerging opportunities. And this is happened due to a sharp increase in foreign trade balance.

The proportion of India's gross domestic product (GDP) that is involved in the international trade of goods and services is one of the important element that are conventionally considered in determining India's openers to the world economy. It is found from the balance of payments ratios that export-GDP ratio shows an increasing trend in the post-reform

TABLE 4.5

**India's Balance of Payments**

| *ITEM* | *1990-91* | *1991-92* | *1992-93* | *1993-94* | *1995-96* | *2000-01* | *2005-06* | *2006-07* | *2007-08* | *2008-09* | *2009-10* |
|---|---|---|---|---|---|---|---|---|---|---|---|
| *(1)* | *(2)* | *(3)* | *(4)* | *(5)* | *(6)* | *(7)* | *(8)* | *(9)* | *(10)* | *(11)* | *(12)* |
| I. Merchandise | | | | | | | | | | | |
| (a) Exports | 18477 | 18266 | 18869 | 22683 | 26855 | 32311 | 34133 | 35680 | 34298 | 37542 | 44894 |
| (b) Imports | 27914 | 21064 | 24316 | 26739 | 35904 | 43670 | 48948 | 51187 | 47544 | 55383 | 59264 |
| (c) Trade Balance (a–b) | -9437 | -2798 | -5447 | -4056 | -9049 | -11359 | -14815 | -15507 | -13246 | -17841 | -14370 |
| II. Invisibles (net) | -243 | 1620 | 1921 | 2898 | 5680 | 5449 | 10196 | 10007 | 9208 | 13143 | 11791 |
| III. Current Account (I + II) | -9680 | -1178 | -3526 | -1158 | -3369 | -5910 | -4619 | -5500 | -4038 | -4698 | -2579 |
| IV. Capital Account (a to f) | 7188 | 3777 | 2936 | 9695 | 9156 | 4689 | 11412 | 10011 | 8260 | 10840 | 8409 |
| (a) Foreign Investment | 103 | 133 | 559 | 4235 | 4807 | 4805 | 6153 | 5390 | 2412 | 5117 | 4588 |
| (i) FDI (net) | 97 | 129 | 315 | 586 | 1314 | 2144 | 2821 | 3557 | 2462 | 2093 | 1828 |
| (ii) FIIs | 0 | 0 | 1 | 1665 | 1503 | 2009 | 1926 | 979 | -390 | 2135 | 1847 |
| (iii) Euro equities and others | 6 | 4 | 243 | 1984 | 1990 | 652 | 1406 | 854 | 340 | 889 | 913 |
| (b) External Assistance | 2210 | 3037 | 1859 | 1901 | 1526 | 883 | 1109 | 907 | 820 | 901 | 427 |

*(Contd.)*

TABLE 4.5 (*Contd.*)

| (1) | (2) | (3) | (4) | (5) | (6) | (7) | (8) | (9) | (10) | (11) | (12) |
|---|---|---|---|---|---|---|---|---|---|---|---|
| (c) Commercial Borrowings (net) | 2248 | 1456 | -359 | 607 | 1030 | 1275 | 2848 | 3999 | 4362 | 313 | 4011 |
| (d) Rupee debt service | -1193 | -1240 | -878 | -1053 | -983 | -952 | -727 | -767 | -802 | -711 | -617 |
| (e) NRI deposits (net) | 1536 | 290 | 2001 | 1205 | 172 | 1103 | 3350 | 1125 | 1742 | 1540 | 2317 |
| (f) Other capital | 2284 | 101 | -245 | 2800 | 2604 | -2425 | -1321 | -643 | -274 | 3940 | -2291 |
| V. Overall Balance (III + IV) | -2492 | 2599 | -590 | 8537 | 5787 | -1221 | 6793 | 4511 | 4222 | 6142 | 5830 |
| VI. IMF (net) | 1214 | 786 | 1288 | 187 | -1143 | -1715 | -975 | -618 | 3829 | -260 | -26 |
| VI. Reserve Use (increase –, decrease +) | 1278 | -3385 | -698 | -8724 | -4644 | 2936 | -5818 | -3893 | -393 | -6142 | -5830 |
| VIII. SDR Allocation | 0 | 0 | 0 | 0 | 0 | 0 | 0 | 0 | 0 | 0 | 0 |

*Source* : Handbook of Statistics on Indian Economy, 2012, Reserve Bank of India, Mumbai.

period than that in the pre-reform period (Table 4.5). In 1980-81, the ratios of exports and imports to GDP were 4.6 and 8.9 respectively. In 1990-91, export ratio raises to 5.8 and import ratio decreased to 8.8. In 2009-10 both export and import ratios to GDP increased to 9.4 and 12.4 respectively. Current account deficit ratio to GDP also improved from –1.5 in 1980-81 to –0.5 in 2009-10.

India started out the opening up in 1970 with a very low level of participation in foreign trade with less than 8 per cent of its GDP. There was a spurt during the 1970s except 1973, triggered, no doubt, by the OPEC oil price hike, which on the one hand made for higher costs of imports, directly and indirectly, but on the other hand also created new markets for Indian goods and services in the West Asia. For about a decade, the share of foreign trade in GDP increased gradually, from 7.57 per cent in 1970 to 15.36 per cent in 1980. The rising share of imports explains this rise more while the share of exports remained largely stagnant. Over the period from 1981 to 1991, there is another spurt, followed by a surge over the next four years, crossing the level of 20 per cent in 1993 and reaching the unprecedented figure of almost 25 per cent in 1995. During 1996-2006 the share remained stable (Table 4.6).

While views may differ over the degree of success of India in participating more actively in the world economy, especially since it had been so insulated from it earlier, it is clear that over last two decades from 1989 to 2010, India's foreign trade in goods and services as a share of its GDP expanded by only 38.32 per cent from 16.57 per cent to 22.92 per cent. The share of imports increased by 29.30 per cent from 9.42 per cent to 12.18 per cent during that period. The share of exports increased by 50.21 per cent from 7.15 per cent to 10.74 per cent during 1989 to 2010. If we consider the year 2010, the share of imports increased by only 1.80 and the share of exports increased by 13.99. In terms of India's own economic past, this extent of increase represents a significant change in its relationship with the world economy. However, the average annual rate of growth of about 5 per cent is only modest and can not be regarded as having the potential for serious destabilizing consequences.

The sharp increase in the share of exports is mainly caused by huge FDI inflows in the post-reform periods. The share of net

TABLE 4.6
**Balance of Payments Ratios**

| *Season* | *Exports/ GDP* | *Imports/ GDP* | *Net Earnings/ GDP* | *Current A/c Deficit/ GDP* | *Net Capital Inflows/ GDP* |
|---|---|---|---|---|---|
| 1980-81 | 4.6 | 8.9 | 2.8 | –1.5 | 1.2 |
| 1981-82 | 4.6 | 8.4 | 2.2 | –1.7 | 0.8 |
| 1982-83 | 4.8 | 8.4 | 1.8 | –1.7 | 1.8 |
| 1983-84 | 4.6 | 7.8 | 1.6 | –1.5 | 2 |
| 1984-85 | 5.2 | 8.1 | 1.7 | –1.2 | 1.4 |
| 1985-86 | 4.1 | 7.6 | 1.3 | –2.3 | 1.9 |
| 1989-90 | 5.8 | 8.3 | 0.2 | –2.3 | 1.9 |
| 1990-91 | 5.8 | 8.8 | –0.1 | –3.1 | 2.6 |
| 1991-92 | 6.9 | 7.9 | 0.7 | –0.3 | 1.8 |
| 1992-93 | 7.3 | 9.6 | 0.6 | –1.7 | 2.1 |
| 1993-94 | 8.3 | 9.8 | 1.1 | –0.4 | 3.3 |
| 1994-95 | 8.4 | 11.2 | 1.8 | –1.0 | 2.3 |
| 1995-96 | 9.2 | 12.4 | 1.6 | –1.7 | 0.7 |
| 1996-97 | 8.9 | 12.8 | 2.7 | –1.2 | 2.9 |
| 1997-98 | 8.7 | 12.5 | 2.5 | –1.4 | 2.3 |
| 2000-01 | 8.2 | 11.4 | 2.2 | –1.0 | 2 |
| 2005-06 | 8.3 | 12.3 | 2.9 | –1.0 | 2.3 |
| 2009-10 | 9.4 | 12.4 | 2.5 | –0.5 | n.a |

*Sources* : (i) *Statistical Outline of India, 2002-03,* Tata Services Limited, Mumbai, p. 90. (ii) *RBI Bulletin,* 2012.

FDI inflows to GDP is increased in large percentage after the implementation of new economic reforms. Just as controls on foreign trade insulated India's economic market from world markets, so did controls on capital movements insulate its financial markets from the world's financial markets. India's stringent restrictions on capital movements were part and parcel of the larger vision of building an autarkic industrial economy, independent of the world's other economies. Outflow of capital from India was simply prohibited, while severe restrictions applied to inflow of foreign capital. FPI was not allowed, while

TABLE 4.7

**India's Foreign Trade and Foreign Investment**

| Year | Exports of Goods and Services (% of GDP) | Imports of Goods and Services (% of GDP) | Total Foreign Trade (as % of GDP) | FDI Net Inflows (US $ Mn.) | FPI Net Inflows (US $ Mn.) | Total Foreign Investment (US $ Mn.) | FDI Net Inflows (% of GDP) |
|---|---|---|---|---|---|---|---|
| (1) | (2) | (3) | (4) | (5) | (6) | (7) | (8) |
| 1980 | 6.04 | 9.32 | 15.36 | 79.00 | 0.00 | 79.00 | 0.04 |
| 1981 | 5.89 | 8.91 | 14.80 | 92.00 | 0.00 | 92.00 | 0.05 |
| 1985 | 5.63 | 8.13 | 13.76 | 72.00 | 0.00 | 72.00 | 0.04 |
| 1986 | 5.68 | 7.80 | 13.48 | 6.00 | 0.00 | 6.00 | Negl. |
| 1989 | 6.28 | 8.44 | 14.72 | 19.00 | 0.00 | 19.00 | 0.01 |
| 1990 | 5.51 | 8.38 | 13.89 | 106.00 | 0.00 | 106.00 | 0.05 |
| 1991 | 5.50 | 8.06 | 13.56 | 118.00 | 192.00 | 310.00 | 0.05 |
| 1995 | 5.84 | 8.22 | 14.06 | 212.00 | 0.00 | 212.00 | 0.08 |
| 1996 | 6.16 | 9.08 | 12.24 | 91.00 | 56.00 | 147.00 | 0.03 |
| 1998 | 7.15 | 9.42 | 16.57 | 252.00 | 168.00 | 420.00 | 0.08 |
| 1999 | 7.14 | 9.76 | 16.90 | 162.00 | 105.00 | 267.00 | 0.05 |
| 2000 | 8.56 | 9.14 | 17.70 | 74.00 | 0.00 | 74.00 | 0.03 |

(Contd.)

TABLE 4.7 (*Contd.*)

| (1) | (2) | (3) | (4) | (5) | (6) | (7) | (8) |
|---|---|---|---|---|---|---|---|
| 2001 | 8.94 | 10.59 | 19.53 | 277.00 | 241.40 | 518.40 | 0.11 |
| 2002 | 10.00 | 11.26 | 21.26 | 550.40 | 1840.40 | 2390.80 | 0.20 |
| 2003 | 9.98 | 12.54 | 22.52 | 973.30 | 4728.70 | 5702.00 | 0.29 |
| 2004 | 10.90 | 14.07 | 24.97 | 2143.60 | 1517.00 | 3660.60 | 0.59 |
| 2005 | 10.48 | 14.02 | 24.50 | 2426.00 | 4397.90 | 6823.90 | 0.61 |
| 2006 | 10.72 | 14.09 | 24.81 | 3577.00 | 2116.10 | 5693.10 | 0.85 |
| 2007 | 11.03 | 13.75 | 24.78 | 2635.00 | 341.60 | 2976.60 | 0.61 |
| 2008 | 9.08 | 12.26 | 21.34 | 2155.00 | 3026.00 | 5181.00 | 0.53 |
| 2009 | 10.74 | 12.18 | 22.92 | 2339.00 | 2760.00 | 5099.00 | 0.54 |
| 2010 | 8.15 | 9.59 | 17.74 | 3904.00 | 2021.00 | 5925.00 | 0.91 |

*Source* : World Bank Indicators Database, Various Years.

FDI was seen only as a tool of the last resort to obtain otherwise inaccessible technology or to bolster exports, rather than as an instrument for augmenting production. The upper limit for FDI in domestically located firms was set at 40 per cent.

The whole picture changed in 1991. The broader shift in economic policy in 1991 had reverberations for policy on capital movements as well. Restrictions were loosened first in respect of trade, current account payment and FDI, followed by liberalization of FPI. A huge investment in the form of FDI now comes to India to invest directly in the production process and in foreign trade. Up to 1991, the share of net FDI inflows in GDP was around 0.05 per cent. In 1992 the share of FDI increases to 0.11 per cent. This trend continued up to 1997 and reaches 0.85 per cent. After some turmoil again the share of FDI increases and reaches it maximum with 0.91 per cent in 2010. As the share of FDI increased by 1037.50 per cent from 0.08 per cent in 1989 to 0.91 per cent in 2001, share of trade also increased by 7.06 per cent from 16.57 per cent in 1989 to 17.74 per cent in 2010 (Table 4.7).

Thus the inflow of FDI should certainly help the country. However, FDI inflow thus far appears to have very substantially gone into consumer goods industries, both durable and non-durable. There is really no major thrust—in the matter of FDI—for exports of manufactures. The WTO arrangements, in fact, rule out any conditionalities either in regard to export or even in regard to domestic manufacturing content. Through increasing trade performance, FDI helped the integration of Indian economy to the global economy.

### IV.II.VI. FDI Inflows and Inequality

Each new advance in civilization is at the same time a new advance in inequality. All institutions set-up by the society, which have arisen civilization turn into the opposite of their original purpose. As economic reform taken place in India, the economy gained a lot in the various fields. With reforms, FDI came into the economy in a larger proportion than before. This inflow helped to better growth, trade performance, enterprise level research and development, social and physical infrastructure, decreased savings-investment gap for the society.

FDI brings many goods for the economy but at the same time it has been shown that the burden of fiscal adjustment has been unequal in that it has led to declining expenditures on social sectors such as education, health and poverty alleviation. In the early post-reform period there is a decline in social sector spending. Hence, concerns have been raised regarding the levels of human development. As far as poverty alleviation is concerned, the decade of 1990s can be termed as a 'decade of lost opportunity'. The inequalities between rich and poor states have increased during the 1990s. In the following sections we shall tried to analyze the cases of inequalities occurred as FDI inflows increased into India (Pan, 2011).

### *(a) Region-wise Inequalities*

FDI inflows a part of which comes in the form of investments in physical infrastructure have lagged behind in the past few years. Major projects involving private participation (including foreign involvement) have been sanctioned in power, expressways, bridges, ports, etc. They have been slow in getting off the ground. While such projects should be promoted and encouraged, they should not be at the cost of public investments in infrastructure and maintenance of existing infrastructure.

After dismantling of the industrial licensing system, there is no mechanism left with the government to channel industrial investment to relatively less developed regions. This might explain the increase in interstate disparities that has been observed during the post-reform period. The government might create a regional development fund which is built up with a cess imposed on the units set-up in more developed states and subsidies the investments in poorer states, among other measures, to bring about regional balance.

Among the Indian states, Maharashtra, Delhi, Tamil Nadu, Karnataka, Goa, West Bengal, Gujarat, Haryana, Kerala and Punjab are the richer states in terms of per capita income. While the all-India average of per capita income in 2009-10 was Rs. 15,562, Delhi (Rs. 39,620), Goa (Rs. 24,309), Punjab (Rs. 23,040), Maharashtra (Rs. 22,604), Haryana (Rs. 21,114), Tamil Nadu (Rs. 19,141), Gujarat (Rs. 18,625), Kerala (Rs. 18,262), Karnataka (Rs. 16,343) and West Bengal (Rs. 15,569) are well ahead of the all-India level. In 1990-91, all-India average of per capita income was Rs. 5,671. At that time also the current richer states became richer. Delhi (Rs. 11,373), Goa (Rs. 8,952), Punjab

(Rs. 8,177), Haryana (Rs. 7,721), Maharashtra (Rs. 7,612) and Gujarat (Rs. 6,343) were well ahead of the national level. Kerala (Rs. 5,110), West Bengal (Rs. 5,072), Tamil Nadu (Rs. 5,541) were also coming closer to the all-India levels.

During 1991 to 2010 period FDI came into India to establish its supremacy into the already richer states. Maharashtra, Tamil Nadu, Delhi, Gujarat, Karnataka and Andhra Pradesh were their favourite states to invest. In Maharashtra Rs. 48,722.40 crore, in Delhi Rs. 33,806.58 crore, in Tamil Nadu Rs. 23,470.30 crore, in Karnataka Rs. 21,945.00 crore, in Gujarat Rs. 18,453.20 crore, in Andhra Pradesh Rs. 13,092.24 crore were invested by multinational firms as FDI. On the other hand, Assam (negligible), Tripura (negligible), Meghalaya (0.02 per cent), Bihar (0.26 per cent), Rajasthan (1.07 per cent), Uttar Pradesh (1.70 per cent), Orissa (2.92 per cent) attracted only a miniscule percentage of FDI. This means, poorer states not getting the benefit of FDI and only richer states (except Andhra Pradesh) which were already richer take the maximum facility of FDI. This means region-wise inequality among the Indian states is increasing and unequal distribution of FDI inflows is also responsible for that (Table 4.8).

### *(b) Class-wise Inequalities*

Policy-makers of India know what to do to remove inequality throughout the economy but they are confused at a loss where to begin. Of course, we have no choice, since the annual budget exercise is a constitutional compulsion. The fact for the moment, however, remains that interest rates have fallen; that there is inadequate aggregate demand and the level of inflation is very low. How can one imagine that under these circumstances economic growth can be brought about, without macro-economic interventions, defies economic logic. Keynesian macrodynamics was designed for an industrial economy in a state of recession. We have a history of adopting interventionism under a semi-controlled economy between 1951 and 1990 and then from 1991 we have adopted a version of free market economies.

During the period 1951-2010 we had low levels of industrialization and a modest growth rate. This is when we were interventionists in our management of macro-economics.

TABLE 4.8
**FDI and Per Capita Income**

| *States* | *Per Capita Income (at current prices)* | | | *FDI (1991-2010)* | | |
|---|---|---|---|---|---|---|
| | *1980-81 (Rs.)* | *1990-91 (Rs.)* | *2009-10 (Rs.)* | *No. of Approvals* | *Amount (Rs. Crore)* | *% of Total* |
| *(1)* | *(2)* | *(3)* | *(4)* | *(5)* | *(6)* | *(7)* |
| 1. Richer States | | | | | | |
| Delhi | 3797 | 11373 | 39620 | 1990 | 33806.58 | 12.02 |
| Goa | 3140 | 8952 | 24309 | 177 | 970.62 | 0.35 |
| Punjab | 2674 | 8177 | 23040 | 183 | 1968.40 | 0.70 |
| Maharashtra | 2435 | 7612 | 22604 | 4002 | 48722.40 | 17.32 |
| Haryana | 2370 | 7721 | 21114 | 784 | 3519.40 | 1.25 |
| Tamil Nadu | 1498 | 5541 | 19141 | 2165 | 23470.30 | 8.34 |
| Gujarat | 1940 | 6343 | 18625 | 1050 | 18435.20 | 6.56 |
| Kerala | 1508 | 5110 | 18262 | 265 | 1527.80 | 0.54 |
| Karnataka | 1527 | 4975 | 16343 | 1973 | 21945.00 | 7.80 |
| West Bengal | 1612 | 5072 | 15569 | 594 | 8808.30 | 3.13 |

| | | | | | | |
|---|---|---|---|---|---|---|
| 2. Poorer States | | | | | | |
| Uttar Pradesh | 1278 | 3937 | 9765 | 740 | 47950.00 | 1.70 |
| Assam | 1317 | 4432 | 9612 | 18 | 1.48 | negl. |
| Orissa | 1314 | 3166 | 9162 | 136 | 8229.00 | 2.92 |
| Bihar | 917 | 2966 | 5540 | 47 | 739.50 | 0.26 |
| Tripura | — | 4240 | 10931 | 2 | 0.68 | negl. |
| Meghalaya | 1361 | 4944 | 13029 | 5 | 52.96 | 0.02 |
| Andhra Pradesh | 1380 | 4816 | 14715 | 1017 | 13092.24 | 4.65 |
| Rajasthan | 1222 | 4883 | 12533 | 320 | 3004.70 | 1.07 |
| All India | 1830 | 5671 | 15562 | 22084 | 281333.60 | — |

*Source* : Calculated from *Statistical Outline of India,* various issues.

After 1997, the rate of economic growth especially in the manufacturing sector has slowed down and there is a general recession in the economy. The service sector is in fact merely an enabler in the circular flow of income. What can it enable if the fundamentals are missing, one wonders. This is when we needed interventionism but we have rejected it and in doing so have effectively thrown the baby out with the baby water. Here increased the inflow of FDI into the economy to give birth to the seek industries. And then, the very same industrialists who were asking for a level playing field in 1985-92 started asking for some sort of state protectionism after 1997.

The central government speaks of free markets and alludes to pump priming in the same breath. FDI allowed to most of the sectors to rebuild and make competitive Indian economy. The facilities of FDI directly goes to the upper class of the society as their profit percentage increasing with the new industries and running the seek one. Lower class also facilitate with getting jobs and more wages than before. The middle class, in the meanwhile, continues to get the cleft stick. The gap between the upper class and middle class of the society has been widened and gap between the middle class and lower class of the society has been shortened. Though the number of people who live below the poverty line is fast increasing, above poverty line lower class get benefited with the new reform policies. The reserve army of the unemployed from the middle class is fast burgeoning and there is no social security net to absorb them. The trickle down effect of development what India achieve with the help of FDI just remained a figment of the economist's vivid imagination.

## IV.III. ELASTICITY OF FOREIGN DIRECT INVESTMENT WITH RESPECT TO ITS DETERMINANTS

The average response of real FDI inflows with respect to its different determinants is known as the elasticity of FDI. As we have discussed in Chapter II that the main determinants of FDI in India are market size, change in market size, openness, infrastructure, composite indicator, exchange rate, rate of inflation, capital formation, etc. Thus, elasticity of foreign direct investment is defined as the proportionate change in the FDI inflows resulting from a proportionate change in the determinant variables of FDI. Symbolically we may write,

$$e_{FDI} = \frac{d(FDI)}{FDI} \Big/ \frac{d(DV)}{DV} = \frac{d(FDI)}{d(DV)} \cdot \frac{DV}{FDI}$$

where, $e_{FDI}$ = elasticity of FDI, d(FDI) = change in FDI inflows, FDI = original FDI inflows, d(DV) = change in determinant variables, DV = original value of determinant variables.

TABLE 4.9

**Elasticity of FDI Inflows in India**

| *Sl. No.* | *Variables* | *Elasticity* | *Relation* |
|---|---|---|---|
| 1. | Gross Domestic Product (GDP) | 11.65 | Positive |
| 2. | Change in the GDP Level | 0.223 | Positive |
| 3. | Infrastructure | 1.0334 | Positive |
| 4. | Exchange Rate | — | Negative |
| 5. | Degree of Openness | –4.3625 | Positive |
| 6. | Composite Indicator | 12.068 | Negative |
| 7. | Domestic Market Size | –1.6633 | Positive |
| 8. | Capital Formation | — | Positive |
| 9. | Debt-Service Ratio | — | Negative |
| 10. | Labour Intensive Production | — | Negative |

*Source* : The calculation of Elasticity for 1 and 2 from Table 4.1; 5 and 8 from Table 4.2; 7 and 10 from Table 4.3; 4, 6 and 9 from Table 4.5.

Taking the main ten determinant variables into consideration we have found that FDI inflows into India is positively related with GDP, change in the GDP level, infrastructure, degree of openness, domestic market size and capital formation but inversely related with exchange rate, composite indicator of FDI, debt-service ratio and labour intensive production process (Table 4.9).

The GDP elasticity co-efficient indicates that for a one per cent increase in the real GDP this year, the real FDI inflows, on the average, increase by 11.65 per cent in the following year. The magnitude of the response of real FDI inflows to the openness is also as high as that with respect of GDP at around 12 per cent and this instantaneous response is indicating the crucial importance of the policy variable in influencing FDI inflows into the country (Table 4.9).

## IV.IV. SUMMARY AND CONCLUSION

This chapter basically highlighted on the real impact of foreign direct investment on Indian economic development. Throughout the process, we have discussed the impact of FDI on GDP growth; trade and balance of payments; production, productivity and efficiency; employment and wage; region-wise and class-wise inequality and on savings-investment gap.

The analysis found that FDI shows a positive trend into the source of GDP. MNC offers more wages than the workers paid in the local level but it can't find any solution for unemployment problem in India in the short-run. Though for long-run the effects should be considerable in nature. FDI closen the gap between the poor countries and rich countries through trade. India also benefited by exporting her product into the world market and coming closure to the developed countries through this process. The inflow of FDI makes a tremendous impact on this. FDI also helped Indian economy to pick up the investment and capital formation when there is dearth of savings. But throughout this process the inequality among the states has increased as rich states become richer by the introduction of new firms.

Thus FDI has a mixed impact on Indian economy. In the next chapter we shall try to find out the anticipated and actual roles of FDI in India.

### END NOTES

1. The Prowess database comprises firm-level data collected by the Center for Monitoring the Indian Economy (CMIE), a private company in India.
2. Coefficients are estimated from a regression of changes in (log) output regressed on changes in (log) materials, skilled labour, unskilled labour, capital stock, changes in FDI at the plant and sector level, and annual time dummies. In column (2) of Table 4.3 shows, tests for equality of coefficients between OLS and OLS with industry dummies. In column (3), tests for equality of coefficients (excluding the time dummies) between specifications in columns (2) and (3). In column (2), the critical 5 per cent value for the $X_2(19) = 30.1$. In column (3), the critical 5 per cent value for the $X_2(7) = 14.1$. A higher value indicates rejection of the test. For details, see *John Dinardo*

*et. al.* (1996).

3. While expressing foreign presence as a share (of labour or of sales) facilitates comparisons between large and small industries, the share's behaviours over time is influenced both by changes in FDI (the numerator) and changes in the size of the industry (the denominator).

## References


Aitken, B.J. and Harison, A.E. (1997), "Do Domestic Firms Benefit from FDI? Evidence from Panel Data", *Mimeo*, Columbia University.

Bhagwati, J. (1998), "The Capital Myth : The Difference between Trade in Widgets and Dollars', *Foreign Affairs*, Vol. 77, pp. 7-12.

Binmore, K.; Rubinstein, A.; Wolinsky. A. (1986), "The Nash Bargaining Solution in Economic Modelling", *Rand Journal of Economics*, Vol. 17, pp. 176-88.

Blomstrom, Magnus (1986), "Foreign Investment and Productive Efficiency: The Case of Mexico", *Journal of Industrial Economics*, Vol. 35, No. 1, September, pp. 97-110.

Borensztein, E.; J. De Gregorio; Lee, J.W. (1998), "How Does Foreign Direct Investment Affect Economic Growth?" *Journal of International Economics*, Vol. 45, No. 1, June, pp. 115-35.

Bughin, J. and Vannini, S. (1995), "Strategic Direct Investment Under Unionised Oligopoly", *International Journal of Industrial Organisation*, Vol. 13, pp. 127-45.

De Mello, L.R.J. (1999), "Foreign Direct Investment-led Growth: Evidence from Time Series and Panel Data", *Oxford Economic Papers*, Vol. 51, pp. 133-51, Oxford University Press.

Dinordo, John; Johnston, Jack and Johnston, John (1996), *Econometric Methods*, New York: McGraw Hill, October.

Fischer, Stanley (1998), "The Asian Crisis: A View from the IMF", *Address at the Midwinter Conference of the Bankers' Association for Foreign Trade*, Washington, DC, January 22.

Government of India (2012), Economic Survey, New Delhi.

Hedge, Dinesh and Sorab Sadri (2001), "India's Economic Reforms : An Examination of the Effect of Liberalization in Selected Segments", *IASSI Quarterly*, Vol. 20, No. 2, pp. 5-29.

Joshi, Vijoy and IMD Little (1996), *India's Economic Reforms, 1991-2000*, Oxford University Press, New Delhi.

Krugman, Paul (1998), "Saving Asia : It's Time to Get Radical", *Fortune*, September 7, pp. 33-38.

Naylor, R. and Santoni, M. (1998), "Wage Bargaining and Foreign Direct Investment", *Working Paper*, University of Warwick.

Pan, S. and Sen, R.K., (2007), *Foreign Direct Investment and Trade in India*, Deep & Deep Publications, New Delhi.

Pan, S. (2011), "State-wise Disparity in Income and Employment in India during the Globalization Era", in D. Mukhopadhyay (ed.):

*Globalization and Inequality*, pp. 215-29, Deep & Deep Publications, New Delhi.

Pedersen, Jorgen Dige (2000), "Explaining Economic Liberalisation in India : State and Society Perspectives", *World Development*, Vol. 28, No. 2, pp. 265-82.

RBI (2002), *Report on Currency and Finance, 2000-01*, Reserve Bank of India, pp. VI1-VI27, Mumbai.

RBI (2012), *Reserve Bank of India Bulletin*, Mumbai, February.

Reis, A.B. (2001), "On the Welfare Effects of Foreign Investment," *Journal of International Economics*, Vol. 54, No. 2, August, pp. 411-27.

Stiglitz, J. (1998), "The Role of International Financial Institutions in the Current Global Economy", *Address to the Chicago Council on Foreign Relations*, Chicago, February 27.

UNCTAD (2000), *Trade and Development Report, 2000*, United Nations, New York and Geneva.

Unel, Bulent (2003), "Productivity Trends in India's Manufacturing Sectors in the Last Two Decades", *IMF Working Paper*, WP/03/22, January.

Zhao, L. (1998), "The Impact of Foreign Direct Investment on Wages and Employment", *Oxford Economic Papers*, Vol. 50, pp. 284-301.

CHAPTER

# 5

# *FDI in India : Their Anticipated and Actual Roles*

## V.I. INTRODUCTION

Throughout the world, most of the foreign investment is made in response to two basic factors: (i) safety of investment, and (ii) opportunity for profit. Macro-economic and political stability is central to a country's attractiveness as a FDI location, because it is considered critically important by foreign investors for both the safety of the investment and the realization of opportunities for profits.

India's development strategy has produced mixed results. It has been successful in transforming a secularly stagnant economy into one growing at persistently positive rates. India has a diversified industrial base and a relatively large and sophisticated financial sector. Mumbai stock exchange is the developing world's fourth largest after Korea's, Malaysia's and Mexico's. In addition, with conservative macro-economic management, inflation remained low and fiscal and balance of payments imbalances seldom persisted. India has never defaulted on its external debt. These successes have been achieved in a very complex society divided along ethnic, linguistic and religious lines. However, India continues to have one of the highest poverty incidences in the developing world and accounts for about one-fourth of the world's absolute poor.

Keeping in above information in mind, throughout this chapter we shall try to find out the actual role of FDI in India. In the decade of 1980s, there had been a growing recognition among India's policy-makers that a more market-oriented approach to economic management would generate higher growth and greater resources for social programmes. While controls on capacity utilization and borrowing were lifted, the investment licensing regime continued to make firm's investment decisions conditional on cumbersome government approvals and resulted in foreign investment levels well below those achieved in other less developed countries. In the next few sections we analyze the gap between approvals and approved FDI in India.

## V.II. FDI APPROVALS AND ACTUAL INFLOWS

Foreign direct investment has been growing more rapidly than world trade since 1990, implying an increase in the integration of the world economy through finance and ownership. The decade of the 1990s, saw a marked shift in the attitude of less developed countries towards FDI. Stimulated by changes in international capital markets and in the determinants of competitiveness in international trade, many less developed countries including India began actively seeking private sources of capital, particularly foreign investment (FDI and FPI), by redefining their development strategies, liberalising their economic and implementing a range of new policies.

### V.II.I. India's Share in Global FDI Inflows : Recent Trend

India's share in FDI inflows among developing countries reached a peak of 1.9 per cent in 1997. It declined sharply to 1 per cent in 2001 and 2005 but has recovered sharply to 1.7 per cent in 2010 (Table 5.1). India's performance on the FDI front has shown a significant improvement since last year. FDI inflows grew by 65 per cent to US $ 3.91 billion during 2009-10 thus exceeding the previous peak of US $ 3.56 billion in 1997-98 (as per BOP accounts of RBI). This growth of 65 per cent is particularly encouraging at a time when global FDI inflows have declined by over 40 per cent. The upward trend in FDI

TABLE 5.1

**FDI Inflows into Developing Countries**

*(Share of Developing Country Total, Per cent)*

| *Host Region/Economy* | *1989-94 annual average* | *1995* | *1996* | *1997* | *2000* | *2001* | *2005* | *2010* |
|---|---|---|---|---|---|---|---|---|
| *(1)* | *(2)* | *(3)* | *(4)* | *(5)* | *(6)* | *(7)* | *(8)* | *(9)* |
| Developing Countries (in billion $) | 59.6 | 113.3 | 152.5 | 187.4 | 188.4 | 222.0 | 240.2 | 225.0 |
| Argentina | 4.5 | 4.5 | 4.5 | 4.9 | 3.9 | 10.9 | 4.7 | — |
| Brazil | 2.5 | 4.9 | 6.9 | 10.0 | 15.1 | 14.1 | 13.9 | 8.9 |
| China | 23.5 | 31.5 | 26.4 | 23.6 | 23.2 | 18.2 | 17.0 | 20.8 |
| Indonesia | 2.5 | 3.8 | 4.1 | 2.5 | –0.2 | –1.2 | –1.9 | — |
| India | 0.7 | 1.9 | 1.7 | 1.9 | 1.4 | 1.0 | 1.0 | 1.7 |
| Malaysia | 6.2 | 5.1 | 4.8 | 3.5 | 1.4 | 1.6 | 2.3 | — |
| South Korea | 1.5 | 1.6 | 1.5 | 1.5 | 2.9 | 4.8 | 4.2 | 4.2 |
| Singapore | 8.1 | 7.8 | 6.8 | 6.9 | 3.3 | 3.2 | 2.7 | — |
| Thailand | 3.2 | 1.8 | 1.5 | 1.9 | 2.7 | 1.6 | 1.0 | — |
| Taiwan | 2.0 | 1.4 | 1.2 | 1.2 | 0.1 | 1.3 | 2.0 | — |
| Vietnam | 1.0 | 2.0 | 1.6 | 1.5 | 1.2 | 0.9 | 0.9 | — |

*Sources* : (i) *World Investment Report*, 2010.
(ii) UNCTAD Press Release, Dated 21st Jan., 2010.
(iii) *RBI Bulletin*, 2012, Govt. of India.

inflows has been sustained during the current financial year with FDI inflows during April-June 2010 about double that during the corresponding period of 2009.[1]

Fiscal 2001-02 witnessed FDI inflows of US$ 4.6 billion (net of ADRs/GDRs). Compared with US $ 2.46 billion received in 2009-10, this represents 66 per cent growth. The upward trend has been sustained during the first quarter of fiscal 2010-11 with FDI inflows of US $ 1.35 billion (net of ADRs/GDRs) as against US$ 0.63 billion (net of ADRs/GDRs) in the corresponding period of fiscal 2009-10, representing 106 per cent growth. It is pertinent to note that this growth has been achieved at a time when global FDI inflows have been experiencing a steep decline of 51 per cent (during 2010).[2]

The cumulative FDI inflows from January 1991 to March 2011 are around US $ 25.02 billion net of ADRs/GDRs. The realisation rate against FDI approvals has risen from 17 per cent in 1992 to 72 per cent in 2010. The sectors that account for maximum FDI are fuel (power, oil refineries, gas); telecom; electronic goods, IT and software; automobiles; and services. The major investing countries are Mauritius (mainly routed from developed countries), USA, Japan, UK, Germany, the Netherlands and South Korea. The states that account for maximum FDI are Maharashtra, Delhi, Tamil Nadu, Karnataka and Gujarat.

Some of the factors that explain the recent spurt in FDI inflows into India are:

(a) Progressive liberalisation of FDI policy has strengthened investor confidence—opening up of new sectors (integrated townships, defence industry, tea plantations, etc.), removal of FDI caps in most sectors, including advertising, airports, private sector oil refining, drugs and pharmaceuticals, etc. and greater degree of automaticity for investment.

(b) Liberalisation of foreign exchange regulations by way of simplification of procedures for making inward and outward remittances.

(c) Sectoral reforms, especially in sectors such as telecom, information technology and automobiles have made them attractive destination for FDI.

(d) Policy to allow foreign companies to set-up wholly owned subsidiaries in India has enabled foreign companies to convert their joint ventures into wholly owned subsidiaries (WOS). The percentage of FDI through merger and acquisition route has increased to around 30 per cent (from around 10 per cent in 2010), which is still much lower than the global percentage of 70-80 per cent.

(e) Public sector disinvestment has finally emerged as an important means to promote FDI.

(f) Liberal policy towards Foreign Venture Capital Investment (FVCI) has given an impetus to investments in technology and infrastructure projects.

(g) Various investment facilitation measures taken by DIPP such as facility for electronic filling of applications, outline chat facility with the applicants, online status on registration/disposal of applications, dedicated e-mail facility for investment-related queries, etc., have also contributed substantially to improving investor confidence. On an average, about 2,000 responses in a year are given to investors and potential investors.

(h) Government has set-up an inter-ministerial committee to examine the extant procedures for investment approvals and implementation of projects, and suggest measures to simplify and expedite the process for both public and private investment. The committee, which was set-up in September 2001, has submitted Part I of its report to the Government. A sub-group of the committee is specifically looking into simplification of procedures relating to private investment. The sub-group will submit its report shortly.

(i) The Foreign Investment Implementation Authority (FIIA) has been activated and now meets at regular intervals to review and resolve investment-related problems. A recent study conducted by FICCI, FIIA acknowledges that has emerged as a problem-solving platform.

### V.II.II. Actual FDI Stock

The policy pursued by the Government towards FDI for more than two decades since independence was cautious. With the result, FDI stock increased by only Rs. 489 crores from Rs. 386 crores in the year 1955 to Rs. 875 crores in 1979. This is evidenced by Table 5.2, revealing a modest growth rate of 3.5 per cent per annum till 1979.

This lower growth of inward FDI stock has been attributed, apart from restrictive policy aspects, to the underdeveloped infrastructural base, limitations of human capital resources, underdeveloped indigenous market coupled with lower purchasing power, absence of domestic leadership for creative destruction, etc. During this phase of inward FDI, a major portion had originated from the UK whereas in terms of rate of growth, countries like Germany, Switzerland, and USA were ahead. During the same period, manufacturing sector was the dominant host of inward FDI stock.

TABLE 5.2

**Compound Growth Rates of FDI Stock and Real FDI Inflows in India**

| *Period* | *Growth Rate of FDI Stock (%)* | *Period* | *Growth Rate of Real FDI Inflows (%) (1980-81 = 100)* |
|---|---|---|---|
| 1964-79 | 3.46 | 1980-81 to 1990-91 | 20.72 |
| 1980-91 | 12.41 | 1991-92 to 2000-01 | 54.87 |
| 1992-2001 | 48.87 | 2001-02 to 2009-10 | 30.92 |
| 2002-10 | 50.74 | 1980-81 to 2009-10 | 41.74 |
| 1964-2010 | 31.87 | — | — |

*Source* : See End Note 3.

The second phase which spanned the decade of eighties was marked by a substantial increase of FDI stock by Rs. 1712 crores, from Rs. 933 crores in 1980 to Rs. 2705 crores in 1990. The period registered a remarkable growth rate of about 12 per cent, nearly quadrupled over that of the preceding period.[3] The partial policy liberalization effected during this period along with the accumulated productive capabilities available in the economy, and further supported by expanding market as well as improved infrastructure, have been identified as the possible factors that gave a push to the propensity of foreign investors to invest in India. This period was also characterized by a relative decline in the share of manufacturing sector in total FDI stock though it continued to be the predominant sector attracting FDI stock. The final stage for inward FDI in India was characterized by a full-fledged liberalization effected during the 1990s, commencing in the year 1991. During 1991-2010, increase in FDI stock was Rs. 47093.3 crores from Rs. 3213 crores in 1991 to Rs. 50306.3 crores in 2010. In fact, there was a distinct break with the former phases as indicated by the impressive growth rate of 49 per cent during this period *vis-a-vis* the growth rates for earlier periods as well as for the period as a whole. This has been mainly attributed to the major policy liberalizations and significant role acquired by financial institutions, trading and other service segments of economy. The relative share of manufacturing sector in FDI stock continued to decline (Table 5.2).

Sectoral distribution of stock of FDI in India (Table 3.12) shows that the percentage share of FDI in the March 1980 was 4.1 per cent for plantation and horticulture. In March 1990, it increased to 9.5 per cent but in March 2010 it decreased to 0.22 per cent. In the mining sector FDI stock as in March 1980 was 0.8 per cent which goes down in March 1990 to 0.3 per cent and shows some improvement in March 2010 period with 1.79 per cent. Actual FDI stock in the petroleum and power sector was 3.9 per cent in March 1980, decreased to 0.1 per cent in March 1990 and increased in huge amount with 32.47 per cent. But in the manufacturing sector stock of FDI shows a downward trend with 86.9 per cent in March 1980, 84.9 per cent in March 1990 and 30.77 per cent in March 2010. Besides petroleum and power sector, service sector also shows an upward trend of FDI stock with 4.1 per cent in March 1980, 5.2 per cent in March 1990 and massive increase to 39.74 per cent in March 2010.

### V.II.III. Actual Inward FDI Flows

During the partial liberalization phase (1980-81 to 1990-91) the real FDI flows exhibited a remarkable growth rate of 20.72

per cent per annum, which went up to 54.87 per cent in the post-reform phase (1991-92 to 2009-10). This quantum jump in the growth rate during the post-reform phase may be attributed to the contributory factors already mentioned in section V.II.I.

FDI flows in the year 1980-81 as a percentage of real GDP is only 0.01 and that of real gross fixed capital formation is 0.04, but these real share risen to 0.03 and 9.4 respectively in the year 1990-91 and further to 0.91 and 9.6 respectively in the year 2010, evidencing the increasing economic significance of FDI to Indian economy.

The relative share of FDI in total foreign investment in the Indian economy has been looking up in the post-reform era. Another significant observation is that the relative share of FDI in total foreign investment in the Indian economy has been looking up in the post-reform era. Whereas this constituted only 13.84 per cent during the year 1993-94, the relative share has gone up to 65.99 per cent in 2000-01 and more than 100 per cent during the year 2005-06 (which signify a negative inflow of portfolio investment) and again goes down to 39.84 in 2009-10 (Table 5.3). It may appear that there has been a decline in the

TABLE 5.3

**Relative Share of FDI (%)**

*(Amount in US $ Mn.)*

| *Year* | *Total Investment* | *FDI (Net)* | *Portfolio Investment* | *% Share of FDI to Total* |
|---|---|---|---|---|
| 1990-91 | 103 | 97 | 6 | 94.17 |
| 1991-92 | 133 | 129 | 4 | 96.17 |
| 1992-93 | 559 | 315 | 244 | 56.35 |
| 1993-94 | 4235 | 586 | 3649 | 13.84 |
| 1994-95 | 4807 | 1314 | 3493 | 27.34 |
| 1995-96 | 4805 | 2144 | 2661 | 44.62 |
| 2000-01 | 5390 | 3557 | 1833 | 65.99 |
| 2005-06 | 2412 | 2462 | –50 | 102.07 |
| 2008-09 | 5117 | 2093 | 3024 | 40.9 |
| 2009-10 | 4588 | 1828 | 2760 | 39.84 |

*Source* : *SIA Newsletter*, 2002 and 2010, various issues.

relative share of FDI after 1992-93; however, a closer examination of Table 5.3 reveals that the absolute quantum of FDI has in fact increased but the massive increase in portfolio investment depressed the relative share of FDI in 1993-94, 1994-95, 2008-09 and in 2009-10.

### V.II.IV. Actual *vs.* Approved FDI

The actual inflow of FDI is lagging far behind approvals granted in India. This undesirable facet of the problem may be stemming from a complex interactive process of several factors like lack of a transparent incentive mechanism, administrative hurdles, political inexpediency, etc. But the foremost bottleneck in infrastructure constraints on production process. Hence, several studies (*Pan and Sen*, 2007; *Pan*, 2011) have pointed out that to attract and maximize the extent of actualization of FDI approved, we should make our administrative process even more transparent, reallocate towards infrastructure sector, and build up a political consensus to ensure a stable FDI policy. With a growing indigenous market, availability of cheap and skilled labour, and political stability once attained, India may soon emerge as a winner in the game of attracting foreign investment.

From Table 5.4 it is found that all FDI approvals are not coming actually into the country. Due to the said reasons, FDI actually has came Rs. 990747.7 million while the amount of approved FDI was Rs. 2840100 million during the period 1991-2010. This means only 34.88 per cent FDI actually came since economic reform has taken into the country. While the approved FDI through SIA and FIPB route was Rs. 2629600 million but in realities only Rs. 602798 million has come. Actual FDI inflows through RBI route shows some improvement with Rs. 304363.9 million while approved FDI amount was Rs. 210500 and this is due to inclusion of RBI automatic approval (under delegated power) with amount of inflows on acquisition of shares. The table also shows that among the approvals of FDI through FIPB and SIA routes only 22.92 per cent has actually come into reality. This means though India widen up her economy to the world, sincere FDI investors struggling here to invest and to do well in

TABLE 5.4

**FDI Approvals vs. Actual FDI Inflows**

(Rs. in Million)

| Year | FDI Approvals | | | | Actual FDI Inflows | | | |
|---|---|---|---|---|---|---|---|---|
| | SIA | FIPB | RBI | Total | SIA, FIPB | RBI | NRI | Total |
| (1) | (2) | (3) | (4) | (5) | (6) | (7) | (8) | (9) |
| 1991 | 3600 | 300 | 1400 | 5300 | 1911.8 | — | 1602.5 | 3514.3 |
| 1992 | 4200 | 26900 | 7800 | 38900 | 4779.5 | 475.4 | 1602.5 | 6751.8 |
| 1993 | 1600 | 80400 | 6600 | 88600 | 9851.6 | 2411 | 5604.5 | 17867.1 |
| 1994 | 3200 | 133400 | 5300 | 141900 | 15007.6 | 3625.8 | 11185.1 | 29818.5 |
| 1995 | 3000 | 312300 | 5400 | 320700 | 38694.4 | 5301.6 | 19705.6 | 63701.6 |
| 1996 | 11800 | 337200 | 12500 | 361500 | 57589.1 | 9234.2 | 20620.4 | 87443.7 |
| 1997 | 3200 | 45300 | 92700 | 548900 | 101284 | 18212.5 | 10396.2 | 129892.7 |
| 1998 | 7200 | 299000 | 1900 | 308100 | 82397.3 | 46700 | 3594.8 | 132692.1 |
| 2000 | 100 | 273600 | 9900 | 283600 | 61894.3 | 27216.4 | 3488.3 | 92599 |
| 2005 | 1900 | 352700 | 15700 | 370300 | 63425.3 | 37498.5 | 3488.2 | 104412 |
| 2009 | 7900 | 237400 | 23500 | 268800 | 96385.9 | 62032.1 | 2292.5 | 160710.5 |
| 2010 | 2200 | 73500 | 27800 | 103500 | 69577.2 | 91656.4 | 110.8 | 161344.4 |
| Total | 49900 | 2579700 | 210500 | 2840100 | 602798 | 304363.9 | 83585.8 | 990747.7 |

*Note* : Since 1996 onwards Actual FDI Inflows through RBI data included RBI Automatic approval (under delegated power) and amount of inflows on acquisition of shares.

*Source* : *SIA Newsletter*, January 2002 and June 2011.

the business. To attract and maximize the extent of actualization of FDI approved, we should make our administrative process transparent reallocate towards infrastructure sector, and build up a political consensus to ensure a stable FDI policy.

FDI inflows reached a peak of US $ 3.56 million in 1997-98. Thereafter, FDI inflows have been below US $ 2.5 billion every year. However, in the ongoing fiscal reform process, FDI inflows are expected to improve significantly. But more important than the amount of approvals, it is the steady improvement in actual inflow that merits attention. With the exception of 1998, the lowest annual growth in FDI inflows over the last eight-years has been about 15 percent.

Even the ratio of actual inflow to approvals continues to improve steadily. Although, the figures in Table 5.4 are strictly not comparable as there is a significant lag in approvals and inflow—which means that inflows for a particular year are not likely to be from the projects approved in that year—the improvement shows that an increasing number of projects are actually taking off.

In the first few years of reforms, large number of projects were being approved but most of these were not taking off. A number of these projects were in the power generation. With ground realities now becoming clear to international investors, there has been a shift in the nature of FDI investment in India. The emphasis has now shifted towards smaller projects in software, electronics and service sector. This is evident in average investment per approval coming down from the peak of Rs. 329.67 million in 1997 to less than half to Rs. 135.62 million in 2010. While in the beginning of reform, actual average investment per approvals was Rs. 12.16 million in 1991, it increased to an all time high of Rs. 111.41 million in 2000 and then slower down to Rs. 53.65 million in 2005 and again improved to Rs. 81.08 million in 2010 (Table 5.5). That seems to suggest that although big ticket of FDI has not come into India, a somewhat less eye-catching but steady FDI inflow is beginning to happen.

TABLE 5.5

**FDI—Small But Certain**

| *Year* | *No. of FDI Approved* | *Amount Approved (Rs. Mn)* | *Amount/No. of Approvals (Rs. Mn)* | *Actual Inflow (Rs. Mn)* | *Amount/ Actual Inflow (Rs. Mn)* |
|---|---|---|---|---|---|
| 1991 | 289 | 5300 | 18.34 | 3514.3 | 12.16 |
| 1992 | 692 | 38900 | 56.21 | 6751.8 | 9.76 |
| 1993 | 785 | 88600 | 112.87 | 17867.1 | 22.76 |
| 1994 | 1062 | 141900 | 133.62 | 29818.5 | 28.08 |
| 1995 | 1355 | 320700 | 236.68 | 63701.6 | 47.01 |
| 1996 | 1559 | 361500 | 231.88 | 87443.7 | 56.09 |
| 1997 | 1665 | 548900 | 329.67 | 129892.7 | 78.01 |
| 2000 | 1191 | 308100 | 258.69 | 132692.1 | 111.41 |
| 2005 | 1726 | 283600 | 164.31 | 92599.0 | 53.65 |
| 2009 | 1726 | 370300 | 214.54 | 104412.0 | 60.49 |
| 2010 | 1982 | 268800 | 135.62 | 160710.5 | 81.08 |

*Sources* : *SIA Newsletter*, December 2002 and December 2011.

## V.III. GENERAL ISSUES RELATED TO APPROVAL AND IMPLEMENTATION OF FDI PROJECTS

In pursuance of the need felt by the Government of India to recast their investment approval and regulation framework with a view to ensuring that the scarce resources are used effectively, the Cabinet Secretariat set-up a Committee.[4] The Committee was set-up to examine the extant procedures for investment approvals and implementation of projects and suggest measures to simplify and expedite the process for both public and private investments.

The report of the Committee has concentrated mainly on the upstream issue relating to government and public sector projects, i.e., issues that arise from the conceptualization to the stage of investment approval. A sub-group was formed who has separately been looking into the downstream issues, i.e., those from stage of investment approval to the implementation of the project and also some of the operational issues. The issues covered under the upstream and downstream categories are:

(a) *Upstream Issues:* The issues that arise from the stage of conceptualization of the project to the investment approval in the case of public projects are covered under upstream issues. These would also include any permission, license, approval, etc., necessary before investment approval.

(b) *Downstream Issues:* Downstream issues, on the other hand, would include all the implementation and operational issues starting from the stage of investment approval in case of a public project or financial closure in case of private project up to the commencement of commercial production. It would also include the various statutory approvals/ clearances required for commissioning the project. Downstream operational issues would include the operational phase of the project after its commissioning.

### Causes behind Poor Quality of Project Decisions and Delays in Implementation

The Government of India and its PSEs together invest almost Rs. 130,000 crores annually in projects and schemes in infrastructure, social development and industrial development sectors. With progressive liberalization of the economy and opening up of a large number of sectors to private and FDI, the private sector has a major role in investment, which will assume even greater significance in the years ahead.

It has, however, been observed that liberalization of the economic policy and changes in the structure of the economy has not translated fully into attracting greater investments due to a variety of reasons. Existing procedures of project formulation, appraisal and approval particularly for government projects, inadequacies in the existing management system and inadequate skills in project formulation, appraisal and management are some of the major reasons behind delays in the investment approvals and implementation of projects. Some of the main upstream factors affecting these projects are:

### *(a) Process Related*

(i) Significant time lag between the grant of 'in principle' approval and submission of detailed feasibility report for appraisal.

(ii) Poor quality of project formulation resulting in delays in decision-making and implementation in many cases. Issues that should have been identified and addressed at the formulation stages, but were missed out, also cause delays in implementation, overruns, need for revision of cost estimates and a fresh set of approval.

(iii) Multiplicity of agencies, viz., DOE, EFC, PIB, etc., for project appraisal leading to delays in decision-making. Many agencies provide inputs at the stage of project appraisal often resulting in overlap and redundancy in their roles.

(iv) Involvement of many agencies at the stage of project formulation and appraisal also makes it difficult to fix responsibility.

(v) Delays in project appraisal and approval beyond the prescribed time.

(vi) Absence of professional project management approaches that have evolved recently, particularly in the private sector. This includes cross-functional teams to determine best project configuration; early identification of key personnel to manage the project, skill-based staffing, continuity of project teams and rigorous evaluation.

(vii) Inadequate use of IT in decision-making.

### *(b) Organisational Issues*

(viii) Weak performance management systems in the government and public sector resulting in lack of urgency to adhere to decision-making time limits or to be held accountable for results weak target setting and evaluation.

### *(c) Capacity Constraints*

(ix) Lack of specialization skills in project formulation and appraisal.

(x) Absence of professional advice on project formulation and appraisal.

(xi) Limited codification of knowledge and maintenance of database, compendium of standard appraisal techniques and documentation formats.

## V.III.I. Procedures for Formulation, Appraisal and Approval of FDI: Policies Adopted During 1992-97

A public sector projects, either of government or its agencies viz. PSEs, etc., has to pass through many stages from its conceptualization to approval before it is taken up for implementation. Private projects on the other hand have to get permissions, as required, and achieve financial closure before these could be taken up for implementation. While there is this difference in the approval mechanism, the subsequent stages for implementation of the project are similar for both public and private projects in terms of the approvals/permissions required and other reporting, record-keeping and statutory requirements.

### *Project Cycle of Public Project—Conceptualization to Implementation*

A project in the public sector would typically go through the following cycle from conceptualization to implementations at the central government level. Similar stages exist at the state level with the approval level being much less than that at the central level. Very often the projects get approved at the level of the Chief Minister and the state finance department usually has a greater say in the appraisal and approval of the projects and the elaborate process of approval at the cabinet level which exists in Government of India is generally non-existent at the State level.

#### *(a) Identification of Project*

A project is identified based on the national and state priorities, sectoral setting and competing claims from other activities and sectors. Concerned Ministries in the centre/state governments identify specific projects with the help of public sector enterprises and other expert agencies. Approval of the Planning Commission and separately of the Administrative Minister/FM/CCEA is required for launching a new plan scheme in the central sector or a new centrally sponsored Scheme. Planning Commission has laid down a two-stage process, first an 'in-principle' approval, followed by a full Planning Commission approval after the project/scheme has been appraised by EFC/PIB. Based on the pre-feasibility report, the project is considered for 'in-principle' approval by the Planning Commission for inclusion in the plan.

*(b) Project Preparation*

Project preparation is the next stage of the project cycle involving analysis of the technical, financial and institutional considerations, alternate strategies and the selection of the best alternative.

For infrastructure projects in power and coal, this exercise is part of Stage-I clearance. For Stage-I clearance, a fair estimate of the cost is prepared after considering technical, financial and institutional parameters. In this stage the project has to obtain all statutory clearances, particularly relating to environment and techno-economic clearance by CEA, CWC, etc. The document thus prepared also referred to as pre-feasibility report.

The feasibility repot is a more detailed exercise and may take up to two or three years depending upon the size and complexity of the project. The feasibility report covers all aspects of the project including a more realistic estimate of cost and benefits, fund flow for the project, etc.

*(c) Project Appraisal*

Appraisal of the project involves a detailed analysis on technical, economic, financial and institutional parameters. All projects above Rs. 15 crores also required appraisal by the Project Appraisal and Monitoring Division (PAMD) of Planning Commission. Ministers/Departments are required to obtain the following approval/clearances before the proposal is submitted for appraisal:

(i) 'In-principle' approval of Planning Commission for inclusion of the project in the Five Year Plan/Annual Plan.

(ii) Provision of adequate funds, required for implementation of the proposal.

(iii) Comments/Concurrence of Financial Adviser of the ministry for proposal is enclosed along with the EFC/PIB memo.

*(d) Project Approval*

After appraisal, the project is taken up for consideration for approval after budgetary provisions have been made. Till February 2002, the Minister of the concerned Ministry was the competent authority to sanction projects/schemes involving outlay of less than Rs. 20 crores. The Minister of the concerned Administrative Ministry and the Finance Minister were the competent authority to sanction projects/schemes with outlay between Rs. 20-50 crores.

*(e) Implementation*

After approval, the project is taken up for implementation. This often requires a number of approvals/permissions, both statutory as well as non-statutory, to be taken from both Central as well as state departments/agencies.

*(f) Evaluation*

With respect to the objectives set out for the project evaluation is carried out by the project authorities in the prescribed format after project's completion. Often these evaluation studies are not systematically used for taking lessons for future projects due to lack of organizational arrangements either in the concerned Ministry or Ministry of Statistics and Programme Implementation (MSPI).

*(g) Approval of Projects at State Level*

The process is almost similar for projects approved at the State level with the Planning and Finance departments normally appraising the projects and the approval at the level of the Chief Minister through the Finance Department.

### V.III.II. Policies Adopted for Appraisal and Approval of FDI during 1997 to 2010

It is seen that apart from the bottlenecks created due to delays in approvals of projects and in obtaining various permissions/approvals, poor quality of project formulation and its appraisal also impact implementation of projects. Inadequacies in the project formulation and appraisal often lead to cost and time overruns and the inevitable requirement of revision in the project cost estimates making a fresh round of approvals necessary, further delaying its implementation.

### *(a) Project Formulation*

While delays in the approval of projects, and in obtaining other permissions necessary for their implementation, continue to be a constraint poor quality of project formulation and its appraisal have been identified as major roadblocks in implementation of projects. Failure to identify any constraints in the availability of essential requirements of land, environmental impact, etc., at the time of project formulation itself could cripple the implementation of the project at a later stage.

Project preparation commences after inclusion of the proposal in the plan. Project formulation, including pre-feasibility studies, and drafting of TORs being specialized jobs, require special skills and expertise. Capacity building measures for the personnel entrusted with the responsibilities of project formulation, therefore, assume special significance. Besides skill up-gradation of such personnel, services of outside experts may be availed as may be necessary.

### *(b) Strengthening the Project Appraisal Mechanism*

The need for creating specialization in the project appraisal mechanism can hardly be over emphasized. Rigorous examination of the project proposal by experts would not only improve the project content but would also ensure best utilization of investment. Multiplicity of schemes with similar objectives leading to the resources getting thinly spread also needs to be avoided. This requires strengthening of the project appraisal process. It is also proposed to provide for an expert appraisal process. It is proposed to provide for an expert body for appraisal of all public sector projects involving investment exceeding Rs. 25 crores by setting up a Project Appraisal Unit (PAU) in the Planning Commission. The financial limits for appraisal of projects by PAU may be made co-terminus with the plan period to be reviewed in every five years.

TABLE 5.6
**Appraisal Authority of FDI**

| *Project/Scheme Outlay* | | *Approval Authority* |
|---|---|---|
| *Earlier Limit (From 1992)* | *Present Limit (From 2002)* | |
| *(1)* | *(2)* | *(3)* |
| Up to Rs. 1.5 Crores | Up to Rs. 5 Crores | Ministry in normal courses |
| About Rs. 1.5 Crores but less than Rs. 15 Crores | Above Rs. 5 Crores but less than Rs. 25 Crores | Standing Finance Committee (SFC) of Ministry |
| Rs. 15 Crores and above but less than Rs. 50 Crores | Rs. 25 Crores and above but less than Rs. 10 Crores | Expenditure Finance Committee (EFC) chaired Secretary. |
| Rs. 50 Crores and above but less than Rs. 100 Crores | Rs. 100 Crores and above but less than Rs. 200 Crores | Expenditure Finance Committee (EFC) chaired by Secretary (Expenditure) |
| Rs. 100 Crores and above | Rs. 200 Crores and above | Public Investment Board/EFC chaired by Secretary (Expenditure). Project Scheme where financial returns are quantifiable will be considered by PIB, others by EFC. |
| Less than Rs. 20 Crores | Less than Rs. 50 Crores | Administrative Minister |
| Rs. 20 Crores and above but less than Rs. 50 Crores | Rs. 50 Crores and above but less than Rs. 100 Crores | Adminstrative Minister and the Finance Minister |
| Rs. 50 Crores and above | Rs. 100 Crores and above | Cabinet/CCEA |

*Source* : *Reports on Investment Appraisal and FDI in India*, New Delhi, 2011.

### *(c) Expecting the Approval Process*

The project proposal after appraisal is taken up for approval at appropriate levels under the prevailing delegation of powers. The Cabinet Secretariat had prescribed guidelines in June 2010 for inter-ministerial consultations after EFC/PIB stage for obtaining investment approval. Delays in these consultations also contribute to delays in approval of projects.

### *(d) Empowered Commissions in Select Ministries*

McKinsey's report has recommended establishing 'Empowered Commissions' in place of the existing Ministry structure in 3-4 high priority sectors with large project investments. The model of converting existing Ministry structure into Commissions has been recommended to provide for faster decision-making, clearer individual roles and greater operational flexibility. Under these recommendations such commissions would have both full time and part time Directors from concerned Ministries apart from professionals and would be authorized to take decisions on individual projects once the overall budget has been finalized.

### *(e) Enhancing the Approval Authority of Ministries*

The Committee had examined at length the need for greater delegation of financial powers at various levels. Under the prevailing procedures, approval authority of a project would depend upon its estimated cost. Till February 2002, projects with investment exceeding Rs. 50 crores required approval by CCEA. This limit applied from 1992 when the Transaction of Business Rules was amended to enhance the outlay limit for investment proposal by CCEA from Rs. 20 corers to Rs. 50 crores. Even when delegation of power for appraisal forum was revised in 1997, no changes in the delegation of power for investment approval were made. The comparative position of the appraisal and investment approval powers applicable from 1992 and revised in February 2002 is shown in Table 5.6.

## V.III.III. Existing Procedure for Approval and Operation of FDI Since 2010

The Industrial Policy Reforms, initiated in 1991, have substantially liberalized the industrial licensing requirements, removed restrictions on investment and expansion, facilitated import of foreign technology and inflow of FDI. Industrial licensing is now virtually abolished except for a few industries, still reserved public sector, and six other industries where it is still considered necessary on strategic/environmental safety considerations.

Simultaneous with the dismantling of the elaborate and complex industrial licensing regime, simplified policies and procedures allowing FDI have also come in force in virtually all sectors except those of strategic concern. FDI for a large number of activities is now permitted through automatic route under powers delegated to RBI. For remaining activities Government approval is granted on the recommendation of FIPB. In almost 95-98 per cent cases, decision is communicated by FIPB within 4-6 weeks of filling the application.

Under FIPB route, projects involving foreign investment with estimated project cost of up to Rs. 600 crores are approved at the level of Commerce and Industry Minister. Cases beyond Rs. 600 crores, are considered by the Cabinet Committee on Economic Affairs (CCEA). There are no restrictions in terms of investment limit under the automatic route.

## Stages a Typical Project has to Pass Through

A project after approval from concerned authorities of the Central and State Governments, as the case may be, has to typically pass through the following stages during its implementation:

| *Sl. No.* | *Type of Clearance* | *Authority* | *Act under which Required* |
|---|---|---|---|
| | *(1)* | *(2)* | *(3)* |
| | **Central Level Clearances** | | |
| 1. | Registration as a Company | Registrar of Companies | The Companies Act, 1956 |
| 2. | Clearance from Coastal Regulation Zone | MOEF | The Environment (Protection) Act, 1986 |
| 3. | Environment Clearance | MOEF | The Environment (Protection) Act, 1986 |
| 4. | Forest Clearance for Diversion of Forest Land | State Forest Department/ MOEF | The Forest (Conservation) Act, 1986 |

(*Contd.*)

| (1) | (2) | (3) |
|---|---|---|
| 5. Explosive License | Controller of Explosives | The Explosives Act, 1884 |
| 6. Certificate of Commencement of Business | Registrar of Companies | The Companies Act, 1956 |
| 7. Rehabilitation and Resettlement Plan | State Government/ MOEF | — |
| 8. Permission for Import of Goods | Director General of Foreign Trade | Exim Policy |
| 9. Pollution Clearance | State Pollution Control Board/ Central Pollution Control Board | The Water (Prevention and Control of Pollution) Act, 1974 and The Air (Prevention and Control of Pollution) Act, 1981 |
| **State Level Clearances** | | |
| 1. Allotment of Land | | |
| a. Allotment of Land/Shed in Industrial Areas | Central Industrial Development Authority | — |
| b. Allotment of Government Land | District Collector/ Revenue Department | State Land Revenue Act |
| c. Acquisition of land | District Collector/ State Government | The Land Acquision Act, 1894 |
| 2. Change in Land Use | | |
| a. Conversion of Land Use to Non-Agriculture Purpose | District Collector/ Revenue Act Department | State Land Revenue |
| b. Change in Land Use in Urban Areas | Town Planning Department | State Urban Improvement/Municipal Act |
| 3. Approval of Building Plan | | |
| a. Approval in Industrial Areas | Concerned Industrial Development Authority | — |
| b. Approval in Other Areas | Local Authorities | Municipal Byelaws |
| 4. 'No Objection' from Fire Department | Fire Service Department | — |

| | | |
|---|---|---|
| 5. Release of Power Connection | State Electricity Board (SEB) or its Successor Entities | — |
| 6. Consent for Setting up Captive Power Plant | SEB/its successor entities | The Electricity (Supply) Act, 1948 |
| 7. Release of Water Connection | | |
| a. In Industrial Areas | Industrial Development Authority | — |
| b. In Other Areas | State Water Supply Department | — |
| 8. Site Clearance Certificate-required in Case of Identified Highly Polluting Industries | State Government | The Factories Act, 1948 |
| 9. Boiler Certification | Chief Inspector of Boilers | The Indian Boilers Act, 1923 |
| 10. Registration as a Factory | Chief Inspector of Factories | The Factories Act, 1948 |
| 11. Sales Tax Registration | Sales Tax Department | State Sales Tax Act |
| 12. Registration under the Trade Union Act, 1926 | Labour Department of State Government | The Trade Unions Act, 1926 |
| 13. Registration Under the Provident Funds Act, 1925 | Labour Department of State Government | The Provident Funds Act, 1925 |
| 14. Registration under Shops and Establishment Act, 1988 | Labour Department of State Government | The Shops and Establishments Act, 1988 |
| 15. Registration under Industrial Disputes Act, 1947 | " | The Industrial Disputes Act, 1947 |
| 16. Registration under Minimum Wages Act | " | The Minimum Wages Act, 1948 |
| 17. Registration under the State Employees Insurance Act, 1948 | " | The State Employees Insurance Act, 1948 |

Besides the above general clearances required for most projects, sector specific projects require additional clearances. In addition to a large number of clearances, the power projects are also required to obtain many approvals/licenses periodically from many agencies during operation of the project.

## V.IV. INSTITUTIONAL ARRANGEMENTS FOR VARIOUS APPROVALS AND FACILITATION OF FDI

Following institutional mechanisms exist for approval of industrial and FDI projects at the level of Government of India:

(a) Foreign Investment Promotion Board (FIPB) for approving foreign investment proposals not falling under the automatic route.

(b) Project Approval Board (PAB) for approving foreign technology transfer proposals not falling under the automatic route.

(c) Licensing Committee (LC) for considering and recommending proposals for grant of industrial license.

(d) Concerned Ministries/Departments issue various approvals as per the allocation of business and various Acts being administered by them.

(e) At the state level, State Investment Promotion Agency and, at the district level, District Industries Centres, generally look after projects. Concerned departments of the state government handle sectoral projects.

At the central government level, Foreign Investment Implementation Authority (FIIA) has been established in the Department of Industrial Policy and Promotion, to assist foreign investors in resolution of their operational difficulties and in getting necessary approvals. Apart from the Ministries of Government of India, senior officials from States and representatives of apex industrial organizations and investors also participate in the meetings of FIIA. Besides, Fast Track Committees (FTCs) have been set up in 30 Ministries/ Departments for close monitoring of projects with estimated investment of Rs. 100 crores and above and for resolution of issues hampering implementation.

## V.V. SUMMARY AND CONCLUSION

Throughout the chapter we have tried to find out the real picture of FDI inflows into the country. Section V.II. shows that the actual FDI inflows are far behind the original approvals of FDI. Thus the expected role of FDI should not be fulfilled properly as the gap between the actual flows and approvals is widening. To find out the reason behind it we have checked the general issues related to approval and implementation of FDI projects in section V.III.

It can be concluded that while overall policy have been liberalized, reforms in institutional mechanism and procedural simplification to translate policy liberalization into ease of doing business have generally lagged behind. A great deal of this lies within the state domain, and therefore any attempt to remove the bottlenecks would necessarily require complete involvement of state governments.

### End Notes

1. *The Economist* issue of June 29, 2009 has also acknowledged last years record inflow of FDI as a promising feature. The EIU report on *'World Investment Prospects, 2010'* projects an annual average FDI inflow of US $ 5.3 billion for India during 2012-16.
2. Data collected from Report of the Committee on Compilation of FDI in India (October 2010), page 325.
3. The growth rate has been calculated by using semi-log of the form, log Y= a+bt, where Y denotes the variable of interest and t is trend. Since FDI stock data were not available for the period 1981-85 and 1996-99, the same have been worked out by adding net inflows to the FDI stock.
4. The Committee was set-up vide its Order No. 212/9/2001-CA.IV dated on 24.09.2001 with Shri V.N. Kaul, Secretary, Ministry of Petroleum and Natural Gas as convener.

### References

Dutta, R. and Sundaram, K.P.M. (2001), *Indian Economy*, pp. 315-35 and 745-58, S. Chand and Company, New Delhi.

Pan, S. and Sen, R.K. (2007), *Foreign Direct Investment and Trade in India*, Deep & Deep Publications Private Limited, New Delhi.

Planning Commission (2002), *Report of the Steering Group on Foreign Direct Investment*, Government of India, New Delhi.

Radhakrishnan, K.G. and Pradhan, J.P. (2000), "Foreign Direct Investment in India: Policy, Trends and Determinants", *Productivity*, Vol. 41, No. 3, October-December, pp. 454-62.

Rangarajan, C. (2002), "Capital Flows: Another Look", *Economic and Political Weekly*, Vol. xxxv, No. 50, December 9-15, pp. 4421-27.

Satyanarayan, B. (1995), "Foreign Direct Investment in Less Developed Countries (With Special Reference to India)", *IASSI Quarterly*, Vol. 13, No. 4, April-June, pp. 73-79.

Tan, J.L.H. (1997), "Singapore's FDI in Indochina and Myanmar: Opportunities and Challenges", *RIS Occasional Paper*, No. 50, New Delhi.

CHAPTER

# 6

# *FDI Inflows into India : Survey Results*

## VI.I. INTRODUCTION

India's FDI inflow estimates, in the balance of payments do not include reinvested earnings (by foreign companies), inter-company debt transactions (subordinated debt) and overseas commercial borrowings by foreign direct investors in foreign invested firms, as per the standard IMF definitions. Methodologically, reinvested earnings are required to be shown nationally as dividends paid out under investment income in current account and as inflow of FDI. The other capital, in turn, covers the borrowing and leading of funds—including debt securities and suppliers' credit—between direct investors and direct investment enterprises. From a technical point of view, it is well recognized that it is quite difficult to capture 'reinvested earnings' through the reporting arrangements for foreign exchange transactions, mainly because such transactions do not take place though it have to be imputed in the balance of payments statistics.

Direct investment, other capital transactions between direct investors and direct investment enterprises, however, pass through the banking channel. There exists, however, the problem of identifying and isolating mutual borrowing and lending of funds among direct investors and direct investment enterprises. Recognizing the above-mentioned constraints, greater reliance needs to be placed on collection of such data through direct investors' survey. The proper coverage of such transactions in India depends, therefore, upon the availability of information through the survey. The data on inward FDI for India at present do not include reinvested earning and 'other direct capital investment.'

In this context, the National Statistical Commission recommended conducting periodical surveys on dividends and profits arising out of foreign direct investment and portfolio investment separately. In pursuance of the recommendation, a survey is being launched by the Reserve Bank of India to collect detailed information on FDI. Some estimate on reinvested earning and other capital would be available from the survey and the data on inward FDI could be subsequently revised to include the data on reinvested earnings and other capital.

With help of the above information, in this chapter we shall concentrate on the analysis of sample survey results of FDI inflows. A comparison also is done between the sample results and the macro-results surveyed by RBI. Then an international comparison of FDI inflows among the countries will be produced also.

## VI.II. RESULTS OF SAMPLE SURVEY

This section will produce the results of sample survey which we have been collected from manufacturing firm running and producing with FDI during the period 1991 and 2010. The following sections give details on collection of data, actual situation of FDI, comparison of the survey results with the macro-results and the chief defects of the policy.

### VI.II.I. Collection of Data

According to the information of Secretariat for Industrial Assistance, Government of India and Department of Commerce and Industry, Government of West Bengal, we have collected data on FDI from allover West Bengal and from a selected part of Tamil Nadu, Kerala, Orissa, Maharashtra and Goa from nearly 250 samples. For West Bengal, the survey has been conducted for 3 categories of FDI in metro cities, middle-towns and villages (both irrigated and non-irrigated areas).

### VI.II.II. Actual Situation of FDI: Sample Study of West Bengal

Though there are some infrastructure problems to enter into Indian home market for MNC but after entrance by somehow they find it profitable to them. Among Indian states, Maharashtra is in the top of the table of State-wise break up of FDI during August 1991 to June 2010 period. West Bengal stands eighth in the table as the state starting late of the reform process of the Centre started in 1991.

From the survey, we have found that West Bengal government has given due importance to the monitoring of FDI proposals. Since 1991, a considerable number of FDI proposals/ approvals have been received for setting up new projects in West Bengal. 571 approvals have been received for units in West Bengal during August 1991 to June 2010. While in Maharashtra, Tamil Nadu, Kerala, Orissa and Goa the approvals goes up to 3689, 2014, 243, 136 and 165 respectively during this period.

Out of 571 approvals for West Bengal, 102 FDI approvals have already been implemented and 19 projects are different stages of implementation. The latest two inclusions of foreign collaborator into the state are from an UK-based NRI and Switzerland. The UK-based NRI set-up their industry to produce footwear with leather uppers and manmade sales at Burdwan and for this invest Rs. 2350 million with 100 per cent equity participation. And the MNC from Switzerland with collaboration with a New Delhi-based Sika Qualcrete Limited set-up industry in Kolkata and engaged themselves for the manufacture of specialist chemicals for various applications in construction, civil engineering building industries and industries in general. The company is investing Rs. 8 million with 100 per cent equity participation also. These two FDI came into the state through SIA (Secretariat for Industrial Assistance) route.

FDI in West Bengal has primarily come in the petrochemicals, power and telecom sectors from the three host regions, namely, Japan, Germany and USA. The best way to woo foreign investors is to match and marry specific sector under consideration with the special advantage the host country enjoys. The Chief Minister of West Bengal visited Japan in 2010 and despite a recession in Japan he was given assurance of further investment in the state. The State Government, on its part, has put in place inventive schemes for mega projects including FDI. Task Forces on sectors like information technology, service sector and agro-industries have also been constituted.

The share of Eastern and North-Eastern India in total FDI has been around seven per cent; the share of West Bengal alone being four per cent. However, whenever a business delegation from outside has been visited India, it is taken on a fixed circuit of Mumbai—Delhi—Bengaluru and Hyderabad to the determinant of equally good locations elsewhere. There is also a need to further improve the international linkages of these regions through increasing flights and airport facilities. West Bengal and Eastern India on the whole have skilled manpower and are rich in natural resources; however, in the absence of requisite infrastructure development these advantages are not able to attract FDI. The State Government may, therefore, be allowed to directly negotiate with multilateral and bilateral agencies for infrastructure developments.

The Government of India could consider laying a gas pipeline from Myanmar to India through the continental self or through Tripura to West Bengal (in India), this would give boost to future investments in this region. The Government of India may, furthermore, remove complexities arising from sectoral caps on foreign equity holding and may also consult the State Governments while framing the FDI policy. As a late starter of the so-called economic globalization, West Bengal is far behind to attract FDI into the state for its infrastructure development. Where other Indian States follows center's decision to open the economy in 1991, West Bengal take four valuable years to realize the importance of openness to the economy in 1994.

Since then West Bengal government has taken several steps to attract FDI, open the door for NRI in a more polite manner, signed MoU with foreign MNCs, organize trade fair and taken some other steps also but it was too late to attract foreign investors into the state. Most of the industrialists left the state for its unhealthy situation; NRIs also are not interested to invest into the state, as they don't get any cooperation from the State Government.

The survey also shows that there are a higher number of approvals of the FDI collaboration into the state but the actual rate is too small to get positive result from FDI. Agricultural sector are not suitable for MNCs to invest here also. Another important observation is that the actual inflow of FDI is lagging far behind approvals granted, ranging from 13 per cent to 47 per cent of approvals granted during the period 1991-2010. This undesirable fact of the problem may be stemming from a complex interactive process of several factors like lack of transparent incentive mechanism, administrative hurdles, political inexpediency, etc. But the foremost bottleneck is infrastructure, construction on production process. Hence, study has pointed out that to attract and maximize the extent of actualization of FDI approved, we should make our administrative process even more transparent, reallocate towards infrastructure sector, and build up a political consensus to ensure a stable FDI policy. With a growing indigenous market, availability of cheap and skilled labour, and political stability once attained, as a recent IMF report predicts, India, especially West Bengal, may soon emerge as a winner in the game of attracting foreign investment.

### VI.II.III. Comparison of Survey Results with Macro Results

A review of the Foreign Direct Investment proposals received in West Bengal during the last 20 years indicates a major change in the industrial structure of the state. The change is likely to be seen in area of non-traditional/sunrise industries like superior grade newsprint project of M/s. Indo-Canadian Papers Limited, at an investment of Rs. 2567 crore. Storage of propane, butane, L.P.G. and evacuation/distribution project of Indian Oil Petronos Private Limited at an investment of Rs. 244.26 crore, bottle grade polyester chips project of South Asian Petrochem Limited at an investment of Rs. 443.05 crore, coal mining project of Integrated Coal Mining Private Limited at an investment of Rs. 552 crore, glass stemware and trumber project of M/s. Louseizer Glass (India) Limited at an investment of Rs. 47.75 crore, refinery project of M/s. TCG Refineries Limited, at an investment of Rs. 4028 crore, coal-bed methane gas exploration project of M/s. Great Energy Cooperation Limited at an investment of Rs. 500 crore, five star hotel project of M/s. Hotel and Resort Venture Private Limited at an investment of Rs. 225 crore.

With a view to extent new type of incentives for promotion of industries in the state, the West Bengal Incentive Scheme, 2000 has been issued. The different incentive to be granted to the eligible industries is following:

(i) State Capital Investment Subsidy;
(ii) Interest Subsidy;
(iii) Waiver of Electricity Duty;
(iv) Employment Generation Subsidy;
(v) Remission of Stamp Duty and Registration Fee;
(vi) Subsidy for conversation for use of piped gas;
(vii) Subsidy for quality improvement in the small scale sector;
(viii) Additional incentive for Information Technology, Electronics, Agro and Food Processing Industries and Haldia Petrochemicals Limited Downstream Projects;
(ix) Incentives for approved expansion project of an existing Unit;
(x) Incentives for Leather Units both in the tanning and manufacturing sectors on relocation accompanied with modernisation; and
(xi) Mega Projects.

The project which symbolises the industrial resurgence of West Bengal is the Haldia Petrochemicals Limited, which has been implemented with an investment of Rs. 5170 crore. Till recently, the state had very limited activity in petrochemical and downstream products, barring a few refineries and small scale units. All its limited product requirements were met through imports and supply from other states of the country. A PAT plant promoted by Mitsubishi Chemical Corporation is another giant project implemented at Haldia. It was commissioned in February 2000 and is currently in full production. This unit represents one of the largest Japanese FDIs in manufacturing in India and has generated employment for 700 persons.

Comparison with other states of the country shows that while Maharashtra, Delhi, Tamil Nadu, Karnataka, Gujarat, Andhra Pradesh have attracted 17.38, 11.96, 8.55, 8.27, 6.49 and 4.61 percentage with total approved FDI respectively, West Bengal able to collect only 3.19 per cent of total approved FDI in India during August 1991 to December 2010. Out of total FDI approved in India amounted Rs. 2896801.58 million, West Bengal attract only a minuscule percentage with Rs. 92538.11 million (Table 3.19).

### VI.II.IV. Chief Defects of the Policy

However, as the experience in India under the British rule has shown, foreign capital has not been of much help. No doubt, many of our industries owe their growth to British multinational firms, but the fact is that such foreign investments have only developed our export items like Darjeeling tea, jute, rubber, etc. where the clientele were foreign and profits were high. Not much was done of poor Indians. The pattern of development that took place was essentially dualistic where some pockets were growing while the rest of the economy remained backward.

Because by nature the Multinational Corporations are big industrial giants, they can exercise their semi-monopoly power to oust local producers and exploit the consumers. They, through massive publicity and propaganda, promote inappropriate products and cause misallocation of country's resources. By using inappropriate technology brought from and suited to their home country resources endowments, cause unemployment to rise and dualistic structure to rigidity. By their sheer money power they can corrupt the politicians and bureaucrats and seek large concessions for themselves. They cause drain on our resources in the form of repatriation of their large profits and export of goods made from raw materials, which may be scarce in the country and hence needed to be preserved for our own development.

***The chief defects of the FDI policy are as following:***

(i) The real problem in West Bengal as well as India lies in the low levels of realization of FDI inflows *vis-a-vis* the proposal cleared. Although the realization rate has improved to 45 per cent in 2010 compared to 21 per cent in 1997, it remains a serious problem.

(ii) The precise reason for the low levels of realization is the post-approval procedures, which has played havoc to project implementation. This leads to loss of investor's confidence despite promises of a considerable market size.

(iii) The number of clearance for a typical power project is 43 at the central government level and 57 at the State government level including the local administration. Similarly, the number of clearance for typical mining projects is 37 at the central government level and 47 at the state government level.

(iv) State investment policies are so far limited to granting concessions and incentives to woo investors rather than streamlining their bureaucracies. There is an immediate need of instituting a single window clearance agency to facilitate faster, implementation of projects. The focus should, therefore, be on developing a suitable structure and process of a single window agency.

(v) The biggest barrier for India is the screening stage itself in the action cycle. Often India looses out at the screening stage itself. This is primarily because we do not get across effectively to the decision-making 'board room' levels of corporate entities where a final decision is taken.

(vi) Our promotional effort is quite often of a general nature and not corporate specific. Moreover, India is multi-cultural society and a large number of multi-national companies do not understand the diversity and the multi-plural nature of the society and the different stakeholders in this country.

(vii) Among the policy problems that have been identified by surveys as acting as additional hurdles for FDI are laws, regulatory systems and government monopolies that do not have contemporary relevance.

(viii) Labour laws also discourage the entry of green field FDI because of the fear that it would not be possible to downsize if and when there is a downturn in business. Labour laws, rules and procedures have led to deterioration in the work culture and the comparative advantage that is even beginning to be recognized by responsible Trade Unions.

(ix) The Urban Land Ceiling Acts and Rent Control Acts in states are a serious constraint on the entire real estate sector. This is another sector that has attracted large amounts of FDI in many countries including China.

(x) Weak credibility of regulatory systems and multiple and conflicting roles of agencies and government has an adverse impact on new FDI investors, which is greater than on domestic investors. All monopolists have a strong self-interest in preventing new entrants who can put competitive pressure.

(xi) Strategy and implementation problems connected with disinvestment created great uncertainty and increased policy/regulatory risk, resetting in a lack of interest of FDI investors in building for these companies.

(xii) In the banking sector, controls on activity dampen FDI inflows. It is alleged that persistent fears of impending 'fiscal crisis' is another constraint, and that a well articulated strategy for medium-term fiscal consolidations would address these concerns.

(xiii) In the chemical sector, the absence of product patents has reduced inflows into the drugs and pharmaceuticals sector.

(xiv) According to Boston Consulting Group, investors find it frustrating to navigate through the tangles of bureaucratic controls and procedures.

(xv) The time taken for application/bidding/approval of FDI projects was too long. Multiple approvals, excessive time taken (2-3 years) such as in food processing and long lead times of up to six months for licenses for duty free exports, lead to "loss of investors' confidence despite promises of a considerable market size."

(xvi) The divide between central and state governments in the treatment of foreign investors could undermine the FDI promotion efforts of the Central Governments. The centre-state duality is creating difficulties at both the approval and project implementation stages.

(xvii) The bureaucracy in general is quite unhelpful in extending infrastructural facilities to any project that is being set-up. This leads to time and cost overruns.

(xviii) In the context of FDI, poor infrastructure has a greater effect on export production than on production for the domestic market. FDI directed at the domestic market suffers the same handicap and additional costs as domestic manufacturers that are competing for the domestic market. Inadequate and poor quality roads, railroads and ports, however raise export costs *vis-a-vis* global competitors having better quality and lower cost infrastructure.

(xix) Taxes levied on transportation of goods from state to state (such as octroi and entry tax) adversely impact the economic environment for export production. Differential sale and excise taxes (state and centre) on small and large companies are found to be a deterrent to FDI in sectors such as textiles.

(xx) Tough India's Anglo Saxon legal system as codified is considered by many legal experts to be superior to that of many other emerging economies it is often found in practice to be an obstacle to investment. One of the reasons for the inordinate delay is the interlocutory procedures that characterise judicial procedures.

(xxi) The 'Rule of Law', which has often been cited as one of the attractive features of the Indian economy for foreign investors, is found to be a significant positive factor by only 3 per cent for FDI in India. In contrast, 26 per cent of all those surveyed cited this as an important factor in their global investment decisions.

Due to these difficulties FDI in Indian economy has not come freely. So, in case of attracting FDI into the country, India lagged behind the other countries. In the next section, we shall make a comparison of India with the rest of the world in the light of channeling FDI into the economy.

## VI.III. INTERNATIONAL COMPARISON OF FDI INFLOWS

FDI liberalisation continues all over the world. Between 1991 and 2010, a total of 11805 regulatory changes were introduced in national FDI regimes, of which 1121 were in the direction of creating a more favourable environment for FDI (Table 6.1). During 2000 alone, a total of 150 regulatory changes were made by 69 countries. Of these, 147 (98 per cent) were more favourable to foreign investors. At the international level, treaty making continues, complementing and reinforcing trends at the national level. The number of bilateral investment treaties (BITs) quintupled during the 1990s and, by end-2000, had reached a total of 1941. During 2000 alone, 78 countries including India concluded 84 BITs. The single greatest number of the new treaties was between developing countries (36), 43 per cent of the total. The number of bilateral treaties for the avoidance of double taxation (DTTs) also increased, reaching a total of 2118 at the end of 2010. During 2010, 57 DTTs were concluded by 59 countries. At the regional and inter-regional levels, the number of investment-related instruments continues to grow, especially in the form of free trade and investment agreements.

TABLE 6.1

**National Regulatory Changes, 1991-2010**

| | *Item* | *1991* | *1995* | *2000* | *2005* | *2010* |
|---|---|---|---|---|---|---|
| I. | Number of countries that introduced changes in their investment regimes | 35 | 64 | 60 | 63 | 69 |
| II. | Number of regulatory changes : of which | 82 | 112 | 145 | 140 | 150 |
| | More Favourable to FDI | 80 | 106 | 136 | 131 | 147 |
| | Less Favourable to FDI | 2 | 6 | 9 | 9 | 3 |

*Source* : UNCTAD, based on national sources.

FDI inflows continued their strong recent growth to reach $ 1.3 trillion in 2010, though the pace was slightly slower than in the previous two years. By all measures (assets, sales, trade and employment of foreign affiliates), FDI rose more rapidly in 2005 and 2010 than such other aggregates as gross domestic product (GDP), domestic investment, licensing payments and trade. It is noteworthy, in particular, that TNC activities have risen rapidly in 2005 (as well as during the preceding three years) when world trade was stagnant, testifying to the growing role of FDI as the main force in international economic integration. The ratio of foreign affiliates' sales to global GDP was almost 50 per cent, with the sales value being over twice as high as the value of world exports of goods and services (Table 6.2).

Looking at the recent past, as many as 65 countries experienced an annual average growth rate of 30 per cent or more between 1986 and 2010 (Table 6.3). Another 29 countries had FDI growth rates of 20-29 per cent. In terms of broad country groups, the developed world continued to attract over three-quarters of global FDI inflows in the past two years.

The global trend of FDI inflows shows increasing movement especially after 1991. In this section we shall produce some comparative study of FDI flows between India and other countries.

### VI.III.I. FDI Flows: India in the World Economy

The last decade has witnessed a huge increase in the mobility of international capital flows. Cross-country trends in capital flows reveal that foreign capital flows now dominate with official capital flows reduced to a trickle. Simultaneously, a rise in portfolio capital was titled the composition of international capital flows towards short-term investments, exposing individual countries to enhanced volatility and sudden withdrawal risks. These trends have been driven by globalization, which has enabled pursuit of higher returns and portfolio diversification, and market-oriented reforms in many countries, which have liberalized access to financial markets.

These issues are significant for India as it gradually opens its capital account as part of its broader financial liberalization strategy. Before 1991, India had a closed capital account with

TABLE 6.2

**Selected Indicators of FDI and International Production, 1982-2010**

| *Item* | *Value at current prices* | | | *Annual Growth Rate (%)* | | | | | |
|---|---|---|---|---|---|---|---|---|---|
| | *1982* | *2000* | *2010* | *1986-90* | *1991-95* | *1996-99* | *2001* | *2005* | *2010* |
| *(1)* | *(2)* | *(3)* | *(4)* | *(5)* | *(6)* | *(7)* | *(8)* | *(9)* | *(10)* |
| FDI Inflows | 57 | 202 | 1271 | 23.0 | 20.8 | 40.8 | 44.9 | 55.2 | 18.2 |
| FDI Outflows | 37 | 235 | 1150 | 26.2 | 16.3 | 37.0 | 52.8 | 41.3 | 14.3 |
| FDI Inward Stock | 719 | 1889 | 6314 | 16.2 | 9.3 | 18.4 | 19.8 | 22.3 | 21.5 |
| FDI Outward Stock | 568 | 1717 | 5976 | 20.5 | 10.8 | 16.4 | 20.9 | 19.5 | 19.4 |
| Cross Border M&As | — | 151 | 1144 | 26.4 | 23.3 | 50.0 | 74.4 | 44.1 | 49.3 |
| Sales of Foreign Affiliates | 2465 | 5467 | 15680 | 15.6 | 10.5 | 10.4 | 18.2 | 17.2 | 18.0 |
| Gross Product of Foreign Affiliates | 565 | 1420 | 3167 | 16.4 | 7.2 | 11.0 | 3.2 | 27.2 | 16.5 |
| Total Assets of Foreign Affiliates | 1888 | 5744 | 21102 | 18.2 | 13.9 | 15.9 | 23.4 | 14.8 | 19.8 |
| Export of Foreign Affiliates | 637 | 1166 | 3572 | 13.2 | 14.0 | 11.0 | 11.8 | 16.1 | 17.9 |
| Employment of Foreign Affiliates (1000) | 17454 | 23721 | 45587 | 5.7 | 5.3 | 7.8 | 16.8 | 5.3 | 12.7 |
| GDP at Factor Cost | 10612 | 21475 | 31895 | 11.7 | 6.3 | 0.7 | -0.9 | 3.4 | 6.1 |
| Gross Fixed Capital Formation | 2236 | 4501 | 6466 | 12.2 | 6.6 | 0.6 | -0.6 | 4.3 | — |
| Royalties and License Fees Receipts | 9 | 27 | 66 | 22.1 | 14.1 | 4.0 | 6.1 | 1.1 | — |
| Export of Goods and Non-Factor Services | 2124 | 4381 | 7036 | 15.4 | 8.6 | 1.9 | -1.5 | 3.9 | — |

*Note* : Value in US $ billion.

*Source* : UNCTAD, based on FDI/TNC database and UNCTAD estimates.

TABLE 6.3
**Annual Average FDI Growth Rate, 1986-2009 (Percentage)**

| *Growth Rate* | *Economy* |
|---|---|
| More than 30% | Total 66 Countries (including India, Brazil, China, Germany, Bangladesh, Japan, South Africa, Croatia, Venezuela) |
| 20-29.9% | Total 30 Countries (including Argentina, Chile, Israel, Hong Kong, Korea, Nepal, Sudan, Belgium) |
| 10-19.9% | Total 47 Countries (including UK, Pakistan, Sri Lanka, Zimbabwe, Canada, Philippines, Saudi Arabia, USA) |
| 0-9.9% | Total 29 Countries (including Australia, Italy, Nigeria, Singapore, Spain, Taiwan, Namibia, Kenya) |
| Decline | Total 21 Countries (including Brunei, Indonesia, Iraq, UAE, Rwanda, Yugoslavia, Fiji, Congo, Liberia) |

*Source* : UNCTAD, FDI/INC Database.

capital mobility being restricted through administrative controls and outright prohibition. The balance of payments situation, exchange rate movements and India's import-substituting pattern of development influenced these controls. In the aftermath of the balance of payments crisis in 1991, India embarked upon an economic reform program aimed at transforming the controlled economy into a market-driven one. Following changes in exchange rate regime as well as trade and investment policies' reform; there was a spurt in capital flows into the country between 1992-93 and 2010.

Portfolio investment flows exceed direct investment (FDI) in the early years of liberalization. FDI catches up later, peaking in 1995 but falls thereafter and again shows an upward trend since 2008. While the total inflows of FDI into the world moves from US $ 173.5 billion in 1990 to US $ 1270.8 billion in 2010, developed countries attracted them in maximum amounts. Inflows of FDI to developed countries increased from US $ 136.6 billion to US $ 1005.2 billion in 2010, while in case of developing countries it rose to US $ 240.2 billion in 2010 from the 1990 figure of US $ 35.3 billion (Table 6.4).

TABLE 6.4

**Inflows of FDI in Selected Countries**

*(in US $ bn.)*

| | *1990* | *1991* | *1992* | *1993* | *1994* | *1995* | *1996* | *1997* | *2000* | *2005* | *2010* |
|---|---|---|---|---|---|---|---|---|---|---|---|
| *(1)* | *(2)* | *(3)* | *(4)* | *(5)* | *(6)* | *(7)* | *(8)* | *(9)* | *(10)* | *(11)* | *(12)* |
| India | 0.2 | 0.2 | 0.3 | 0.6 | 1.0 | 2.1 | 2.6 | 3.6 | 2.6 | 2.2 | 2.3 |
| China | 3.5 | 4.4 | 11.2 | 27.5 | 33.8 | 35.8 | 40.2 | 44.2 | 43.8 | 40.3 | 40.8 |
| Mexico | 2.6 | 4.8 | 4.9 | 4.9 | 12.4 | 9.5 | 9.9 | 13.8 | 11.6 | 11.9 | 13.2 |
| Argentina | 1.8 | 2.4 | 4.2 | 6.3 | 3.4 | 5.3 | 6.9 | 9.2 | 7.3 | 24.1 | 11.2 |
| Malaysia | 2.3 | 4.0 | 5.2 | 5.2 | 4.3 | 4.2 | 7.3 | 6.5 | 2.7 | 3.5 | 5.5 |
| Hungary | — | 1.5 | 1.5 | 2.3 | 1.1 | 4.5 | 2.3 | 2.2 | 2.0 | 1.9 | 2.0 |
| Pakistan | 0.2 | 0.3 | 0.2 | 0.3 | 0.4 | 0.7 | 0.9 | 0.7 | 0.5 | 0.5 | 0.3 |
| Colombia | 0.5 | 0.6 | 0.8 | 0.9 | 1.4 | 1.0 | 1.9 | 2.9 | 4.2 | 4.0 | 0.3 |
| Philippines | 0.6 | 0.5 | 0.7 | 0.9 | 1.6 | 1.5 | 1.5 | 1.2 | 1.8 | 0.7 | 1.5 |
| Korea, Rep. | 0.7 | 1.1 | 0.6 | 0.5 | 0.8 | 1.8 | 2.3 | 2.8 | 5.4 | 10.6 | 10.2 |
| Venezuela | 0.4 | 1.9 | 0.7 | 0.4 | 0.8 | 1.0 | 2.2 | 5.5 | 4.5 | 3.2 | 4.1 |
| Turkey | 0.7 | 0.9 | 0.9 | 0.7 | 0.6 | 0.9 | 0.7 | 0.8 | 0.9 | 0.8 | 1.0 |
| Nigeria | 0.6 | 0.7 | 0.9 | 0.7 | 2.0 | 1.1 | 1.6 | 1.5 | 1.1 | 1.0 | 1.0 |
| Chile | 0.8 | 0.9 | 1.0 | 1.2 | 2.6 | 3.0 | 4.7 | 5.2 | 4.6 | 9.2 | 3.7 |
| Egypt | 0.7 | 0.3 | 0.5 | 0.5 | 1.3 | 0.6 | 0.6 | 0.8 | 1.1 | 1.1 | 1.2 |
| Developing Countries | 35.3 | 46.9 | 59.6 | 83.4 | 101.2 | 111.9 | 152.5 | 187.4 | 188.4 | 222.0 | 240.2 |
| Developed Countries | 136.6 | 140.1 | 137.1 | 140.3 | 146.4 | 208.4 | 219.7 | 271.4 | 483.2 | 829.8 | 1005.2 |
| World | 173.5 | 190.6 | 200.1 | 230.6 | 253.5 | 328.9 | 384.9 | 477.9 | 692.5 | 1075.0 | 1270.8 |

*Source* : *Statistical Outline of India*, TATA Service Limited, Mumbai, various years.

In case of India, Table 6.4 shows that inflows of FDI in 1990 was US $ 0.2 billion only which rose to a maximum of US $ 3.6 billion in 1997 and then decline to US $ 2.3 billion in 2010. In case of China, Mexico, Argentina, Malaysia, Korean Republic, Venezuela and Chile inflows of FDI is more than India with US $ 40.8 billion, US $ 13.2 billion, US $ 11.2 billion, US $ 5.5 billion, US $ 10.2 billion, US $ 4.1 billion and US $ 3.7 billion respectively in 2010. On the other, FDI inflows is lesser amount than India to Hungary, Pakistan, Colombia, Philippines, Turkey, Nigeria and Egypt with US $ 2.0 billion, US $ 0.3 billion, US $ 1.5 billion, US $ 1.0 billion, US $ 1.0 billion and US $ 1.2 billion respectively in 2010. This means conditions and facilities to attract FDI into India is better than that of Hungary, Pakistan, Colombia, Philippines, Turkey, Nigeria and Egypt.

In case of outward FDI by home region and economy, India supplied only US $ 7 million at an average between 1988 and 1993 and better her position in the world with US $ 167 million in 2010 compared to other developing countries (Table 6.5). The share of total outflows for developing countries has down warded from 10.62 (on average) per cent during 1988-93 to 8.21 per cent in 2010. Out of these shares in developing countries for outward FDI flows, South, East and South-East Asian countries' share was 62.42 per cent (on average) during 1988-93 but it also declined to 54.41 per cent. India stands tenth in case of outward FDI flows among the South, East and South-East Asian countries.

### VI.III.II. FDI Performance: India *vs.* China

It appears that at the start of the reform process in 1978, China was not evidently better placed to attract large amounts of FDI than India which shared a number of characteristics with China (Table 6.6). Both countries had relatively closed economies, with low income levels and a large share of the population dependent on agriculture. Neither China nor India was receiving significant amounts of FDI. This picture has changed dramatically since then, as a result of China's economic reforms and 'open door' policy. While India's GDP per capita more than doubled between 1978 and 2000, China's GDP per capita quadrupled (in constant U.S. dollar terms). India still remains a fairly closed economy while China has become more integrated into the global economy.

The success of economic reforms in China has prompted many analysts to compare the experiences with those in India, which too is in the phase of economic transition. India also boasts of a large overseas community that could perhaps be similarly drawn to invest in their own country if the right policy prescriptions were to be applied. What really are the implications of the nature and pattern of FDI flows into China for tapping similar flows into India by NRIs?

The following factors need to be borne in mind for getting positive results from FDI:

(a) In understanding policy differences in the shaping of responses it has been suggested that the Chinese FDI policy regime, like the Chinese economic policy generally, has been more decentralized, allowing the overseas Chinese to avoid largely the bureaucratic delays of the central and provincial bureaucracies and aided by the *guanxi* system. Such a comparable regime does not yet effectively exist in India although procedures such as introduction of automatic approvals within ninety days for investments below US $ 2 million in basic and capital goods industries or 100 per cent export-oriented units has helped check this problem.

(b) The character of the typical NRI—usually a salaried professional in the West or wage-earning labourer in the mid-East—is averse to risk, as against the entrepreneurial character of the Chinese diasporas.

(c) The NRI community, from the Mittals, Hindujas, Pauls and Bagris to the Gujaratis of East Africa, Chettiyars of South-East Asia and Sindhis of Hong Kong, do not have the experience of managing export production with low wage labour. Hong Kong and South-East Asian Chinese passed through such a learning experience in the sixties and seventies, something that is unavailable to the NRIs.

Thus, strict analogies are difficult to draw between replicating the experience of China and India. It is said that,

Table 6.5

**FDI Outflows by Home Region and Economy**

*(Million of Dollars)*

| | *1988-1993 (annual average)* | *1994* | *1995* | *1998* | *2000* | *2005* | *2010* |
|---|---|---|---|---|---|---|---|
| *(1)* | *(2)* | *(3)* | *(4)* | *(5)* | *(6)* | *(7)* | *(8)* |
| World | 22357 | 282902 | 357537 | 390776 | 471906 | 687111 | 799928 |
| Developing Countries | 197581 | 240487 | 306822 | 3331963 | 404153 | 651873 | 731765 |
| European Union | 107220 | 120684 | 158990 | 182226 | 223662 | 425495 | 509824 |
| Share of EU | 48.44 | 42.66 | 44.47 | 46.63 | 47.40 | 61.93 | 63.73 |
| United States | 39323 | 73252 | 52074 | 84426 | 99517 | 146052 | 150901 |
| Share of US | 17.77 | 25.89 | 25.75 | 21.61 | 21.09 | 21.28 | 18.86 |
| Japan | 32472 | 18089 | 22508 | 23442 | 26059 | 24152 | 22743 |
| Share of Japan | 14.67 | 6.39 | 6.30 | 6.00 | 5.52 | 3.52 | 2.84 |
| Developing Countries | 23509 | 42124 | 50259 | 57763 | 64335 | 33035 | 65638 |
| % Share in Total Outflows | 10.62 | 14.89 | 14.06 | 14.78 | 13.63 | 4.81 | 8.21 |
| South, East & South-East Asia | 14671 | 36708 | 43442 | 49479 | 47703 | 27000 | 35716 |
| % Share in Developing Countries | 62.41 | 87.14 | 8S.44 | 85.66 | 74.15 | 81.71 | 54.41 |
| Hong Kong, China | 6086 | 21437 | 25000 | 26531 | 24407 | 16973 | 19895 |

| | | | | | | | |
|---|---|---|---|---|---|---|---|
| Taiwan | 3825 | 2640 | 2983 | 3843 | 5243 | 3836 | 4420 |
| Singapore | 1171 | 4577 | 6281 | 6935 | 8859 | —1525 | 3943 |
| China | 1962 | 2000 | 2000 | 2114 | 2563 | 2634 | 2500 |
| Republic of Korea | 966 | 2300 | 3072 | 4249 | 3230 | 3893 | 2548 |
| Malaysia | 326 | 2329 | 2488 | 3768 | 2626 | 785 | 1640 |
| Thailand | 132 | 422 | 835 | 932 | 367 | 134 | 368 |
| Philippines | 91 | 302 | 98 | 182 | 136 | 160 | 128 |
| Indonesia | 78 | 609 | 603 | 600 | 178 | 44 | 72 |
| India | 7 | 83 | 117 | 239 | 113 | 48 | 167 |

*Source* : Calculated from *World Investment Report*, UNCTAD.

Table 6.6
**China and India : Selected Economic Indicators**

| | *1978* | | *2010* | |
|---|---|---|---|---|
| | *India* | *China* | *India* | *China* |
| GDP per capita (in constant US dollar) | 196.8 | 225.1 | 467.4 | 855.0 |
| | (In percent of GDP) | | | |
| External Trade and Investment: | | | | |
| Current Account Balance | 0.1 | 0.3 | —0.7 | 1.9 |
| Exports of Goods | 5.1 | 4.6 | 9.2 | 19.1 |
| Imports of Goods | 6.8 | 5.2 | 12.4 | 23.1 |
| Net Inward FDI Flows | 0.0 | 0.0 | 0.4 | 3.6 |
| Net Outward FDI Flows (in % of total investment) | 0.1 | 0.0 | 1.9 | 9.8 |
| Composition of Output: | | | | |
| Primary Sector Value Added | 38.6 | 28.1 | 25.9 | 15.9 |
| Secondary Sector Value Added | 25.6 | 48.2 | 26.1 | 50.9 |
| Tertiary Sector Value Added | 35.7 | 23.7 | 48.0 | 33.2 |

*Source* : *International Financial Statistics*, and China Statistical Yearbook.

NRIs have carved an important niche in the services sector and in information technology across the world. It is in these sectors perhaps that the Indian Government can look at creative policy responses that, while maintaining a level playing field, seek to turn India into an attractive investment destination for NRIs.

### VI.III.III. FDI Flows : India in Indian Sub-Continent

While FDI has become a dominant source of private flows to developing economies, it has been thus far highly concentrated. Asia has been the most successful region in attracting and maintaining FDI flows. This experience may be attributed to the comparative success of many countries in the region in avoiding high inflation and high levels of external debt, to maintaining skilled, motivated and cost-efficient labour and to liberalization of the investment regime.

Aggregate net flows to South Asian countries as a group has increased steadily since the mid-1980s. During the 1980s, however, the growth pattern of various sources of external flows shows a marked difference. India and Pakistan resorted to attracting foreign exchange deposits from their non-residents. India also expand its commercial bank and bond financing. FDI remains an insignificant source of capital flows to these countries. Here are some information on some South-Asian and South-East Asian countries as following:

(a) *Bangladesh*—The country is heavily dependent on foreign capital for its investment. Some 70 per cent of gross domestic investment is still financed from external resources, despite the fact that the level of these flows has remained stagnant and has declined in real terms.

(b) *Pakistan*—Long-term external flows to Pakistan have been stagnant for most of the 1980s, although the 1989 figure of US $ 1.6 billion was the highest level achieved during the 1980s in nominal terms. Inflows of FDI in Pakistan were US $ 0.2 billion in 1990 which was increased to US $ 0.9 billion in 1996 and then decreased to US $ 0.3 billion in 2010.

(c) *Sri Lanka*—Total net inflows to the country have not grown during the recent decade, and they actually fell since the peak of 1982. Considerable declines in all major components of private flows more than offset steady increases in official flows.

(d) *Indonesia*—Significant growth was registered in official flows to the country during the 1980s. Virtually all components of official flows expanded, and multilateral non-concessional loans experienced the faster growth.

(e) *Malaysia*—From the 1982 peak of US $ 5.3 billion, capital flows to Malaysia have shown a declining trend; reaching US $ 1.2 billion in 1989. This trend has been reinforced by steadily declining official flows and large drops in private loans due to substantial prepayments in some years. FDI inflows go up from US $ 2.3 billion in 1990 to US $ 5.5 billion in 2010.

(f) *Thailand*—The sound macro-economic performance helped improve the country's access to international capital markets and enhanced its attractiveness as a FDI destination. FDI inflows have increased dramatically, from a $ 200-300 million level during early to mid-1980s to $ 1.7 billion in 1989, reflecting more than anything else economic and political stability maintained through the period.

(g) *India*—From the low levels of the early 1980s the country received steady increase in external resources, reaching about $ 5 billion in 1989, an increase of two and a half times the 1980 level. This increase was due to an expansion in commercial bank credits, non-resident deposits and new bond issues, despite generally unfavourable market conditions for developing countries during the period. Then in 1991, taken economic reforms and FDI inflows in creased from $ 0.2 billion in 1990 to $12.37 billion in 2010.

(h) *Singapore*—The Singapore government sees the "first-mover advantage with the accompanying risks, of taking initiative from FDI investors. It also helps developing countries with its outward FDI.

These South-Asian and South-East Asian countries outflows 54.41 per cent FDI out of the share of outflows by developing countries (Table 6.5). India stands 8$^{th}$ in 2010 among these countries in FDI outflows with $ 239 million in 1996 and $ 167 million in 1999.

A comparison of India with these countries reveals that external capital flows have made a positive contribution in fostering growth and improving living standards. Except for the Philippines, all other countries avoided the debt crisis that characterized Latin America and Africa in the 1980s. The only difference between India and other South-East and South Asian countries is that India strongly maintained the capital control with a fixed percentage permitted for FDI while the other countries failed.

## VI.IV. SUMMARY AND CONCLUSION

Throughout this chapter we have analyzed the actually found survey results which are basically collected from West Bengal. Comparing this survey results with macro-results we have found that FDI inflows in India are still negligible and most of FDI projects still under recommendation. Then we have analyzed India's FDI inflows-outflows with other developing countries and with the countries of Asian Subcontinents.

In the next chapter we shall produce some suggestions, total outlay of this study, policy prescriptions for future study and its likely knowledge to India's economic development.

### References

Choudhary, Biplove (2001), "Role of FDI in the Chinese Economy with Special Reference to the Overseas Chinese: Its Implication for India", *China Report—A Journal of East Asian Studies;* Vol. 37, No. 4, October-December.

Howard, Michael and Arindam Banik (2001), "Private Capital Inflows to the Caribbean—Trends, Assessments and Determinants," *Economic and Political Weekly,* Vol. XXXVI, No. 29, July 21-27, pp. 2773-78.

Pan, S. and Sen, R.K. (2007), *Foreign Direct Investment and Trade in India,* Deep & Deep Publication Private Limited, New Delhi.

RBI (2002), *Report on Currency and Finance, 2000-01,* Reserve Bank of India, Mumbai.

RBI (2012), *Reserve Bank of India Bulletin,* February.

UNCTAD (2002), *World Investment Report.*

CHAPTER

# 7

# *Conclusions and Policy Prescriptions*

## VII.I. INTRODUCTION

Throughout Chapter-II to Chapter-VI, we have analyzed the importance of FDI to developing countries with respect to India, nature and magnitude of FDI flows in India, impact of FDI on Indian economy, anticipated and actual roles of FDI in India and survey results with international comparison. These analysis and presentation gave some results for different aspects.

In the last chapter of our study, we now present the total outlay of this book followed by some policy prescriptions. What we have found throughout this study is presented in the next section. The main objective of this chapter is to present the major findings, conclusions and important policy implications of this study.

## VII.II. MAJOR FINDINGS AND CONCLUSIONS

The major findings and conclusions from the detailed descriptive and empirical analysis in different chapters of this study are summarized below.

(1) This study has forged the links between FDI policy, FDI liberalization measures, inward and outward FDI policy and FDI in the reforms period. The study finds that FDI has an important role in India's economic development.

(2) This study aimed at empirical assessment of the impact of FDI on Indian economy. The study finds that the FDI flows have helped boosting the growth of Indian economy.

(3) In the recent past, the FDI policy reforms in India can be traced back to the start of national economic reforms in July 1991. Since then, the reforms have been formulated and implemented at the national and state level reforms. The study finds that FDI flow seems to have provided one mechanism for helping to integrate poorer countries into the global economy.

(4) In essence, the reforms were initiated as a response to overcome the falling economic growth, rising domestic price inflation, rising current account deficit and the budget deficit of the Union Government, declining foreign exchange reserves, etc. To overcome from these situations, this study finds that, the FDI seems to have supplemented the scarcity of domestic savings for financing domestic investment.

(5) From the analysis it is found that productivity of the firm should be increased if FDI is used. It seems that foreign equity participation is positively correlated with plant productivity and foreign investment negatively affects the productivity of domestically owned plants.

(6) The study also finds that FDI is expected to boost long-run growth in the recipient economy via technological upgrading and knowledge spillovers, it is shown that the extent to which FDI is growth-enhancing depends on the degree of complementarity and substitution between FDI and domestic investment.

(7) The heavy reliance on portfolio investment by the East Asian countries has led them to face currency crisis. In contrast, India has followed a slow but

steady adoption of reform measures—the proportion of portfolio investment has remained low than that of FDI inflow in total foreign investment.

(8) There lies no rivalry between exchange entitlement and economic reforms, rather they are complementary—though the complementarity should be guided by social sector reforms to offer social opportunity, freedom and public action. This study finds that 100 per cent foreign equity allowed in several infrastructural areas under the automatic route, subject to a ceiling of Rs. 1500 crores. Also found that permission of FDI up to 100 per cent for development of integrated townships, including housing, commercial premises, hotels and resorts, city and regional level urban infrastructure facilities such as roads and bridges, mass rapid transit systems and manufacture of building materials.

(9) Even though the relation between market-oriented reforms and foreign capital-led growth is a much debated issue, a general consensus is that there lies a positive association between the two since reforms offer a large exposure for the later.

(10) The Chinese experiment suggests that a proper combination of reforms measure and government's guidance coverage can promote economic growth for an economy. Analysis suggest that economic reforms, started by China in 1978 and by India in 1985 (partly)/1991 (full-fledge), encourage foreign investors to come to these two countries for infrastructural development and economic growth.

(11) FDI is attracted into countries for different reasons such as in order for a country to be more attractive to investors, there is a need to create an enabling environment by reducing 59-called hassle costs.

(12) Today FDI is seen as an instrument to facilitate and support domestic investment for achieving a higher level of economic development. Study shows that net FDI inflows increased from 0.03 per cent of GDP in 1990-91 to 0.9 per cent of GDP in 2009-10.

(13) From the study it is also found that FDI creates 'primary' employment for workers engaged directly in new capital goods projects and their spending gives rise to 'secondary' employment in the industries producing consumer goods on the one hand and intermediate goods required for the capital and consumer goods on the other.

(14) According to WTO arrangements, in regard to export or even in regard to domestic manufacturing content it ruled out any conditionality. A huge FDI inflow in the post-reform periods increased the share of exports sharply.

(15) The study also shows that though FDI brings many good for the economy but at the same time the burden of fiscal adjustment has been unequal in that it has led to declining expenditures on social sectors. Actually FDI inflows strongly support the theorem of unequal growth, i.e. the theorem of unbalanced growth. It makes some states richer with its facilities and some states poorer on the other.

(16) The study also finds that to channeling a new project of FDI at least 17 general clearances must have to be passed. So it is a strong delayed procedure as besides these general clearances, sector specific projects also required some additional clearances.

(17) To broaden the scope of impact of FDI policy reforms on domestic welfare, the combined role and effect of FDI and FPI (as total foreign investment) are also attempted in this study. For this purpose, several models are formulated to find out the relationship between FDI with GDP growth; production, productivity and efficiency; balance of payments and trade; inequality; employment and savings-investment gap.

(18) The empirical results in this study are both comparable and distinct as compares to other studies in the literature. However, this study has obtained comparable results under entirely different empirical analysis in regard to specifications of variables, data used, etc. as compared to the other studies.

(19) In 2007 the world economy faced a global financial meltdown which affects the American and European countries badly. Though India crossed the same path but she was quite capable to manage the situation strongly. With restricted FDI inflows and outflows India overcoming from that stupendous phenomena of meltdown.

(20) It is very much true that most of the FDI came into developing countries including India does not possess all the legal barriers of environmental clause. Investment authorities also cleared most of the projects without proper checking the feasibility of the project. This affects Indian economy badly and causes a huge harm to the nation.

(21) Finally, a few words about the problems that the host country usually faces due to the FDI inflow. It is obvious that foreign investors invest in India for her huge domestic demand and weak competitors. Usually four types of problems are created by FDI, viz., mergers and acquisitions, area of investment, political impact and cultural impacts.

(a) It is usually observed that as FDI increases, technology and efficiency of a firm also increase. But so far as the productivity situation of Indian industries is concerned this did not happen. Most of the Indian companies are now being purchased by MNCs. The soft drinks industries in India are an example of such acquisitions. It was also expected that FDI will help to improve competition among firms. But the result shows that the local technology is vanishing gradually and the MNCs are establishing business monopoly in collaboration with Indian firms.

(b) As the government is withdrawing from many sectors of the economy and the gap is being filled up by FDI. But most of this hot money is employed in the less priority sectors to earn quick and high profits. For FDI in core sectors they require double guaranteed returns and the case of Enron is an example in point.

(c) Through FDI foreign control of the economy is increased in all spheres. For example, poultry farm business in South India controlled by the MNCs, prevented the growth of local agriculture.

(d) Through controlling media MNCs are now influencing Indian traditional culture and preference pattern. This is a real danger that is considered by many as more harmful than their economy vices.

## VII.III. POLICY PRESCRIPTIONS OF THE STUDY

Since this study has focused on the analysis of key FDI policy reforms and their impacts on the Indian economy particularly on human development, domestic market and welfare during 1991 to 2010, several useful policy prescriptions are recommended from the major descriptive and empirical findings and conclusions above. The recommendations are summarized below :

(i) In spite of some steps taken by government, the availability of adequate power still seemed to be a distant dream. Its inadequate availablility worked as a dampener on inflow of FDI. There is a need to achieve, quantum jump in the production/generation of electricity.

(ii) Simplification of the procedures for approvals/ clearances would also require basic changes in the regulatory process prescribed under relevant legislations. Detailed examination of each approval requirement under different Acts, rules and regulations would need to be carried out for re-engineering of the regulatory process.

(iii) Independent evaluation of selected projects with expenditure of Rs. 100 crores and above and other priority projects must be carried out by MSPI to identify deficiencies in formulation, appraisal and implementation of projects.

(iv) There was a need to effect attitudinal change in the bureaucracy, so that they act as facilitators of foreign investment, rather than the obstructers.

(v) A coherent tax system should be evolved. Greater transparency and immediate actions are required in the domain of tax regime. The process of realisation of tax should be simple and transparent. The duties should be rationalised so that investing in India becomes a lucrative proposition.

(vi) Foreign investment in Indian venture capital is presently not being captured in the FDI data, as the reporting of the same is not in place. RBI may device a suitable reporting mechanism to capture these data either through the entities themselves or through authorized dealers.

(vii) The states enacting a special Investment Law covering infrastructure investment. The law would apply to both domestic and foreign investment.

(viii) While capacity-building initiatives would be an ongoing exercise, measures to address the deficiencies in the existing set-up need to be completed in a time bound manner, say one year.

(ix) A time limit, of say 4 weeks, may be prescribed within which the concerned authorities need to respond to periodical returns submitted to them for any further clarifications. After this time-limit, the information given should be deemed to have accepted and approved.

(x) In a developing country like India, the FDI policy should focus on maximization of its contribution to India's development, rather than maximisation of the magnitude of inflows by itself.

(xi) Government should strive to set-up a single body for dealing with FDI matters, so as to negate the confusion/complexity of foreign investors, who want to invest in the country.

(xii) Ever since the process of liberalisation and structural reforms was launched a decade ago, the inflow of foreign capital has never matched the targets envisaged. Instead of liberalising the FDI policies further, government should try to change the mindset of State governments, which still had not changed with the times.

(xiii) The Department should accentuate its policy on FDI, so as to facilitate and attract foreign investors towards export-oriented FDI, so as to boost the level of FDI, as in China, where large amount of FDI inflow was in the form of export-oriented FDI.

(xiv) The Department of Revenue may be persuaded to set-up a mechanism to receive feedback from the perspective investors so that various tax laws are updated continuously to make them investor-friendly.

(xv) The FDI inflows in India were too meager. Till now, India had attracted less than one per cent of its GDP, in terms of FDI, ever since the reforms process was set in motion. The macro-economic and organizational framework should be improved, so that the FDI policy looks more coherent.

Foreign direct investment is not a cure-all but if properly used it could be a handy aid and give positive response for Indian economic development.

# *Bibliography*

Agarwal, J.P. (1979), "FDI in Natural Resources of Developing Countries—Review and Prospects", *The Indian Economic Journal,* Vol. 27, No. 2, Oct.-Dec., pp. 48-62.

Aggarwal, Mangat Ram (1984), "Devaluation, International Trade Flow and Payments Imbalances", *Economic Journal,* Vol. 31, No. 3, Jan.-Mar., pp. 24-33.

Ahluwalia, Isher J. (1992), *Trade Policy and Industrialistion in India,* Export-Import Bank of India, Mumbai.

Ahluwalia, M.S. (2000), "Economic Performance of States in Post-Reform Period," *Economic and Political Weekly,* May 6, pp. 1637-48.

———, (2002), "Economic Reforms in India Since 1991: Has Gradualism Worked?" *Journal of Economic Perspectives,* Vol. 16, No. 3, Summer, pp. 67-88.

Aitken, B.; G.H. Hanson and A. Harrison (1997), "Spillovers, Foreign Investment and Export Behavior," *Journal of International Economics,* Vol. 43, pp. 103-32.

Aitken, B.J. and A. Harrison (1991), "Are There Spillovers from FDI? Evidence from Panel Data for Venezuela", *Mimeo,* Boston: MIT.

Alfaro, Laura, Areendam Chanda, Sebnem Kalemli-Ozcan and Selin Sayek (2003), "FDI Spillovers, Financial Markets and Economic Development", *IMF Working Paper,* WP/03/186.

Alguacil, M.T., A. Cuadros and V. Orts (2002), "FDI Exports and Domestic Performance in Mexico: A Causality Analysis", *Economic Letters,* Vol. 77, No. 3, Nov., pp. 371-76.

Alti (2003), "How Sensitive is Investment, to Cash Flow When Financing is Frictionless?" *The Journal of Finance,* Vol. 58, No. 2, April, pp. 707-22.

Bagchi, A.K., *Private Investment in India,* 1903-39.

Bagchi, Amiya Kumar (1999), "Globalisation, Liberalisation and Vulnerability: India and Third World", *Economic and Political Weekly,* Vol. XXXIV, No. 45, November 6-12, pp. 3219-30.

Balakrishnan, Pulapre (2003), "Globalisation, Growth and Justice," *Economic and Political Weekly,* Vol. XXXVIII, No. 30, pp. 3166-72, July 26-Aug. 1.

Balasubramanian, N. (2000), "FDI: Some Corporate Governance Issues in Host Countries", *Productivity,* Vol. 40, No. 4, Jan.-March 2000, pp. 535-43.

Balasubramanyam, Salisu and Sapsford (1996), "FDI and Growth in EP and IS Countries", *The Economic Journal,* Vol. 106, pp. 92-105.

———, (1999), "FDI as an Engine of Growth", *Journal of International Trade and Economic Development,* Vol. 8, No. 1, pp. 27-40.

Baldwin, Robert E. (1979), "Determinants of Trade and Foreign Investment", *The Review of Economics and Statistics,* Vol. 1, February.

Banerjee, Sudeshna Ghosh and Dennis A. Rondinelli (2003), "Does Foreign Aid Promote Privatisation? Empirical Evidence from Developing Countries", *World Development,* Vol. 31, No. 9, pp. 1527-48, September.

Barrell, Ray and Nigel Pain (1997), "FDI, Technological Change, and Economic Growth within Europe", *The Economic Journal,* Vol. 107, November, pp. 1770-86.

Barro, R. and Sala-l-Martin (1995), *Economic Growth,* Cambridge, Massachusetts: McGraw Hill.

Barry and Bradley (1997), "FDI and Trade: The Irish Host-Country Experience", *The Economic Journal,* Vol. 107, No. 445, pp. 1798-1811.

Basu, Anupam and Krishna Srinivasan (2002), "FDI in Africa : Some Case Studies", *IMF Working Paper, WP/02/61,* March.

Bayoumi, Tamim and Gabrielle Lipworth (1997), "Japan's Foreign Direct Investment and Regional Trade", *IMF Working Paper, WP/97/103,* August.

Bhagwati, Jagadish and Srinivasan, T.N. (1975), *Foreign Trade Regimes and Economic Development: India*, National Bureau of Economic Research, New York.

Bhalla, A.S. (1999), "The Impact of Globalisation on China and India, in *50 Years of Development Economics* by A. Vasudevan, D.M. Nachane, A.V. Karnik, Himalaya Publishing House, New Delhi.

Bhatia, D.P. (1996), "Tuning the Economy for a Steep Rise in FDI", *Economic Growth and Social Change*, March, p. 52.

Bhattacharya, Amar, Peter J. Montiel and Sunil Sharma (1999), "Private Capital Flows to Sub-Saharan Africa: An Overview of Trends and Determinants", in Zubair Iqbal and Ravi Kanbur (eds.): *External Finance for Low-Income Countries*, IMP.

Bhattacharya, R. (1976), "Multinational Corporations", *The Economic Studies*, Vol. 17, No. 3, pp. 167-72, September.

Billington (1999), "The Location of FDI: An Empirical Analysis", *Applied Economics*, Vol. 31, pp. 65-76.

Blomstrom, M. and Kokko (1997), "Regional Integration and FDI", *NBER Working Paper*, No. 6019.

Blonigen, Bruce A. (1997), "Firm-specific Assets and Link between Exchange Rates and FDI," *The American Economic Review*, Vol. 87, No. 3, June, pp. 447-65.

Brealey, Richard A. and Myres, Stuart C. (1998), *Principles of Corporate Finance*, 5th Edition, Tata McGraw Hill.

Buckley, Peter, J. (1995), *Foreign Direct Investment and Multinational Enterprises*, MacMillan Press Ltd.

Callen, Tim and Paul Cashin (2001), "Assessing India's External Position", in *India at the Crossroads: Sustaining Growth and Reducing Poverty*, by Tim Callen, Patricia Reynolds, Christopher Tow (eds.), pp. 28-49, IMF.

Calvo, Guillermo A. and Carmen M. Reinhart (2000), "When Capital Inflows Suddenly Stop: Consequences and Policy Option", in Peter Kenen and Swoboda, *Reforming the International Monetary and Financial System*, IMF, pp. 175-201.

Campos, Nauro F. and Fabrizio Coricelli (2002), "Growth in Transition : What We Know, What We Don't and What We should", *Journal of Economic Literature*, Vol. XL, No. 3, Sept., pp. 793-836.

Caves, Richard E. (1971), "International Corporations: The Industrial Economics of Foreign Investment", *Economica,* Vol. 38, No. 149, pp. 1-27.

Chalapati Rao, K.S., M.R. Murthy and K.V.K. Ranganathan (1999), "FDIs in the Post-Liberalisation Period: An Overview", *Journal of Indian School of Political Economy,* Vol. 11, No. 3, July-September.

Chandra, Nirmal Kumar (1999), "FDI and Domestic Neoliberalism in China", *Economic and Political Weekly,* No. 45, pp. 3195-3212, Nov 6-12.

Chen, Zhaohui and Mohsin S. Khan (1997), "Patterns of Capital Flows to Emerging Markets: A Theoretical Perspective", *IMF Working Paper, WP/97/13,* January.

Cheng, Leonard K. and Yum K. Kwan (2000), "What are The Determinants of the Location of FDI? The Chinese Experience," *Journal of International Economics,* Vol. 51, No. 2, August.

Cherian, Joseph A. and Enrico Perotti (2001), "Option Pricing and Foreign Investment under Political Risk", *Journal of International Economics,* Vol. 55, pp. 359-77.

Chia, Siow Yue (1993), "FDIs in ASEAN Countries", *Asian Development Review,* Vol. 11.1, pp. 60-102.

Cushman, David O. (1987), "The Effects of Real Wages and Labour Productivity on FDI", *Southern Economic Journal,* Vol. 54, No. 1, pp. 174-85, July.

CUTS (2002), "FDI in Developing Countries: What Economists (Don't) Know and Policy-makers Should (Not) Do!" *Investment for Development,* 2nd National Reference Group (INDIA) Meeting, Chennai, June 1.

Demurger, S. (2000), *Economic Opening and Growth in China,* Development Centre of the Organisation of Economic Co-operation and Development, Paris.

Das, S.P (2002), "FDI and the Relative Wage in a Developing Economy", *Journal of Developmental Economics,* Vol. 67, No. 1, Feb., pp. 55-78.

Datar, M.K. (1999), DFIs in an Era of Developing Capital Markets, *Economic and Political Weekly,* June 19, pp. 1640-42.

De Mello, Luiz R. (1996), "FDI, International Knowledge Endogenous Growth : Time Series Evidence", *Mimeo*, Kent, England.

De Mello Jr., Luiz R. (1997), "FDI in Developing Countries and Growth: A Selective Study", *Journal of Development Studies*, Vol. 34, No. 1, October.

Dees (1998), "FDI in China: Determinants and Effects", *Economics of Planning*, Vol. 31, pp. 175-94.

Dhar, Biswajit and Chaturvedi, Sachin (1998), "Multilateral Agreement on Investment: An Analysis," *Economic and Political Weekly*, April 11-17, Vol. XXXIII, No. 15, pp. 837-49.

Dhar, Biswajit and Saikat Sinha Roy (1996), "FDI and Domestic Savings—Investment Behaviour: Developing Countries Experience", *Economic and Political Weekly*, Vol. 31, Nos. 35, 36 and 37, p. 2548.

Dua, P. and Rashid, A.I. (1998), "FDI and Economic Activity in India", *Indian Economic Review*, Vol. XXXIII, No. 2.

Dunning, John H. (1998), *Globalisation, Trade and Foreign Direct Investment*, Elsevier, pp. XI + 291.

Dutta, R.C., *Economic History of India*, Vols. 1 and 2.

Fabre, Guilhem (1999), "China in the East Asian Crisis", *Economic and Political Weekly*, Vol. XXXIV, No. 45, pp. 3191-94, Nov. 6-12.

Findley, Ronald (1978), "Relative Backwardness, Direct Foreign Investment and Transfer of Technology: A Simple Dynamic Model", *Quarterly Journal of Economics*, Vol. 92, pp. 1-16.

Fredriksson, Per G., John A. List and Daniel L. Millinet (2003), "Bureaucratic Corruption, Environmental Policy and Inbound US FDI: Theory and Evidence", *Journal of Public Economics*, Vol. 87, Nos. 7-8, pp. 1407-31, August.

Froot, K. and J. Stein (1991), "Exchange Rates and Foreign Direct Investment: An Imperfect Capital Market Approach", *Quarterly Journal of Economics*, Vol. 106, pp. 1191-1217.

Ganesh, S. (1997), "Who is Afraid of Foreign Firms?—Current Trends in FDI in India", *Economic and Political Weekly*, May.

Garibaldi, Pietro, Nada Mora, Ratna Sahay and Jeromin Zettelmeyer (2002), "What Moves Capital to Transition Economics"? IMF, *WP/02/64*, April.

Gaziglou, S. and W.D. McCausland (2001), "An International Economic Analysis of FDI and International Indebtedness," *The Indian Economic Journal,* Vol. 48, No. 4, April-June, pp. 82-91.

Glass, A.J. and Kamal Saggi (1998), "International Technology Transfer and the Technology Gap", *Journal of Developmental Economics,* Vol. 55, pp. 363-98.

———, (1999), "Foreign Direct Investments and the Nature of R&D", *Canadian Journal of Economics,* Vol. 32 pp. 92-117.

Glass, Anny Jocelyn and Kamal Saggi (2002), "Licensing *versus* Direct Investment: Implications for Economic Growth", *Journal of International Economics,* Vol. 56, pp. 131-53.

GOI (2001), *Economic Survey, 2000-01,* Ministry of Finance, GOI, Economic Division, pp. 118-27, 168-70.

Goldar, Biswanath and Ishigami, Etsuro (1999), "Foreign Direct Investment in Asia", *Economic and Political Weekly,* Vol. XXIV, No. 22, pp. M50-M60, May 29-June 4.

Gopinath, T. (1997), "Foreign Investment in India: Policy Issue, Trends and Prospects", *RBI Occasional Papers,* Vol. 18, Nos. 2 and. 3, June-September, pp. 453-70.

Government of India (1999), *India's External Debt: A Status Report,* Government of India Printer, New Delhi.

———, (2002), *India 2002: Investment,* pp. 328-32, Ministry of Information and Broadcasting, New Delhi.

Graham, E.G. (1995), "Foreign Direct Investment in the World Economy", *IMF Working Paper, WP/95/59.*

Gropp, Reint and Kristina Kostial (2000), "The Disappearing is Foreign Direct Investment (FDI) Eroding Corporate Income Taxes?" *WP/00/173, IMF Working Paper,* October.

———, (2001), "FDI and Corporate Tax Revenue: Tax Harmonisation or Competition?" *Finance and Development,* Vol. 38, No. 2, June, IMF, pp. 19-13.

Gupta, Subrata (2003), "Role of Foreign Direct Investment and Multinational Corporations—The Indian Context", *Artha Beekshan,* Vol. II, No. 4, March, pp. 24-37.

Habermeier, Karl (2000), "India—Experience with the Liberalisation of Capital Flows since 1991", in A. Ariyoshi, K. Habermeier, B. Laurens, and Otker—Robe, J.I. Canales—Kriljenko and A. Kirilenko (eds.)—*Capital Controls: Country Experience with their Use and Liberalisation,* IMF, Chapter II.

Hajra, Sujan and Sinate, David L. (1997), "Fifty Years of India's Foreign Trade: Issues and Perspectives", *RBI Occasional Papers,* Vol. 18, Nos. 2 and 3, June-September, pp. 421-52.

Hasan, Rana (2002), "The Impact of Imported Technologies on the Productivity of Firms: Panel Data of Indian Manufacturing Firms", *Journal of Development,* Vol. 69, No. 1, October, pp. 23-49.

Hattori, Tamio (1999), "Economic Development and Technology Accumulation—Experience of South Korea", *Economic and Political Weekly,* Vol. XXXIV, No. 22, pp. M78-M84, May 29-June 4.

Head, Keith and John Ries (2002), "Offshore Production and Skill Upgrading by Japanese Manufacturing Firms", *Journal of International Economics,* Vol. 58, No. 1, October, pp. 81-105.

Hernandez, Leonardo, Pamela Mellado, Rodrigo Valdes (2001), "Determinants of Private Capital Flows in the 1970s and 1990s: Is there Evidence of Contagion?" *IMF Working Paper, WP/01/64,* May.

Hewko, John (2002), "Foreign Direct Investment: Does the Role of Law Matter?" *The World Bank: Transition Newsletter,* Vol. 11. No. 2, March-April, pp. 11-13.

Horstman, I.J., J.R. Markusen (1987), "Licensing *versus* Direct Investment: A Model of Internationalisation by the Multinational Enterprise", *Canadian Journal of Economics,* Vol. 20, pp. 464-81.

Huang, Yasheng (2002), *Selling China: Foreign Direct Investment during the Reform Era,* Cambridge University Press.

Hymer, S.H. (1976), *The International Operations of National Firms: A Study of Direct Foreign Investment,* Cambridge, MA: IT Press.

ISAE (2001), "The Impact of Taxation on FDI Flows in the European Union Member-States", *Istituto Di Studi E Analist Economica,* June, Annual Report on the State of the European Union.

Itoh, Motoshige (2000), "FDI, International Trade and Transfer of Technology: A Case Study in South-East Asia," in John Piggot and Alan Woodland (eds.), *International Trade Policy and The Pacific Rim,* International Economic Association, Vol. 120, Sydney.

Jalan, Bimal (1992), "Balance of Payments, 1956-91", in Bimal Jalan (ed.)—*The Indian Economy: Problems and Prospects,* New Delhi, India.

Jana, Siuli (2003), "A Model on Foreign Direct Investment in the Developing Countries", *Artha Beekshan,* Vol. II, No. 4, March, pp. 38-43.

Jang-Yuan Lee (1997), "Prospect for Increasing Foreign Direct Investment in Low-Income Countries," in Zubair Iqbal and Ravi Kanbur's (eds.), *External Finance for Low-Income Countries,* IMF, pp. 194-206.

Jha, Shikha and Vinaya Swaroop (1999), "Foreign Aid to India—What does it Finance?" *Economic and Political Weekly,* Vol. XIV, No. 19, pp. 1142-46, May 8-14.

Joshi, Himanshu (1995), "Stock Market Risk and Foreign Portfolio Investments—An Empirical Investigation", *RBI Occasional Papers,* Vol. 16, No. 4, December, pp. 301-12.

Joshi, Vijoy and I.M.D. Little (1998), *India's Economic Reforms, 1991-2001,* Oxford University Press, New Delhi.

Khanna, Sushil (1999, "Financial Reforms and Industrial Sector in India", *Economic and Political Weekly,* Vol. XXXIV, No. 5, November 6-12, pp. 3231-41.

Khatkar, R.K.; S.D. Chamola and R.C. Hasija (1997), Globalisation: Multinational Corporation in India", *Kautilya: The Journal of Haryana Economic Association,* Vol. XVII, Nos. 1 and 2, pp. 53-60.

Kindleberger, C.P. (1969), *American Business Abroad:* Six *Lectures on Direct Investment,* New Haven: Yale University Press.

Klein, Michael W. and Rosengren, Eric S. (1994), "The Real Exchange Rate and FDI in the US: Relative Wealth *vs.* Relative Wage Effects", *Journal of International Economics,* Vol. 36 (3-4), pp. 313-89, May.

Klien, Michael W., Joe Peak and Eric S. Rosengren (2002), "Troubled Banks, Impaired FDI: The Role of Relative Access to Credit", *The American Economic Review,* Vol. 92, No. 3, pp. 664-82, June.

Kohli, Renu (2003), "Capital Flows and Domestic Financial Sector in India", *Economic and Political Weekly,* Vol. XXXVIII, No. 8, pp. 761-68, February 22-28.

Kojima, K. (1978), *Direct Foreign Investment,* London: Croo Helm.

Koutsoyannis, A. (1977), *Econometrics,* ELBS, Hampshire.

Kumar, Nagesh (2001), "WTO Regime, Host Country Policies and Global Patterns of MNE Activity: Recent Quantitative Studies and India's Strategic Response," *Economic and Political Weekly,* Vol. XXXVI, No. 1, pp. 39-50, January 6-12.

———, (1995), "Industrialisation, Liberalisation and Two way Flows of FDI, Case of India", *Economic and Political Weekly.*

Kumar, Nagesh (2001), *FDI, Regional Economic Integration and Industrial Restructuring in Asia: Trends, Patterns and Prospects,* No. 62, New Delhi.

———, (2003), "Investment on WTO Agenda: A Developing Country Perspective and Way Forward for Cancun Ministerial Conference," *Economic and Political Weekly,* Vol. XXXVIII, No. 30, pp. 3177, July 26-Aug. 1.

Kust, Mathew J. (1964), *Foreign Enterprises in India: Laws and Policies,* Oxford University Press.

Kumar, P. Vinod (2002), "Maharashtra Tops in FDI Approvals since *1991", The Financial Express,* 23.12.2002, Chennai.

Lakdawala, D.T. (1968), "Development and Foreign Aid", *Indian Economic Journal,* Vol. XV, No. 3, Jan.-Mar., pp. 320-32.

Lall, S. (1980), "Vertical Interfirm Linkages in LDCs: An Empirical Study", *Oxford Bulletin of Economics and Statistics,* Vol. 42, pp. 203-26.

Lehmann, Alexander (2002), "FDI in Emerging Markets: Income Repatriations and Financial Vulnerabilities", *IMF Working Paper, WP/02/47,* March.

Levi, Maurice D. (1990), *International Finance: The Markets and Financial Management of Multinational Business,* International Edition.

Li, Wei (1994), "A Tale of Two Reforms", *Mimeo*-Mimeograph Fuqua School of Business, Duke University.

Lim, Ewe-Ghee (2001), "Determinants of and the Relation between Foreign Direct Investment and Growth: A Summary of the Recent Literature", *IMF Working Paper,* WP/01/175.

Lipschitz, Leslie, Timothy Lane and Alex Mourmouras (2000), "Capital Flows to Transition Economies: Master or Servant"? *IMF Working Paper, WP/02/11,* January.

Lizondo, J. Saul (1990), "Foreign Direct Investment", *IMF Working Paper, WP/90/63.*

Loungani, Prakash and Assaf Razin (2001), "How Beneficial is FDI for Developing Countries?" *Finance and Development*, Vol. 38, No. 2, IMF, pp. 6-9, June.

Lucas, B. Robert (1993), "On the Determinants of FDI: Evidence from East and South-east Asia", *World Development*, Vol. 21, No. 3.

Malhotra, Anju and Dhesi, Autar S. (1985), "FDI in Manufacturing from an LDC : India", *The Indian Economic Journal*, Vol. 32, No. 3, Jan.-March, pp. 36-41.

Mariotti, Sergio, Marco Mutinelli and Lucia Piscitello (2003), "Home Country Employment and FDI: Evidence from the Italian Case", *Cambridge Journal of Economics*, Vol. 27, No. 3, May, pp. 419-31.

Markusen, J.R., A.J. Venables, D.E. Konam and K.H. Zhan (1996), "A Unified Treatment of Horizontal Direct Investment, Vertical Direct Investment, and the Pattern of Trade in Goods and Services", *NBER Working Paper*, No. 5696.

Markusen, J.R. (2001), "Contracts, Intellectual Property Rights and Multinational Investment in Developing Countries", *Journal of International Economics*, Vol. 53, pp. 189-204.

Mehta, Surender and Khatri, Randhir (1997), "Socio-Cultural Environment and Role of Multinational Corporation in Indian Economic Development", *Kautilya : The Journal of Haryana Economic Association*, Vol. XVII, Nos. 1 and 2, pp. 67-81.

Mehta, G.L. (1968), "Development and Foreign Collaboration", *The Indian Economic Journal*, Vol. XV, No. 3, Jan.-Mar., pp. 43-376.

Mien, Bernard Tai Khium (1999), "Foreign Direct Investment and Pattern of Trade: Malayasian Experience", *Economic and Political Weekly*, Vol. XXXIV, No. 22, pp. M72-M77, May 29-June 4.

Mishra, Deepak; Ashoka Mody and Antu Panini Murshid (2001), "Private Capital Flows and Growth", *Finance and Development*, Vol. 38, No. 2, June, IMF, pp. 2-5.

Misra, S.K. and V.K. Puri (2010), *Indian Economy*, Himalaya Publishing House, New Delhi.

Mody, A. and F. Wang (1997), "Explaining Industrial Growth in Coastal China: Economic Reforms .... and What Else?" *The*

*World Bank Economic Review,* May, Vol. 11, No. 2, pp. 293-325.

Mody, Ashoka and Kinoshita, Yuko (2001), "Private Information for Foreign Investment in Emerging Economies", *Canadian Journal of Economics,* Vol. 34, No. 2, pp. 448-64.

Mody, Ashoka and Antu Panini Murshid (2002), "Growing Up with Capital Flows", *IMF Working Paper, WP/02/75,* April.

Molyneux, P. (2002), "The Determinants of Cross-Border Margers in European Banking", Presented at Deutsche Bundesbank Conference on *'FDI in the Real and Financial Sectors of Industrial Countries',* Eltville, May.

Moran, T.R. (1998), "Foreign Direct Investment and Development: The New Policy Agenda for Developing Countries and Economies in Transition", *Institute for International Economics,* Washington D.C.

Muhleisen, Martin (1997), "Improving India's Saving Performance", *IMF Working Paper, WP/97/4,* January.

Mussa, Michael, Alexander K. Swoboda, Jeromin Zettelmeyer and Oliver Jeanne (2000), "Moderating Fluctuations in Capita Flows to Emerging Market Economies", in Peter Kenen and Alexander Swaoboda(eds.): *Reforming the International Monetary and Financial System,* IMF, pp. 75-142, 155-74.

Nagraj, R. (1997), "What has Happened since 1991? Assessment of Indian Economic Reforms", *Economic and Political Weekly,* Nov. 8, pp. 2869-79.

Nagraj, R. (2003), "Foreign Direct Investment in India in the 1990s—Trends and Issues," *Economic and Political Weekly,* April 2-May 2, Vol. XXXVIII, No. 17, pp. 1701-12.

Nair-Richert, Usha and Diana Weinhold (2001), "Causalty Tests for Cross-Country Panels: A New Look at FDI and Economic Growth in Developing Countries", *Oxford Bulletin of Economics and Statistics,* Vol. 63, No. 2, May, pp. 153-71.

Nayar, Baldev Raj (2001), "Opening Up and Openness of Indian Economy", *Economic and Political Weekly,* Vol. XXXI, No. 37, September 15-21, pp. 3529-37.

Neogi, C. and B. Ghosh (1998), "Impact of Liberalisation on Indian Industries: A Firm-Level Study", *Economic and Political Weekly,* Feb. 28, M16-M24.

Pan, S. (2001), " Impact of Globalization on Indian Agriculture", *Conferende Volume*, No. 84, p. 207, IEA, Vellore.

———, (2002), "Globalization of Trade in Food Items, FDI and Welfare in West Bengal during 1991-2001", *Occasional Papers*, Vol. X, pp. 21-28, March, Department of Economics, R.B.U., Kolkata.

———, "FDI in India: Problems and Prospects", *Bihar Economic Journal*, Vol. 8, pp. 471-90, Dhanbad.

———, (2005), Globalization, FDI and Indian Economy", *Occasional Papers*, Vol. XIII, pp. 29-35, R.B.U., Kolkata.

———, (2007), "West Bengal as a Deslenation of FDI", in R.K. Sen and A. Dasgupta (eds.): *West Bengal Today : Twenty-five Years of Economic Development*, Deep & Deep Publications, New Delhi.

———, (2007a), " international Competitiveness: How FDI Helps India under Globalization", *Conference Volume*, IEA, No. 90, pp. 998-1004, Sri Nagar.

———, (2008), "FDI and India's External Sector Development", in F. Raj (ed.): *Indian Econocy: Economic Ideas, Development and Financial Reforms*, pp. 200-13, Deep & Deep Publications (P) Ltd., New Delhi.

———,(2008a), "SEZ and Green Technology: Measuring Productivity with Inflow of FDI", *Industrial Ecology, pp. 1339*, ICFAI University Press, Hyderabad.

———, (2009), "FDI in BRIC Economies: How Important", in P.K. Pal (ed.): *Contemporary Issues in Development Economics—Models and Applications*, pp. , 407-25. Regal Publications, New Delhi.

———, (2011), "State-wise Disparity in Income and Employment in India during the Globalization Era", in D. Mukhopadhyay (ed.): *Globalization and Inequality*, pp. 215-29, Deep & Deep Publications, New Delhi.

———, (2011a), "How FDI Affects the Environment in India: Consequences from Recent Performance", in R.K. Sen (ed.): *Environment and Sustainable Development in India*, Deep & Deep Publications, New Delhi.

———, (2011b), "Realizing Sustainable Growth Using Water Resources in India," *The Indian Economic Journal*, Special Issue, December, pp. 120-29, Pune.

Pan, S., (2011c), "Is Globalization Reducing Poverty and Inequality in India? A Theoretical Overview," in R.K. Sen (ed.): *Modern Indian Economy,* pp. 236-59, Deep & Deep Publications, New Delhi.

Panchamukhi, P.R. (2000), "Social Impact of Economic Reforms in India—A Critical Appraisal", *Economic and Political Weekly,* Vol. XXV, No. 10, pp. 836-47, March 4-10.

Patel, Meena (1984), "Private Foreign Investment and Balance of Payments Effects in India during 1960-70", *The India Economic Journal,* Vol. 31, No. 3, Jan.-Mar., pp. 62-69.

RBI (2012), *Reserve Bank of India Bulletin,* February.

Rob, Rafael and Nikolaos Vettas (2003), "Foreign Direct Investment and Export with Growing Demand", *The Review of Economic Studies,* Vol. 70(3), No. 244, pp. 629-48, July.

Root, Franklin and Ahmed (1979), "Empirical Determinants of Manufacturing DFI in Developing Countries", *Economic Development and Cultural Change,* Vol. 27, No. 4.

Roy, Subhas C. (2000), "Did India's Economic Reforms Improve Efficiency and Productivity? A Non-parametric Analysis of the Initial Evidence from Manufacturing", *Indian Economic Review,* Vol. XXXVII, No. 1, pp. 23-57, January-June.

Sadka Efrain, Razin, Assaf and Chi-Wa Yuen (2000), "An Information Based Model of FDI: The Gains from Trade Revisited" in Isard, Razin and Rose (eds.)—*International Finance and Financial Crisis* (Essays in Honour of Robert P. Flood, Jr.), IMF, Kluwer Academic Publishers, pp. 95-120.

Saggi, K. (1999), "Foreign Direct Investment, Licensing and Incentives for Innovation," *Review of International Economics,* Vol. 4, pp. 99-104.

Sarkar, Abhirup (2003), "Videshi Biniyog Swagata Yadi Raftani Bare, Tabei", *Anandabazar Patrika,* 26 June.

Sarkar, N.K. (1976), *Foreign Investment and Economic Development in Asia,* Edited Volume.

Schneider and Frey (1985), "Economic and Political Determinants of FDI", *World Development,* Vol. 13, pp. 161-75.

Seid, Sherif H. (2002), *Global Regulation of Foreign Direct Investment,* Ashgate Publishing Ltd., Hampshire, England.

Sen, Raj Kumar (2003), "The EU-India Economic Relations: An Analysis", *Artha Beekshan,* Vol. II, No. 4, March, pp. 44-61.

Sen, Raj Kumar and Suvranshu Pan (2003), "Globalisation, Trade and FDI in Food Items in West Bengal," in R.K. Sen (ed): *Economic Reforms and Development,* Deep and Deep Publications (P) Ltd., New Delhi, pp. 313-26.

Siegel, Philip H. (1973), "Foreign Aid and Economic Development", *Economic Affairs,* Vol. 18, Nos. 1-2, pp. 41-53.

Singh, Kavaljit (1997), *The Reality of Foreign Investments,* Books, New Delhi.

Sjoholmn (1999), "Technology Gap, Competition and Spillovers from DFI: Evidence form Establishment Data", *Journal of Development Studies,* Vol. 36, No. 1, pp. 53-73.

Skaksen, Mette Yde and Jan Rose Sorensen (2001), "Should Trade Unions Appreciate Foreign Direct Investment"? *Journal of International Economics,* Vol. 55, pp. 379-90.

Srivastava, Sadhana (2003), "What is the True Level of FD Flows to India?" *Economic and Political Weekly,* Vol. XXXVIII, No. 7, pp. 608-10, 15-21 February.

Subramanian, K.K., D. Sastry, Sitikantha Pattnaik and Sujan Hajra (1996), "Foreign Collaboration under Liberalisation Policy", *Development Research Group Study,* 14, RBI.

Swaminathan, S.A. Aiyar (2003), Unanticipated Consequences of FDI, *The Times of India,* 22.06.2003, Kolkata.

Tewari, Madan Mohan (1976), "Role of Foreign Aid in India's Growth and Self-Reliance", *The Economic Studies,* Sept., Vol. 17, No. 3, pp. 185-88.

Thavaraj, M.J.K. (1967), "External Economics and Investment Programmes", *The Indian Economic Journal,* Vol. XV, No. 1, Jul.-Sept., pp. 14-42.

Thomas, J. and T. Worrall (1994), "Foreign Direct Investment and the Risk of Expropriation", *Review of Economic Studies,* Vol. 61, pp. 81-108.

UNCTAD (1992), *The Determinants of FDI: A Survey of the Evidence,* United Nations, New York.

————, (1993), *Explaining and Forecasting Regional Flows of FDI,* United Nations, New York.

UNCTAD (1995), *World Investment Report: Transnational Corporations and Competitiveness.*

———, (1999), "FDI Rises to $ 4 Trillion in 1998, Growth is Driven by Mergers and Acquisitions", *IMF Survey,* Vol. 28, No. 19, Oct. 11, p. 333.

———, (1999), "FDI to Developing Asia is Buoyant Despite Crisis", *IMF Survey,* Vol. 28, No. 10, May 24, p. 175.

———, (1999), "FDI Flows to Asian Crisis Countries Prove Resilient", *IMF Survey,* Vol. 28, No. 6, March 22, pp. 93-96.

———, (1999), "Global FDI Surged in 1998", *IMF Survey,* Vol. 28, No. 14, July 19, pp. 232-33.

———, (2001), "FDI Flows Soar in 2000, But are Likely to Decline Sharply in this Year", *IMF Survey,* Vol. 30, No. 19, Oct. 8, pp. 314-15.

———, (2002), *World Development Report.*

Unni, Jeemol, N. Lalitha and Uma Rani (2001), "Economic Reforms and Productivity Trends in Indian Manufacturing", *Economic and Political Weekly,* Vol. XXXVI, No. 4, pp. 3914- 22, Oct. 13-19.

Vernon, R. (1966), "International Investment and International Trade in the Product Cycle", *Quarterly Journal of Economics,* Vol. 80, pp. 190-207.

Virmani, Arvind (2003), "India's External Reforms: Modest Globalisation, Significant Gains," *Economic and Political Weekly,* Vol. XXXVIII, No. 32, pp. 3373-90, August 9-15.

Walz, U. (1997), "Innovation, FDI and Growth", *Economica,* Vol. 64, pp. 63-79.

Wang, J.Y., Blomstrom, M. (1992), "Foreign Investment and Technology Transfer: A Simple Model", *European Economic Review,* Vol. 36, pp. 137-55.

WEF (2000), *The Global Competitiveness Report:* Economic Forum, Harvard University.

Wei, S. (1994), "The Open Door Policy and China's Rapid Growth: Evidence from City Level Data" in *Growth Theories in Light of the East Asian Experience,* Krueger (eds.), University of Chicago Press, Chicago.

World Bank (2001), *Improving the Investment Climate in India,* An Investment Climate Assessment Prepared by the World Bank Group in Collaboration with the Confederation of Indian Industries.

Yeaple, Stephen Ross (2003), "The Complex Integration Strategies of Multinationals and Cross-Country Dependencies in the Structure of FDI," *Journal of International Economics,* Vol. 60, Issue 2, August, pp. 293-314.

Zhang, K. (1999), "FDI and Economic Growth: Evidence from Ten East Asian Economies", *Journal of International Economics,* Vol. 54, No. 4, pp. 517-35, November.

Zhao, L. (1995), "Cross-hauling Direct Foreign Investment and Uniconized Oligopoly", *European Economic Review,* Vol. 9, pp. 1237-53.

# Index